Better Homes and Gardens®

quick-fix
FAMILY FAVORITES

Meredith® Books
Des Moines, Iowa

Better Homes and Gardens® Quick-Fix Family Favorites
Contributing Editor: Janet Figg
Contributing Designer: Rachael Thompson
Copy Chief: Doug Kouma
Copy Editor: Kevin Cox
Editorial Assistant: Sheri Cord
Book Production Managers: Marjorie J. Schenkelberg,
  Mark Weaver
Contributing Copy Editor: Marcia Kramer
Contributing Proofreaders: Maria Duryée, Sarah Enticknap, Shawn Simmons
Test Kitchen Director: Lynn Blanchard
Test Kitchen Culinary Specialists: Marilyn Cornelius, Juliana Hale,
  Maryellyn Krantz, Jill Moberly, Colleen Weeden, Lori Wilson
Test Kitchen Nutrition Specialists: Elizabeth Burt, R.D., L.D.;
  Laura Marzen, R.D., L.D.

Meredith® Books
Editorial Director: John Riha
Deputy Editor: Jennifer Darling
Managing Editor: Kathleen Armentrout
Brand Manager: Janell Pittman
Group Editor: Jan Miller
Associate Designer: Erin Burns

Executive Director, Sales: Ken Zagor
Director, Operations: George A. Susral
Director, Production: Douglas M. Johnston
Business Director: Janice Croat

Vice President and General Manager, SIM: Jeff Myers

Better Homes and Gardens® **Magazine**
Editor in Chief: Gayle Goodson Butler
Deputy Editor, Food and Entertaining: Nancy Wall Hopkins

Meredith Publishing Group
President: Jack Griffin
Executive Vice President: Doug Olson

Meredith Corporation
Chairman of the Board: William T. Kerr
President and Chief Executive Officer: Stephen M. Lacy

In Memoriam: E. T. Meredith III (1933–2003)

All of us at Meredith® Books are dedicated to providing you with the information and ideas you need to create delicious foods. We welcome your comments and suggestions.
Write to us at: Meredith Books, Cookbook Editorial Department, 1716 Locust St., Des Moines, IA 50309-3023.

Our seal assures you that every recipe in *Quick-Fix Family Favorites* has been tested in the Better Homes and Gardens® Test Kitchen. This means that each recipe is practical and reliable and meets our high standards of taste appeal. We guarantee your satisfaction with this book for as long as you own it.

table of contents

Better Homes and Gardens
quick-fix
FAMILY FAVORITES

354 EASY RECIPES!

On the cover: Easy Chicken Pot Pie (recipe, page 8)
Photographer: Andy Lyons
Food stylist: Jill Lust

92

110

176

introduction

What's the answer to the weeknight meal hassle? There's no single solution; you may need to use a different strategy every night.

If your family is like most, you have a calendar posted by the phone or on the kitchen wall to track family members' activities. And if your family is like most, that calendar is packed full of things to do and places to go.

It's often tough to get all family members together for a meal and even more difficult to plan and prepare meals when there are countless demands on the cook's time.

We've gathered great-tasting recipes that fit some of the most popular—and practical—weeknight dinner solutions. One night you may have just 20 minutes to put dinner together. Check out pages 6–25 for recipe possibilities. The next day you may prefer to toss meat and vegetables into your slow cooker in the morning and have a savory hot meal waiting when you walk in the door. See the main dishes on pages 92–109. If guests are coming, you may want a selection of appetizers (pages 110–121) or a special but simple entrée such as those on pages 122–135.

In addition to the main-dish recipes, we've included a selection of quick vegetables, side-dish salads, and breads, and another of easy desserts.

In the busy months ahead, make this book your go-to source for great family meals.

Chicken and
Lemon-Broccoli Alfredo

20minute
meals

On weeknights, when every minute of meal *prep time counts,* turn to these recipes. Every one of them is ready for the table *just 20 minutes* after you start to fix dinner.

Chicken and Lemon-Broccoli Alfredo

Start to Finish: 20 minutes

- 4 small skinless, boneless chicken breast halves
  Salt and ground black pepper
- 8 ounces mushrooms, halved
- 1 tablespoon olive oil or cooking oil
- 1 lemon
- 3 cups fresh broccoli florets
- 1 10-ounce container refrigerated light Alfredo pasta sauce
- $1/8$ teaspoon ground black pepper

1. Season chicken with salt and pepper. In a large skillet, cook chicken and mushrooms in hot oil over medium heat for 4 minutes, turning chicken once.

2. Meanwhile, shred 2 teaspoons lemon peel; set aside. Slice lemon. Add broccoli and lemon slices to skillet. Cook, covered, for 8 minutes or until chicken is no longer pink (170°F). Place chicken and vegetables on four plates. Add Alfredo sauce, lemon peel, and $1/8$ teaspoon pepper to skillet; heat through. Serve sauce with chicken. Makes 4 servings.

Per serving: 231 cal., 11 g fat (4 g sat. fat), 20 mg chol., 496 mg sodium, 25 g carbo., 6 g fiber, 12 g pro.

Triple Mango Chicken

Start to Finish: 20 minutes

- 4 small skinless, boneless chicken breast halves
- 1 tablespoon olive oil
- 1 mango, seeded, peeled, and cubed
- $1/2$ cup mango-blend fruit drink
- $1/4$ cup mango chutney
- 2 medium zucchini, thinly sliced lengthwise
  Salt and crushed red pepper

1. In a very large skillet, cook chicken in hot oil over medium heat for 6 minutes. Turn chicken; add mango cubes, mango drink, and chutney. Cook for 4 to 6 minutes more or until chicken is no longer pink (170°F).

2. Meanwhile, place zucchini and $1/4$ cup *water* in a microwave-safe 2-quart dish. Cover with vented plastic wrap. Microwave on 100% power (high) for 2 to 3 minutes, stirring once; drain. Divide zucchini among four plates. Place chicken and mango on top of zucchini. Season with salt and crushed red pepper. Makes 4 servings.

Per serving: 274 cal., 9 g fat (1 g sat. fat), 66 mg chol., 277 mg sodium, 22 g carbo., 2 g fiber, 28 g pro.

> **Is it done yet?** *Cook chicken breasts* until an instant-read thermometer inserted in the center reads 170°F.

Asian Chicken Salad

Start to Finish: 15 minutes

1	10-ounce package torn mixed salad greens
8	ounces cooked chicken, cut into bite-size pieces
1/3	cup bottled Asian vinaigrette salad dressing
1	11-ounce can mandarin orange sections, drained
3	tablespoons sliced almonds, toasted

1. In a large bowl, combine greens and chicken. Add salad dressing; toss to coat. Divide greens mixture among four salad plates. Top with mandarin orange sections and almonds. Serve immediately. Makes 4 servings.

Per serving: 218 cal., 9 g fat (1 g sat. fat), 50 mg chol., 502 mg sodium, 15 g carbo., 2 g fiber, 19 g pro.

Easy Chicken Pot Pie

Start to Finish: 20 minutes   Oven: 450°F

1/2	cup all-purpose flour
1/2	teaspoon ground sage
1/4	teaspoon salt
1/4	teaspoon ground black pepper
12	ounces skinless, boneless chicken breast halves
2	tablespoons cooking oil
2	cups frozen mixed vegetables
1	14-ounce can reduced-sodium chicken broth
1/2	cup milk
1	11.5-ounce package (8) refrigerated corn bread twists
1/2	cup shredded Mexican cheese blend

1. Preheat oven to 450°F. In a large resealable plastic bag, combine flour, sage, salt, and pepper. Cut chicken into bite-size pieces. Add chicken to bag; seal bag and shake to coat.

2. In a skillet, brown chicken over medium-high heat for 2 minutes, stirring to brown evenly (chicken will not be completely cooked). In a colander, run cold water over vegetables to thaw. Add vegetables, broth, and milk to skillet. Bring to boiling, stirring once. Divide chicken mixture among four 16-ounce baking dishes.

3. Separate corn bread twists into 16 pieces. Place four strips over the chicken mixture in each baking dish. Sprinkle with cheese. Bake for 9 to 10 minutes or until corn bread is brown. Makes 4 servings.

Per serving: 612 cal., 25 g fat (7 g sat. fat), 64 mg chol., 1,259 mg sodium, 60 g carbo., 3 g fiber, 34 g pro.

Quick Chicken Fajitas

Start to Finish: 20 minutes   Oven: 350°F

8	7- to 8-inch flour tortillas
1/4	cup bottled Italian salad dressing
2	medium red, yellow, and/or green sweet peppers, cut into bite-size strips
1	medium onion, halved lengthwise and sliced
2	6-ounce packages refrigerated Southwestern-style cooked chicken breast strips
	Bottled salsa, dairy sour cream, guacamole, and/or sliced fresh jalapeño chile peppers*

1. Preheat oven to 350°F. Wrap tortillas in foil. Heat in oven for 10 to 15 minutes or until heated through..

2. In a large skillet, heat 2 tablespoons of the salad dressing over medium-high heat. Add sweet peppers and onion; cook and stir for 2 to 3 minutes or until vegetables are crisp-tender. Add chicken strips and remaining 2 tablespoons salad dressing to skillet; cook and stir for 2 to 3 minutes or until heated through.

3. Spoon the chicken mixture onto warmed tortillas. Top with salsa, sour cream, guacamole, and/or jalapeño peppers. Roll up. Makes 4 servings.

Per serving: 425 cal., 10 g fat (2 g sat. fat), 40 mg chol., 1,232 mg sodium, 58 g carbo., 4 g fiber, 23 g pro.

*Note: Chile peppers contain volatile oils that can burn your skin and eyes; avoid direct contact with them as much as possible. When working with chile peppers, wear plastic or rubber gloves. If your bare hands do touch the peppers, wash your hands and nails well with soap and water.

Creamy Ranch Chicken

Start to Finish: 20 minutes

6	slices bacon
4	skinless, boneless chicken breast halves, cut into bite-size pieces
2	tablespoons all-purpose flour
2	tablespoons ranch dry salad dressing mix
1¼	cups milk
3	cups dried medium noodles
1	tablespoon finely shredded Parmesan cheese

1. Cut bacon into narrow strips. In a large skillet, cook bacon over medium heat until crisp. Drain bacon on paper towels; discard all but 2 tablespoons drippings.

2. In the same skillet, cook chicken in reserved drippings until no longer pink (170°F), turning to brown evenly. Sprinkle flour and salad dressing mix over chicken; stir well. Stir in milk. Cook and stir until thickened and bubbly. Cook and stir 1 minute more. Stir in bacon.

3. Meanwhile, cook noodles according to package directions. Serve chicken mixture with noodles; sprinkle with Parmesan. Makes 4 servings.

Per serving: 488 cal., 18 g fat (7 g sat. fat), 137 mg chol., 574 mg sodium, 27 g carbo., 1 g fiber, 45 g pro.

Turkey Spinach Toss

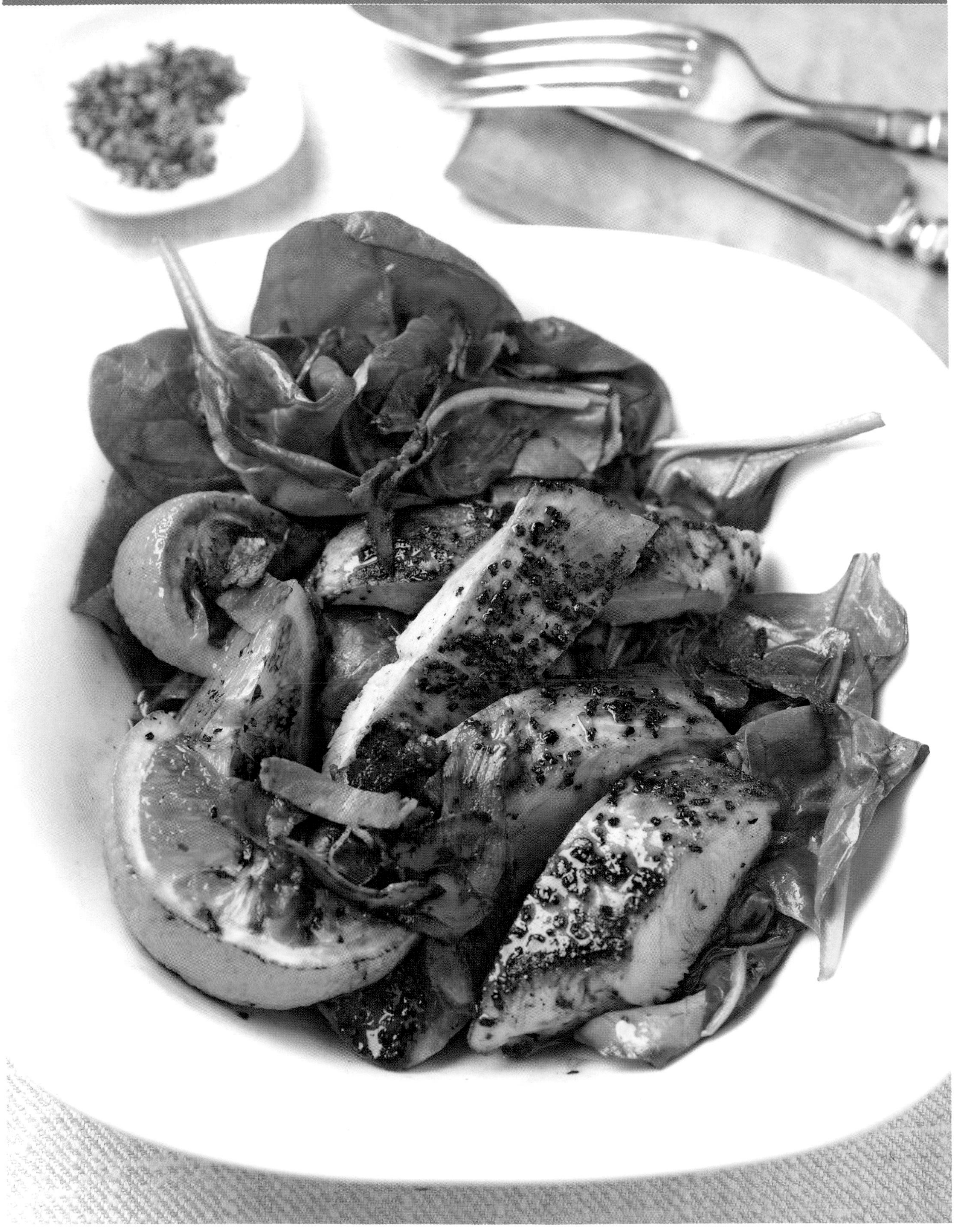

Turkey Spinach Toss

Start to Finish: 20 minutes

2 turkey breast tenderloins, split in half horizontally (about 1 pound)
2 tablespoons butter
2 ounces thinly sliced deli ham
1/2 cup orange juice
2 9- to 10-ounce packages fresh spinach
1 orange, cut into wedges

1. Season turkey with *ground black pepper.* In a very large skillet, cook turkey in hot butter over medium-high heat for 12 minutes or until no longer pink (170°F), turning once. Remove turkey from skillet. Slice into strips; cover and keep warm.

2. Add ham to skillet; cook and stir for 1 minute or until heated and starting to crisp. Remove ham from skillet. Add juice; bring to boiling. Add spinach, half at a time; cook for 1 minute. Add orange wedges with second batch of spinach. Using tongs, remove spinach from skillet; divide among plates. Sprinkle with *salt* and *pepper.* Top with turkey and ham. Drizzle with juices from skillet. Makes 4 servings.

Per serving: 244 cal., 8 g fat (4 g sat. fat), 94 mg chol., 528 mg sodium, 9 g carbo., 3 g fiber, 34 g pro.

Cajun Turkey and Melon Salad

Start to Finish: 18 minutes

2 turkey breast tenderloins, split in half horizontally (about 1 pound)
1 tablespoon olive oil
1 1/2 teaspoons Cajun seasoning
6 cups torn mixed greens
1 1/2 cups sliced cantaloupe
1 cup fresh blueberries
Desired bottled salad dressing

1. Brush turkey pieces with olive oil. Sprinkle with Cajun seasoning. For a charcoal grill, grill turkey on the rack of an uncovered grill directly over medium coals for 12 to 15 minutes or until turkey is no longer pink (170°F), turning once halfway through grilling. (For a gas grill, preheat grill. Reduce heat to medium. Place turkey on grill rack over heat. Cover; grill as above.) Slice turkey into strips.

2. Arrange greens on four plates. Top with turkey, melon, and berries. Pass dressing. Makes 4 servings.

Per serving: 359 cal., 22 g fat (4 g sat. fat), 68 mg chol., 161 mg sodium, 14 g carbo., 3 g fiber, 29 g pro.

Pesto Penne with Roasted Chicken

Start to Finish: 20 minutes

8 ounces dried penne, mostaccioli, or bow tie pasta (4 cups)
2 cups broccoli florets
1 7-ounce container purchased basil pesto
2 1/2 cups bite-size slices purchased roasted chicken or leftover roasted chicken
1 7-ounce jar roasted red sweet peppers, drained and cut into strips
1/4 cup finely shredded Parmesan cheese
Finely shredded Parmesan cheese (optional)
1/2 teaspoon coarsely ground black pepper

1. Cook pasta according to the package directions, adding broccoli for the last 2 minutes of cooking. Drain, reserving 1/2 cup of the pasta water. Return drained pasta and broccoli to the saucepan.

2. In a small bowl, combine pesto and reserved pasta water. Add chicken, roasted red peppers, and pesto mixture to pasta in saucepan. Toss gently to coat. Heat through over medium heat. Add 1/4 cup Parmesan cheese to pasta mixture and toss to combine.

3. Divide pasta among four warm pasta bowls. If desired, top with additional Parmesan cheese. Sprinkle with black pepper. Makes 4 servings.

Per serving: 672 cal., 35 g fat (7 g sat. fat), 93 mg chol., 857 mg sodium, 53 g carbo., 3 g fiber, 37 g pro.

Tequila-Lime Chicken

Start to Finish: 15 minutes

1 9-ounce package refrigerated fettuccine
1 lime
1 10-ounce container refrigerated regular or light Alfredo sauce
1/4 cup tequila or milk
1 9-ounce package refrigerated cooked grilled chicken breast strips

1. Cook the fettuccine according to package directions; drain. Meanwhile, finely shred enough peel from the lime to equal 1 teaspoon. Cut lime into wedges; set aside.

2. In a medium saucepan, heat and stir Alfredo sauce, peel, and tequila just to boiling. Stir in chicken strips; heat through. Toss sauce with hot fettuccine. Serve with lime wedges. Makes 4 servings.

Per serving: 528 cal., 24 g fat (1 g sat. fat), 123 mg chol., 853 mg sodium, 39 g carbo., 2 g fiber, 11 g pro.

Chili Chicken and Pasta

Start to Finish: 20 minutes

- 6 ounces dried angel hair pasta
- 3 fresh ears of sweet corn
- 4 small skinless, boneless chicken breast halves
- 1 1/2 teaspoons chili powder
- 1/4 cup olive oil or cooking oil
- 2 medium tomatoes, sliced
- 3 tablespoons lime or lemon juice

1. Cook pasta and corn in lightly salted boiling water according to pasta package directions. Drain in colander; rinse with cold water.

2. Meanwhile, sprinkle chicken with 1 teaspoon of the chili powder, 1/4 teaspoon *salt,* and 1/4 teaspoon *ground black pepper.* In a large skillet, cook chicken in 1 tablespoon hot oil over medium heat for 8 to 10 minutes or until chicken is no longer pink (170°F), turning once.

3. For dressing, in a screw-top jar, combine remaining 3 tablespoons oil, remaining 1/2 teaspoon chili powder, and lime juice; shake to combine. Cut corn from cob.

4. Divide chicken, corn, tomatoes, and pasta among four dinner plates. Drizzle with dressing; sprinkle lightly with *salt* and *pepper.* Makes 4 servings.

Per serving: 490 cal., 17 g fat (3 g sat. fat), 66 mg chol., 232 mg sodium, 49 g carbo., 4 g fiber, 35 g pro.

Fettuccine with Cherry Tomatoes

Start to Finish: 20 minutes

- 1 9-ounce package refrigerated fettuccine, cut into thirds
- 1/2 cup shredded Parmesan cheese
- 2 tablespoons olive oil or cooking oil
- 1 6- to 9-ounce package refrigerated or frozen Italian-flavor cooked chicken breast strips, thawed if frozen
- 1 pint cherry tomatoes, halved
- 1/2 cup pitted ripe olives, halved
    Salt and freshly ground black pepper

1. In a Dutch oven, cook pasta according to package directions. Drain and return to pan.

2. Add cheese, oil, and chicken to pan. Return to low heat. Toss to coat and heat through. Remove from heat. Add tomatoes and olives. Season with salt and pepper and toss again. Serve immediately. Makes 4 servings.

Per serving: 371 cal., 15 g fat (4 g sat. fat), 76 mg chol., 866 mg sodium, 39 g carbo., 3 g fiber, 22 g pro.

Fettuccine with Cherry Tomatoes

Hearty Italian Stew

Start to Finish: 15 minutes

    1   teaspoon bottled minced garlic
    1   tablespoon olive oil
    2   14.5-ounce cans diced tomatoes with
        basil, garlic, and oregano, undrained
    1   14-ounce can beef broth
1³/₄   cups water
    1   16-ounce package frozen cooked
        Italian-style meatballs
 ¹/₂   of a 16-ounce package frozen yellow,
        green, and red peppers and onion
        stir-fry vegetables
    1   9-ounce package refrigerated
        three-cheese tortellini
 ¹/₂   of a 10-ounce package shredded cabbage
        (about 3 cups)
        Grated Parmesan cheese

1. In a 4- to 5-quart Dutch oven, cook garlic in hot oil over medium heat for 30 seconds. Stir in undrained tomatoes, beef broth, and the water. Add meatballs and frozen pepper blend. Bring mixture to boiling over medium-high heat. Stir in tortellini and cabbage. Cook, covered, for 5 minutes more. Ladle stew into bowls; sprinkle with Parmesan cheese. Makes 6 servings.

Per serving: 459 cal., 23 g fat (10 g sat. fat), 71 mg chol., 1,705 mg sodium, 40 g carbo., 4 g fiber, 23 g pro.

Greek-Style Burgers

Start to Finish: 20 minutes

    4   4-ounce purchased ground beef patties or
        ground turkey patties
        Salt and ground black pepper
 ¹/₃   cup bottled cucumber ranch salad
        dressing
 ¹/₂   cup crumbled feta cheese (2 ounces)
    1   tablespoon snipped fresh mint
    4   lettuce leaves
    4   kaiser rolls, split and toasted
    4   tomato slices

1. Measure thickness of patties; sprinkle patties lightly with salt and pepper. For a charcoal grill, place patties on the greased rack of an uncovered grill. Grill directly over medium coals until done (160°F), turning once. Allow about 10 minutes for ¹/₂-inch patties or 14 to 18 minutes for ³/₄-inch patties, turning once halfway through grilling. (For a gas grill, preheat grill. Reduce heat to medium. Place patties on grill rack over heat. Cover and grill as above.)

2. Meanwhile, for cucumber sauce, in a small bowl, combine salad dressing, feta, and mint.

3. Place lettuce on bottom halves of rolls. Top with patties, tomato, and cucumber sauce. Cover with roll tops. Makes 4 servings.

Per burger: 542 cal., 33 g fat (11 g sat. fat), 88 mg chol., 837 mg sodium, 33 g carbo., 2 g fiber, 29 g pro.

Southwestern Steak Chili

Start to Finish: 20 minutes

    1   cup frozen whole kernel corn, thawed
    1   to 1¹/₂ teaspoons chili powder
    1   tablespoon cooking oil
    1   17-ounce package refrigerated cooked
        beef sirloin tips
    1   16-ounce jar mild or medium thick and
        chunky salsa
    1   14- to 16-ounce can pinto or red beans,
        rinsed and drained
 ¹/₄   cup hickory-flavor barbecue sauce
 ¹/₄   cup dairy sour cream

1. In a large saucepan or Dutch oven, cook corn and chili powder in hot oil over medium heat for 3 minutes, stirring frequently. Stir in beef tips with gravy, salsa, beans, and barbecue sauce. Bring to boiling, stirring occasionally to break up beef slightly. Reduce heat. Simmer, covered, for 5 minutes. Top each serving with a tablespoon of sour cream. Makes 4 servings.

Per serving: 354 cal., 11 g fat (3 g sat. fat), 47 mg chol., 1,834 mg sodium, 42 g carbo., 7 g fiber, 25 g pro.

savvy shopping

Easy meals begin with smart grocery shopping. Look for ingredients that contain the flavor of several ingredients, such as bottled Asian sauces or seasoned canned tomatoes. Keep an eye out for ingredients, such as purchased ground beef patties and refrigerated cooked beef, that let you skip an entire preparation step. These products save time and allow plenty of culinary creativity.

Garlicky Steak and Asparagus

Prep: 15 minutes   Grill: 3 minutes

  1   or 2 large cloves garlic, coarsely chopped
$1/2$ teaspoon cracked or coarsely ground
       black pepper
$1/4$ teaspoon salt
  1   12- to 14-ounce boneless beef top loin
       (strip) steak, cut about $3/4$ inch thick
  8   to 10 thin asparagus spears, trimmed
       (6 ounces)
  2   teaspoons garlic-flavor or regular olive oil
$1/2$ cup beef broth
  1   tablespoon dry white wine
$1/4$ teaspoon Dijon-style mustard

  1. In a small bowl, combine garlic, pepper, and salt. Rub mixture on both sides of steak, pressing in the mixture with your fingers. Place asparagus in a shallow dish and drizzle with oil. For sauce, in a medium skillet, stir together broth and wine. Cook over high heat for 4 to 5 minutes or until mixture is reduced to $1/4$ cup. Whisk in mustard; keep warm.
  2. Preheat an indoor electric grill on high setting, if available. Place steak on grill rack. If using a covered grill, close lid. Grill until steak reaches desired doneness. For a covered grill, allow 3 to 4 minutes for medium-rare (145°F) or 5 to 7 minutes for medium (160°F). For an uncovered grill, allow 6 to 8 minutes for medium-rare or 8 to 10 minutes for medium, turning steak once. If space allows, add asparagus to covered grill for the last 2 to 3 minutes. For an uncovered grill, add asparagus during the last 4 to 5 minutes. For smaller grills, grill steak, then asparagus. Cook asparagus until crisp-tender.
  3. Cut steak in half crosswise. Serve steak with sauce and asparagus. Makes 2 servings.
  Per serving: 458 cal., 32 g fat (11 g sat. fat), 110 mg chol., 549 mg sodium, 3 g carbo., 1 g fiber, 37 g pro.

Ham and Rye Salad

Prep: 10 minutes   Bake: 10 minutes   Oven: 350°F

  6   slices rye bread
  3   tablespoons butter, melted
  1   10-ounce package torn mixed salad greens
       with carrot
  1   8-ounce boneless cooked ham slice, cubed
$2/3$ cup bottled honey-mustard salad dressing

  1. Preheat oven to 350°F. Cut rye bread slices into $3/4$-inch cubes (you should have 4 cups); place in a large bowl. Add melted butter and toss to coat. Arrange bread cubes in an even layer in a shallow baking pan. Bake for 10 to 15 minutes or until toasted, turning once. Cool.
  2. In a large salad bowl, toss together bread cubes, greens, cubed ham, and salad dressing. Makes 4 to 6 servings.
  Per serving: 503 cal., 36 g fat (10 g sat. fat), 65 mg chol., 1,602 mg sodium, 29 g carbo., 4 g fiber, 18 g pro.

Lamb Chops with Tomatoes

Start to Finish: 20 minutes

  8   lamb loin chops, cut 1 inch thick
       Salt and ground black pepper
  1   8.8-ounce pouch cooked long grain rice
  4   medium roma tomatoes, cut up
  4   green onions, cut into 1-inch pieces
  1   tablespoon snipped fresh oregano
  1   tablespoon balsamic vinegar

  1. Season chops with salt and pepper. For a charcoal grill, grill chops on the rack of an uncovered grill directly over medium coals for 12 to 14 minutes for medium-rare (145°F) or 15 to 17 minutes for medium (160°F), turning once halfway through grilling. (For a gas grill, preheat grill. Reduce heat to medium. Place chops on grill rack over heat. Cover; grill as above.)
  2. Meanwhile, microwave rice according to the package directions. In a food processor, combine tomatoes, green onions, and oregano; process with on/off turns until coarsely chopped. Transfer to a bowl; stir in vinegar. Season with additional salt and pepper. On four dinner plates, arrange chops on rice; top with tomato mixture. Makes 4 servings.
  Per serving: 273 cal., 7 g fat (2 g sat. fat), 70 mg chol., 153 mg sodium, 26 g carbo., 3 g fiber, 25 g pro.

When buying lamb chops, look for meat with a *pinkish-red color* and bones that are red, moist, and porous.

Smoked Pork Chops with Curried Fruit

Start to Finish: 20 minutes

- 4 cooked smoked pork chops, cut $3/4$ inch thick
- 1 tablespoon cooking oil
- 1 8-ounce can pineapple chunks (juice pack)
- $1/3$ cup chopped onion (1 small)
- 1 tablespoon butter
- $1^1/2$ teaspoons curry powder
- $3/4$ cup orange juice
- 1 tablespoon cornstarch
- 1 cup fresh cranberries
- 1 11-ounce can mandarin orange sections, drained
- 2 cups hot cooked couscous or basmati rice (optional)

1. Trim fat from meat. In a 12-inch skillet, cook chops in hot oil for 8 to 10 minutes or until hot, turning once.

2. Meanwhile, for sauce, drain pineapple, reserving juice. In a medium saucepan, cook onion in hot butter until tender. Stir in curry powder. Cook and stir for 1 minute. Stir together reserved pineapple juice, orange juice, and cornstarch. Stir into saucepan. Add cranberries. Cook and stir over medium heat until thickened and bubbly. Cook and stir for 2 minutes more. Gently stir in pineapple and mandarin oranges; heat through. Serve sauce over pork chops. If desired, serve with couscous or rice. Makes 4 servings.

Per serving: 422 cal., 20 g fat (7 g sat. fat), 92 mg chol., 2,162 mg sodium, 28 g carbo., 3 g fiber, 33 g pro.

Smoked Pork Chop Skillet

Start to Finish: 20 minutes

- 4 cooked smoked pork chops, cut $3/4$ inch thick
- 1 16-ounce package frozen French-style green beans
- $1/4$ cup water
- $1^1/2$ teaspoons snipped fresh sage or $1/2$ teaspoon dried leaf sage, crushed
- $1/2$ cup balsamic vinegar

1. In a large nonstick skillet, cook chops over medium heat for 3 to 5 minutes on each side or until light brown. Remove from skillet; keep warm. Add beans, the water, and sage to skillet; return chops to skillet. Cook, covered, over medium heat for 5 minutes.

2. Meanwhile, in a small saucepan, boil vinegar gently about 5 minutes or until reduced to $1/4$ cup. Brush chops with vinegar; drizzle remaining vinegar over bean mixture. Makes 6 servings.

Per serving: 363 cal., 15 g fat (5 g sat. fat), 115 mg chol., 2,682 mg sodium, 14 g carbo., 1 g fiber, 38 g pro.

Jerk Pork Chops

Start to Finish: 20 minutes

- 4 boneless pork loin chops, cut $1/2$ inch thick
- 3 tablespoons orange juice or grapefruit juice
- 2 teaspoons Jamaican jerk or steak seasoning
- 1 tablespoon cooking oil
- 2 tablespoons Dijon-style mustard
- $1/3$ cup orange marmalade

1. Brush both sides of pork chops with 1 tablespoon of the orange juice. Sprinkle both sides with seasoning. In a large nonstick skillet, cook chops in hot oil over medium heat for 9 to 11 minutes or until slightly pink in the center, turning once halfway through cooking. Transfer chops to a platter.

2. Remove pan from heat. Stir mustard into pan drippings. Whisk in marmalade and remaining 2 tablespoons orange juice. Return to heat. Cook and stir just until boiling. Pour sauce over chops. Makes 4 servings.

Per serving: 342 cal., 11 g fat (3 g sat. fat), 107 mg chol., 435 mg sodium, 20 g carbo., 0 g fiber, 39 g pro.

Sausage and Orzo

Start to Finish: 16 minutes

1 pound cooked sausage, halved lengthwise and cut into 2-inch pieces
1 tablespoon cooking oil
1 cup dried orzo
1 14-ounce can low-sodium beef broth
1 teaspoon dried Italian seasoning
2 medium zucchini, halved lengthwise and coarsely chopped ($2^1/_2$ cups)
$^1/_4$ cup chopped red sweet pepper
2 green onions cut into 1-inch pieces
   Salt and ground black pepper

1. In a large skillet, brown sausage in hot oil for 2 minutes; stir in orzo. Cook and stir for 1 minute. Stir in broth, $^1/_4$ cup *water*, and seasoning. Bring to boiling; reduce heat. Simmer, covered, for 8 minutes or until orzo is tender. Add zucchini the last 4 minutes of cooking. Stir in sweet pepper and green onions. Season with salt and pepper. Makes 4 servings.

Per serving: 467 cal., 24 g fat (8 g sat. fat), 79 mg chol., 1,630 mg sodium, 40 g carbo., 3 g fiber, 23 g pro.

Tuna-Potato Cakes

Start to Finish: 18 minutes

1 cup packaged refrigerated mashed potatoes with garlic*
1 12-ounce can tuna (water pack), drained and broken into chunks
1/3 cup seasoned fine dry bread crumbs
1/2 cup finely chopped celery
1/4 teaspoon ground black pepper
2 tablespoons cooking oil

1. In a medium bowl, combine potatoes, tuna, bread crumbs, celery, and pepper.

2. In a small skillet, heat oil over medium heat. Drop about 1/3 cup potato mixture into hot oil; flatten into a 1/2-inch patty. Cook for 4 minutes or until bottom is brown. Carefully turn; cook 4 minutes more. Repeat with remaining mixture. Makes 4 servings.

*Test Kitchen Tip: Instead of packaged refrigerated mashed potatoes, use leftover mashed potatoes plus 1/4 teaspoon garlic powder.

Per serving (2 cakes): 267 cal., 14 g fat (2 g sat. fat), 22 mg chol., 621 mg sodium, 16 g carbo., 1 g fiber, 19 g pro.

Quick Cioppino

Start to Finish: 20 minutes

6 ounces fresh or frozen cod fillets
6 ounces fresh or frozen peeled and deveined shrimp
1 medium green sweet pepper, cut into thin bite-size strips
1 large onion, chopped (1 cup)
1 teaspoon bottled minced garlic
1 tablespoon olive oil or cooking oil
2 14.5-ounce cans Italian-style stewed tomatoes, undrained
1/2 cup water
3 tablespoons snipped fresh basil

1. Thaw cod and shrimp, if frozen. Cut cod into 1-inch pieces. Rinse cod and shrimp; pat dry and set aside.

2. In a large saucepan, cook sweet pepper, onion, and garlic in hot oil over medium heat until tender. Stir in undrained tomatoes and the water. Bring to boiling. Stir in cod and shrimp. Return to boiling; reduce heat. Simmer, covered, for 2 to 3 minutes or until the cod flakes easily and shrimp are opaque. Stir in basil. Makes 4 servings.

Per serving: 222 cal., 6 g fat (1 g sat. fat), 85 mg chol., 538 mg sodium, 19 g carbo., 3 g fiber, 19 g pro.

Tilapia with Ginger-Marinated Cucumbers

Start to Finish: 20 minutes

1/2 cup cider vinegar
1/4 cup packed brown sugar
2 teaspoons grated fresh ginger
1/2 teaspoon salt
2 medium cucumbers, sliced (about 3 1/2 cups)
2 tablespoons coarsely chopped fresh mint
Nonstick cooking spray
4 4-ounce tilapia fillets, 1/2 to 3/4 inch thick
1 6-ounce carton plain yogurt
1 teaspoon packed brown sugar
Lemon peel strips (optional)
Cracked black pepper

1. Preheat the broiler. In a medium bowl, stir together vinegar, 1/4 cup brown sugar, ginger, and salt until sugar dissolves. Set aside 1/4 cup of the mixture. Add cucumbers and half of the mint to remaining mixture; toss to coat and set aside.

2. Rinse fish; pat dry with paper towels. Lightly coat the rack of an unheated broiler pan with cooking spray; add tilapia. Brush the 1/4 cup vinegar mixture over fish. Broil 4 inches from the heat for 4 to 6 minutes or until fish flakes easily when tested with a fork.

3. Meanwhile, in another small bowl, combine yogurt, remaining mint, and 1 teaspoon brown sugar.

4. Use a slotted spoon to place cucumbers on plates. Top with fish and yogurt mixture. Sprinkle with lemon peel strips, if desired, and cracked pepper. Makes 4 servings.

Per serving: 210 cal., 3 g fat (1 g sat. fat), 59 mg chol., 388 mg sodium, 23 g carbo., 0 g fiber, 26 g pro.

fish facts

Fish are marketed in several forms. A fillet, the form usually called for in quick-to-fix recipes such as these, is a boneless piece cut from the side and away from the backbone. Most fillets are skinless, although salmon fillets sometimes are marketed with the skin on. Fillet cooking times are based on their thickness; allow 4 to 6 minutes for each 1/2 inch of thickness.

Salmon in Parchment

Start to Finish: 20 minutes   Oven: 375°F

4	12-inch squares parchment paper
4	skinless salmon fillets (about 1¼ pounds total)
1	tablespoon olive oil or cooking oil
⅛	teaspoon ground black pepper
1	tablespoon snipped fresh mint
1	tablespoon snipped fresh dill or 1 teaspoon dried dillweed
4	thin slices lemon, quartered
1	tablespoon drained capers
	Dill sprigs and/or lemon wedges (optional)

1. Preheat oven to 375°F. Rinse fish; pat dry with paper towels. Place one fish portion in the middle of each parchment square. Drizzle with olive oil and sprinkle with pepper. Top each with mint, dill, lemon pieces, and capers. Bring up two opposite sides of parchment and fold several times over fish. Fold remaining ends of parchment and tuck under. Place fish packets in a shallow baking pan.

2. Bake for 13 to 15 minutes or until fish flakes easily when tested with a fork, carefully opening one packet to test doneness. Carefully open each packet to serve. If desired, garnish with fresh dill sprigs and/or lemon wedges. Makes 4 servings.

Per serving: 292 cal., 19 g fat (4 g sat. fat), 84 mg chol., 148 mg sodium, 1 g carbo., 0 g fiber, 28 g pro.

Fish Fillets with Salsa Verde

Start to Finish: 20 minutes

1	pound fresh or frozen cod or orange roughy fillets
1	tablespoon lime juice
1	tablespoon olive oil
$^1/_8$	teaspoon salt
$^1/_8$	teaspoon ground black pepper
$^1/_2$	cup bottled salsa verde
3	tablespoons snipped fresh cilantro

1. Thaw fish, if frozen. Rinse fish; pat dry with paper towels. Preheat broiler. In a small bowl, combine lime juice, oil, salt, and pepper. Brush fish with lime juice mixture.

2. Measure thickness of fish. Place fish on the greased unheated rack of a broiler pan. Tuck under any thin edges. Broil 4 inches from heat until fish flakes easily when tested with a fork. (Allow 4 to 6 minutes per $^1/_2$-inch thickness of fish. If fillets are 1 inch or more thick, turn once halfway through broiling.)

3. Meanwhile, stir together salsa verde and 2 tablespoons of the cilantro. Top fish with salsa mixture; sprinkle with remaining 1 tablespoon cilantro. Makes 4 servings.

Per serving: 125 cal., 4 g fat (1 g sat. fat), 42 mg chol., 157 mg sodium, 1 g carbo., 0 g fiber, 20 g pro.

Tilapia with Grape Chutney

Start to Finish: 20 minutes

4	4-ounce fresh or frozen tilapia or sole fillets
	Salt and ground black pepper
2	tablespoons cooking oil
1	cup seedless green grapes, halved
$^1/_2$	cup tropical blend mixed dried fruit bits
$^1/_3$	cup sliced green onions
$^1/_3$	cup apricot spreadable fruit

1. Thaw fish, if frozen. Rinse fish; pat dry with paper towels. Season with salt and pepper.

2. In a 12-inch skillet, cook fish in hot oil over medium-high heat for 3 to 4 minutes or until fish flakes easily when tested with a fork, turning once.

3. Transfer fish to a platter; keep warm. Add grapes, fruit bits, onions, and spreadable fruit to skillet; cook and stir for 2 minutes. Season to taste with salt and pepper. Serve sauce over fish. Makes 4 servings.

Per serving: 305 cal., 9 g fat (1 g sat. fat), 57 mg chol., 208 mg sodium, 37 g carbo., 2 g fiber, 24 g pro.

Cheesy Tuna and Noodles

Start to Finish: 20 minutes

1	12-ounce package dried egg noodles (6 cups)
1	10.75-ounce can condensed cream of celery soup
6	ounces American cheese, cubed, or process Swiss cheese slices, torn
$^1/_2$	cup milk
1	12-ounce can solid white tuna (water pack), drained

1. In a 4-quart Dutch oven, cook noodles according to package directions; drain and set aside. In the same pan, combine soup, cheese, and milk. Cook and stir over medium heat until bubbly. Stir in tuna. Gently stir in cooked noodles; cook 2 to 3 minutes more until heated through. Makes 4 to 6 servings.

Per serving: 645 cal., 23 g fat (11 g sat. fat), 162 mg chol., 1,476 mg sodium, 68 g carbo., 3 g fiber, 40 g pro.

Tuna Salad with Capers

Start to Finish: 20 minutes

$^1/_2$	cup mayonnaise or salad dressing
2	tablespoons capers, drained
2	tablespoons lemon juice
1	tablespoon snipped fresh tarragon
1	teaspoon Cajun seasoning or pepper blend
1	12-ounce can solid white tuna, drained
2	tablespoons milk
1	10-ounce package torn mixed greens (romaine blend) or 8 cups torn romaine
2	cups packaged coleslaw mix
3	small tomatoes, cut into wedges

1. In a small bowl, combine mayonnaise, capers, lemon juice, tarragon, and Cajun seasoning. In a large bowl, flake tuna into large chunks; toss with 3 tablespoons of the mayonnaise mixture. Stir milk into remaining mayonnaise mixture. Divide greens among six plates; top with coleslaw mix, tuna, and tomato wedges. Serve with dressing. Makes 6 servings.

Per serving: 228 cal., 17 g fat (3 g sat. fat), 38 mg chol., 455 mg sodium, 5 g carbo., 2 g fiber, 15 g pro.

Citrus Scallops

Start to Finish: 15 minutes

1	pound fresh or frozen sea scallops
1	medium orange
1	tablespoon olive oil
2	cloves garlic, minced, or 1 teaspoon bottled minced garlic
1/2	teaspoon snipped fresh thyme
	Salt and ground black pepper

1. Thaw scallops, if frozen. Rinse scallops; pat dry with paper towels. Set scallops aside. Finely shred 1 teaspoon peel from the orange. Cut orange in half; squeeze to get 1/3 cup juice.

2. In a large skillet, cook scallops in hot oil over medium-high heat for 2 to 3 minutes or until scallops are opaque, stirring frequently. Transfer scallops to a serving platter; keep warm.

3. For sauce, add garlic to skillet; cook and stir for 30 seconds (add more oil to skillet if necessary). Add orange peel, orange juice, and thyme to skillet. Bring to boiling; reduce heat. Simmer, uncovered, for 1 to 2 minutes or until desired consistency. Season with salt and pepper. Pour over scallops. Makes 4 servings.

Per serving: 142 cal., 4 g fat (1 g sat. fat), 37 mg chol., 218 mg sodium, 5 g carbo., 0 g fiber, 19 g pro.

Saucy Shrimp and Veggies

Start to Finish: 20 minutes

1	12-ounce package peeled fresh baby carrots
8	ounces broccoli, trimmed and cut up (3 cups)
1	pound peeled and deveined medium shrimp
1	cup cherry tomatoes
1	tablespoon cooking oil
1/3	cup honey
2	tablespoons bottled chili-garlic sauce
2	tablespoons orange juice

1. In a large saucepan, cook carrots, covered, in lightly salted boiling water for 5 minutes. Add broccoli; cook for 3 to 4 minutes more or just until vegetables are tender. Drain.

2. Meanwhile, rinse shrimp; pat dry with paper towels. In a large skillet, cook and stir shrimp and tomatoes in hot oil for 3 to 4 minutes or until shrimp are opaque. Transfer to serving platter with vegetables. For sauce, in the skillet, combine honey, chili sauce, and orange juice; heat through. Spoon over shrimp and vegetables. Makes 4 servings.

Per serving: 319 cal., 6 g fat (1 g sat. fat), 172 mg chol., 361 mg sodium, 43 g carbo., 5 g fiber, 26 g pro.

Salsa, Bean, and Cheese Pizza

Start to Finish: 20 minutes   Oven: 425°F

4	6-inch corn tortillas*
4	teaspoons olive oil
1	medium onion, chopped (1/2 cup)
1	fresh jalapeño chile pepper, seeded and finely chopped*
1	clove garlic, minced
1	cup rinsed and drained canned black beans
1	cup chopped, seeded tomato
4	ounces Monterey Jack, cheddar, or mozzarella cheese, shredded (1 cup)
2	tablespoons chopped fresh cilantro

1. Preheat the oven to 425°F. Place tortillas on an ungreased baking sheet. Lightly brush tortillas on both sides with 1 teaspoon of the olive oil. Bake about 3 minutes on each side or until light brown and crisp.

2. Meanwhile, in a large skillet, cook onion, chile pepper, and garlic in the remaining 3 teaspoons oil over medium-high heat until onion is tender. Stir in black beans and tomato; heat through.

3. Sprinkle tortillas with half of the cheese. Spoon bean mixture over cheese. Sprinkle with remaining cheese. Bake about 4 minutes or until cheese melts. Sprinkle with cilantro. Makes 4 servings.

*Test Kitchen Tips: If you prefer, substitute purchased tostada shells for the corn tortillas; reduce the amount of oil to 3 teaspoons and omit Step 1.

When working with chile peppers, wear plastic or rubber gloves. If your bare hands do touch the peppers, wash your hands and nails well with soap and warm water.

Per serving: 231 cal., 11 g fat (4 g sat. fat), 20 mg chol., 496 mg sodium, 25 g carbo., 6 g fiber, 12 g pro.

Ravioli with Zucchini
Start to Finish: 18 minutes

- 1 9-ounce package refrigerated whole wheat cheese-filled ravioli
- 1/2 cup walnuts, coarsely chopped
- 2 tablespoons olive oil
- 2 medium zucchini, halved lengthwise and sliced
- 6 green onions, diagonally sliced 1/4 inch thick
- 1/2 cup milk
- 1 cup finely shredded Parmesan cheese (4 ounces)
- 1/8 teaspoon salt
- 1/8 teaspoon ground black pepper

1. Cook ravioli in boiling salted water for 6 to 8 minutes or until tender; drain.

2. Meanwhile, in a large skillet, cook walnuts in hot oil over medium heat for 2 to 3 minutes; remove with a slotted spoon. Add zucchini and green onion to skillet. Cook and stir for 2 to 3 minutes or until vegetables are crisp-tender.

3. Add pasta, walnuts, milk, and 3/4 cup of the cheese to the pan. Cook and toss for 1 minute. Season with salt and pepper. Transfer to serving bowls; sprinkle with remaining cheese. Makes 4 servings.

Per serving: 466 cal., 29 g fat (9 g sat. fat), 59 mg chol., 859 mg sodium, 33 g carbo., 6 g fiber, 21 g pro.

Noodle Big Bowls with Spinach and Tofu
Start to Finish: 20 minutes

- Nonstick cooking spray
- 1 16-ounce package extra-firm or firm tofu, drained
- 1 7.25-ounce jar hoisin sauce (2/3 cup)
- 4 14-ounce cans chicken broth with roasted garlic*
- 12 ounces dried udon noodles or linguine, broken
- 2 6-ounce packages fresh baby spinach

1. Preheat broiler. Lightly coat the unheated rack of a broiler pan with nonstick cooking spray. Cut the tofu crosswise into six slices and pat dry. Arrange in a single layer on the prepared rack of the broiler pan; brush tops of slices with 3 tablespoons of the hoisin sauce. Broil 4 to 6 inches from heat, without turning, about 8 to 10 minutes or until hoisin is bubbly.

2. Meanwhile, in a 4- to 6-quart Dutch oven, combine chicken broth and remaining hoisin sauce. Bring to boiling. Add noodles and cook according to package directions, adding spinach the last 2 minutes of cooking time. Divide mixture among four large, deep soup bowls.

3. Cut tofu into cubes or strips; serve on top of noodle mixture. Makes 6 servings.

*Test Kitchen Tip: You may substitute four 14-ounce cans reduced-sodium chicken broth and 1 tablespoon bottled minced roasted garlic.

Per serving: 340 cal., 6 g fat (1 g sat. fat), 3 mg chol., 1,573 mg sodium, 55 g carbo., 4 g fiber, 16 g pro.

a word about tofu

> Before cooking tofu (bean curd), drain, slice or cube it, and blot with paper towels to remove excess water. This allows marinades and seasoning mixtures to be better absorbed. Choose *extra-firm* tofu for broiling, frying, or crumbling. *Firm* tofu is good for frying and sautéing but retains some delicacy that extra-firm lacks. Marinated, ready-to-use tofu also is available.

Skillet Pot Roast with Mushrooms and Cherries

open a
package

Grab a package of frozen hash browns, cooked shrimp, or meatballs; refrigerated cooked beef or polenta; filled pasta; or a roasted chicken and you can have *dinner on the table in a snap.*

Skillet Pot Roast with Mushrooms and Cherries
Start to Finish: 30 minutes

1   12-ounce package frozen unsweetened pitted dark sweet cherries
8   ounces fresh button mushrooms, halved
1   medium red sweet pepper, cut into strips
1   large onion, chopped (1 cup)
2   teaspoons dried sage or thyme, crushed
1   tablespoon olive oil or cooking oil
2   16- to 17-ounce packages refrigerated cooked beef pot roast with juices
2   tablespoons balsamic vinegar

1. Place frozen cherries in a colander. Run cold water over cherries to partially thaw. Set aside; drain well.

2. In a 12-inch skillet, cook mushrooms, sweet pepper, onion, and 1 tablespoon fresh herb or all of dried herb in hot oil over medium heat about 7 minutes or until tender. Add pot roasts and juices, cherries, and balsamic vinegar to skillet. Bring to boiling; reduce heat. Simmer, uncovered, for 10 minutes or until heated through and juices thicken slightly, stirring occasionally. Sprinkle with remaining fresh herb; stir to combine. Makes 4 to 6 servings.

Per serving: 420 cal., 17 g fat (5 g sat. fat), 104 mg chol., 1,174 mg sodium, 31 g carbo., 3 g fiber, 40 g pro.

Beef Tips with Cornichons
Start to Finish: 35 minutes

$\frac{1}{2}$ cup chopped onion (1 medium)
1   teaspoon bottled minced garlic (2 cloves)
1   tablespoon cooking oil
$\frac{1}{4}$ cup dry white wine
1   17-ounce package refrigerated cooked beef tips with gravy
$\frac{1}{3}$ cup cornichons,* sliced lengthwise
$\frac{1}{2}$ teaspoon dried tarragon, crushed
$\frac{1}{2}$ cup dairy sour cream
    Hot cooked noodles or rice

1. In a large skillet, cook and stir onion and garlic in hot oil over medium heat until onion is tender. Add white wine. Bring to boiling; reduce heat. Simmer, uncovered, until reduced by half.

2. Add beef tips with gravy, cornichons, and tarragon to skillet; cook until heated through. Stir in sour cream. Serve immediately over hot cooked noodles or rice. Makes 4 servings.

*Note: Look for cornichons (small sour pickles) with other pickles at your supermarket or food specialty store.

Per serving: 347 cal., 16 g fat (6 g sat. fat), 84 mg chol., 828 mg sodium, 28 g carbo., 2 g fiber, 22 g pro.

Beef Ragout

Start to Finish: 25 minutes

- 10 ounces dried wide egg noodles
- 1 17-ounce package refrigerated cooked beef tips with gravy
- 1 10.75-ounce can condensed cheddar cheese soup
- 1 9-ounce package frozen Italian-style green beans
- 1 4.5-ounce jar (drained weight) whole mushrooms, drained
- ½ cup water
- 3 tablespoons tomato paste
- 2 tablespoons dried minced onion
- ½ cup dairy sour cream

1. Prepare noodles according to package directions. Drain and keep warm.

2. Meanwhile, in a 4-quart Dutch oven, combine beef tips with gravy, soup, green beans, mushrooms, the water, tomato paste, and dried minced onion. Bring to boiling; reduce heat. Simmer, covered, for 10 to 15 minutes or until green beans are crisp-tender, stirring occasionally. Stir in sour cream; cook for 2 to 3 minutes more or until heated through (do not boil). Serve over hot cooked noodles. Makes 6 servings.

Per serving: 378 cal., 13 g fat (5 g sat. fat), 90 mg chol., 954 mg sodium, 49 g carbo., 4 g fiber, 22 g pro.

Beef Roast with Vegetables

Start to Finish: 35 minutes

- 1 17-ounce package refrigerated cooked beef roast au jus
- 1½ cups packaged peeled baby carrots
- 8 ounces tiny new potatoes, quartered
- 2 stalks celery, cut into 1-inch pieces
- ¼ cup water
- ½ teaspoon dried thyme, crushed
- ½ teaspoon garlic pepper seasoning

1. Transfer liquid from beef roast package to a large skillet. Cut any large carrots in half lengthwise. Add carrots, potatoes, celery, and the water to skillet. Place beef roast on top of vegetables. Sprinkle thyme and garlic pepper seasoning over all. Bring to boiling; reduce heat. Simmer, covered, about 20 minutes or until vegetables are tender and meat is heated through. Makes 4 servings.

Per serving: 239 cal., 9 g fat (4 g sat. fat), 64 mg chol., 591 mg sodium, 18 g carbo., 3 g fiber, 25 g pro.

Southwestern Pot Roast

Start to Finish: 25 minutes

- 1 16- or 17-ounce package refrigerated cooked beef pot roast with juices
- 1½ cups sliced fresh mushrooms
- 1 cup bottled picante sauce
- 1 14-ounce can chicken broth
- 1 cup quick-cooking couscous
- 2 tablespoons snipped fresh cilantro

1. Transfer liquid from pot roast package to a large skillet; add mushrooms and picante sauce. Cut pot roast into 1- to 1½-inch pieces; add to skillet. Bring to boiling; reduce heat. Simmer, covered, for 10 minutes.

2. Meanwhile, in a medium saucepan, bring broth to boiling. Stir in couscous; cover and remove from heat. Let stand about 5 minutes or until liquid is absorbed. Fluff couscous with a fork. Stir in cilantro.

3. Place couscous mixture on serving platter. Spoon pot roast mixture over couscous mixture. Serve immediately. Makes 4 servings.

Per serving: 479 cal., 13 g fat (4 g sat. fat), 120 mg chol., 1,000 mg sodium, 43 g carbo., 3 g fiber, 46 g pro.

Simple Beef and Noodles

Prep: 15 minutes   Cook: 20 minutes

- 1 17-ounce package refrigerated cooked beef tips with gravy
- ½ teaspoon dried basil, crushed
- ¼ teaspoon ground black pepper
- 1 10.75-ounce can condensed golden mushroom soup
- ½ cup beef broth
- 1½ cups sliced fresh mushrooms
- 1 cup packaged peeled baby carrots, halved lengthwise
- 1 cup loose-pack frozen small whole onions
- 12 ounces dried wide egg noodles

1. In a large saucepan, combine beef tips with gravy, basil, and pepper. Stir in soup and broth. Bring to boiling. Add mushrooms, carrots, and onions. Return to boiling; reduce heat to low. Simmer, covered, for 20 to 25 minutes or until vegetables are tender, stirring frequently.

2. Meanwhile, cook noodles according to package directions; drain. Serve meat mixture over noodles. Makes 6 servings.

Per serving: 364 cal., 8 g fat (2 g sat. fat), 87 mg chol., 903 mg sodium, 51 g carbo., 4 g fiber, 22 g pro.

Easy Shepherd's Pie

Prep: 20 minutes   Bake: 20 minutes
Stand: 10 minutes   Oven: 375°F

1   17-ounce package refrigerated cooked beef tips with gravy
2   cups frozen mixed vegetables
1   11-ounce can condensed tomato bisque soup
1   tablespoon Worcestershire sauce
1   teaspoon dried minced onion
½   teaspoon dried thyme, crushed
⅛   teaspoon ground black pepper
1   24-ounce package refrigerated mashed potatoes
½   cup shredded cheddar cheese (2 ounces)

1. Preheat oven to 375°F. Lightly grease four 16-ounce individual casserole dishes or a 2-quart square baking dish; set aside. In a large saucepan, combine beef tips with gravy, vegetables, soup, Worcestershire sauce, onion, thyme, and pepper. Bring to boiling over medium heat, stirring occasionally. Transfer mixture to prepared baking dishes or dish.

2. In a large bowl, stir potatoes until nearly smooth. Spoon a mound of potatoes onto each individual dish or spoon into six mounds on top of meat mixture in square baking dish.

3. Bake, uncovered, for 20 to 25 minutes or until bubbly around edges. Sprinkle with cheese. Let stand for 10 minutes before serving. Makes 4 servings.

Per serving: 463 cal., 16 g fat (6 g sat. fat), 65 mg chol., 1,624 mg sodium, 53 g carbo., 6 g fiber, 28 g pro.

easiest-ever beef

When you want a hearty beef dish with slow-simmered flavor but are short on time, open a package of refrigerated cooked beef. Beef roast au jus, beef tips with gravy, and beef pot roast with juices are ready to heat and eat right from the package. They can be the start of a bounty of easy, great-tasting beef dinners.

Linguine with Garlic Shrimp

Start to Finish: 25 minutes

- 8 ounces refrigerated linguine or fettuccine
- ½ cup chicken broth
- 2 teaspoons cornstarch
- 1 tablespoon snipped fresh basil or ½ teaspoon dried basil, crushed
- 2 cups sliced fresh mushrooms
- 1 cup chopped yellow or green sweet pepper
- 2 tablespoons bottled minced garlic
- 1 tablespoon olive oil
- 1 14.5 ounce can Italian-style stewed tomatoes, undrained
- 8 ounces frozen peeled, cooked shrimp, thawed
- ¼ cup finely shredded Parmesan cheese (1 ounce)
- Fresh basil leaves (optional)

1. Cook pasta according to package directions; drain and keep warm. In a small bowl, combine chicken broth, cornstarch, and basil; set aside.

2. Meanwhile, in a large skillet, cook mushrooms, sweet pepper, and garlic in hot oil about 3 minutes or until pepper is just tender. Add broth mixture and undrained tomatoes; cook and stir until bubbly. Add shrimp; simmer, covered about 2 minutes or until heated through.

3. To serve, spoon shrimp mixture over pasta. Top with Parmesan cheese. If desired, garnish with fresh basil leaves. Makes 4 servings.

Per serving: 420 cal., 9 g fat (2 g sat. fat), 92 mg chol., 482 mg sodium, 59 g carbo., 3 g fiber, 25 g pro.

Shortcut Shrimp Risotto

Prep: 10 minutes   Cook: 26 minutes

- 2 14.5-ounce cans reduced-sodium chicken broth
- 1⅓ cups Arborio rice or short grain white rice
- 1 medium onion, finely chopped (½ cup)
- ¾ teaspoon dried basil, crushed, or 1 tablespoon snipped fresh basil
- 1 12-ounce package frozen peeled, cooked shrimp, thawed
- 1½ cups frozen loose-pack peas, thawed
- ¼ cup grated Parmesan cheese

1. In a large saucepan, combine broth, rice, onion, and, if using, dried basil. Bring mixture to boiling; reduce heat. Simmer, covered, for 18 minutes.

2. Stir in shrimp and peas. Cook, covered, for 3 minutes more (do not lift cover). Stir in fresh basil, if using. Sprinkle with Parmesan cheese. Makes 4 servings.

Per serving: 325 cal., 3 g fat (1 g sat. fat), 171 mg chol., 842 mg sodium, 45 g carbo., 3 g fiber, 29 g pro.

Shrimp Alfredo

Start to Finish: 25 minutes

- 1 cup milk
- ¼ cup butter or margarine
- 2 4.4-ounce packages noodles with Alfredo-style sauce
- 2½ cups thinly sliced zucchini (2 medium)
- 1 12-ounce package frozen peeled, cooked shrimp, thawed

1. In a large saucepan, combine 3 cups *water,* milk, and butter. Bring to boiling. Stir in noodle mix. Return to boiling; reduce heat. Simmer, uncovered, for 5 minutes.

2. Stir in zucchini. Return to a gentle boil; cook, uncovered, about 3 minutes more or until noodles are tender.

3. Gently stir in shrimp. Heat through. Remove from heat; let stand for 3 to 5 minutes or until slightly thickened. Makes 4 servings.

Per serving: 486 cal., 21 g fat (12 g sat. fat), 264 mg chol., 1,279 mg sodium, 44 g carbo., 2 g fiber, 30 g pro.

Shrimp-Artichoke Skillet

Start to Finish: 25 minutes

- 1 14-ounce can artichoke hearts, drained
- ⅓ cup chopped onion (1 small)
- 1 tablespoon butter
- 1 10.75-ounce can condensed golden mushroom soup
- ¾ cup half-and-half or light cream
- ¼ cup dry sherry
- ½ cup shredded Parmesan cheese
- 1 12-ounce package frozen peeled, cooked shrimp, thawed
- 2 cups hot cooked rice

1. Quarter artichoke hearts; set aside. In a large skillet, cook onion in hot butter over medium heat until tender. Add soup, half-and-half, and sherry, stirring until smooth. Add Parmesan cheese; heat and stir until melted.

2. Add artichoke hearts and shrimp; heat through. Serve over hot cooked rice. Makes 4 servings.

Per serving: 422 cal., 14 g fat (8 g sat. fat), 202 mg chol., 1,349 mg sodium, 38 g carbo., 4 g fiber, 28 g pro.

Shrimp and Asparagus Salad
Start to Finish: 20 minutes

- 12   ounces fresh asparagus spears, trimmed
- 6   cups watercress, tough stems removed
- 1   16-ounce package frozen peeled, cooked shrimp with tails, thawed
- 2   cups cherry tomatoes, halved
- ½   cup bottled raspberry or berry vinaigrette salad dressing
    Cracked black pepper
    Cracker bread (optional)

1. In a large skillet, cook asparagus, covered, in a small amount of boiling salted water for 3 minutes or until crisp-tender; drain in a colander. Run under cold water until cool.

2. Divide asparagus among four dinner plates; top with watercress, shrimp, and cherry tomatoes. Drizzle with dressing. Sprinkle with cracked black pepper. If desired, serve wtih cracker bread. Makes 4 servings.

Per serving: 257 cal., 8 g fat (1 g sat. fat), 227 mg chol., 360 mg sodium, 14 g carbo., 2 g fiber, 33 g pro.

Ravioli Skillet Lasagna

Start to Finish: 25 minutes

- 2 **cups purchased chunk-style pasta sauce**
- ⅓ **cup water**
- 1 **9-ounce package refrigerated meat- or cheese-filled ravioli**
- 1 **egg, slightly beaten**
- 1 **15-ounce carton ricotta cheese**
- ¼ **cup grated Romano or Parmesan cheese**
- 1 **10-ounce package frozen chopped spinach, thawed and drained**

Grated Romano or Parmesan cheese

1. In a large skillet, combine pasta sauce and the water. Bring to boiling. Stir in ravioli. Cook, covered, over medium heat about 5 minutes or until ravioli are nearly tender, stirring once to prevent sticking.

2. In a medium bowl, combine egg, ricotta cheese, and ¼ cup Romano cheese. Dot ravioli mixture with spinach. Spoon ricotta mixture on top of spinach. Cook, covered, over low heat about 10 minutes more or until ricotta layer is set and pasta is just tender. Sprinkle with additional grated Romano. Makes 4 servings.

Per serving: 433 cal., 14 g fat (3 g sat. fat), 131 mg chol., 501 mg sodium, 49 g carbo., 3 g fiber, 36 g pro.

Tortellini-Vegetable Chowder

Start to Finish: 30 minutes

2   14.5-ounce cans reduced-sodium chicken broth
1   16-ounce package loose-pack frozen broccoli, cauliflower, and carrots
1   9-ounce package refrigerated cheese- or meat-filled tortellini
2   cups milk
¼   cup all-purpose flour
1   tablespoon snipped fresh basil or 1 teaspoon dried basil, crushed
1   cup shredded process smoked Gouda cheese (4 ounces)
     Ground black pepper (optional)

1. In a large saucepan, combine broth and frozen vegetables. Bring to boiling; add tortellini. Return to boiling; reduce heat. Simmer, uncovered, about 4 minutes or until vegetables are just tender.

2. Meanwhile, in a screw-top jar, combine about half of the milk and all of the flour; cover and shake well. Add to saucepan; add remaining milk and dried basil, if using. Cook and stir until thickened and bubbly. Cook and stir for 1 minute more. Stir in cheese and fresh basil, if using, until cheese melts. If desired, season with pepper. Makes 6 servings.

Per serving: 302 cal., 10 g fat (5 g sat. fat), 41 mg chol., 878 mg sodium, 39 g carbo., 3 g fiber, 17 g pro.

Tortellini Stir-Fry

Start to Finish: 20 minutes

1   9-ounce package refrigerated cheese-filled tortellini
1   16-ounce package fresh cut or frozen stir-fry vegetables (such as broccoli, pea pods, carrots, and celery)
1   tablespoon cooking oil
¾   cup peanut stir-fry sauce
¼   cup chopped dry-roasted cashews

1. Cook tortellini according to package directions. Drain and set aside.

2. In a wok or large skillet, stir-fry vegetables in hot oil over medium-high heat for 3 to 5 minutes (7 to 8 minutes for frozen vegetables) or until crisp-tender. Add pasta and stir-fry sauce; toss gently to coat. Heat through. Sprinkle with cashews; serve immediately. Makes 4 servings.

Per serving: 400 cal., 16 g fat (3 g sat. fat), 30 mg chol., 1,256 mg sodium, 48 g carbo., 4 g fiber, 18 g pro.

Smoked Turkey and Tortellini Salad

Start to Finish: 20 minutes

1   9-ounce package refrigerated cheese-filled tortellini or one 7- to 8-ounce package dried cheese-filled tortellini
1   cup chopped smoked turkey, cooked ham, or cooked chicken
8   cherry tomatoes, quartered
½   cup coarsely chopped green sweet pepper
¼   cup sliced pitted ripe olives (optional)
¼   cup bottled Italian vinaigrette or balsamic vinaigrette salad dressing
     Ground black pepper

1. Cook tortellini according to package directions; drain. Rinse with cold water; drain again.

2. In a large bowl, combine tortellini, turkey, tomatoes, sweet pepper, and, if desired, olives. Drizzle salad dressing over mixture; toss to coat. Season with pepper. Serve immediately. Makes 4 servings.

Per serving: 330 cal., 15 g fat (2 g sat. fat), 20 mg chol., 897 mg sodium, 32 g carbo., 1 g fiber, 17 g pro.

Tortellini and Peas

Start to Finish: 20 minutes

1   9-ounce package refrigerated cheese-filled tortellini or ravioli
1   cup frozen peas
2   tablespoons all-purpose flour
⅛   teaspoon ground black pepper
1   cup half-and-half, light cream, or milk
1   14.5-ounce can diced tomatoes with basil, garlic, and oregano, undrained
     Salt and freshly ground black pepper
2   tablespoons shredded Parmesan cheese

1. Cook tortellini according to package directions, adding peas the last minute of cooking. Drain. Return tortellini mixture to pan; cover to keep warm.

2. Meanwhile, for sauce, in a medium saucepan, stir together flour and ⅛ teaspoon pepper. Gradually stir in half-and-half. Cook and stir over medium heat until thickened and bubbly. Cook and stir for 1 minute more. Gradually stir in undrained tomatoes. Season with additional salt and pepper.

3. Pour sauce over tortellini mixture; toss gently to coat. Sprinkle with Parmesan cheese. Makes 4 servings.

Per serving: 410 cal., 13 g fat (7 g sat. fat), 54 mg chol., 998 mg sodium, 57 g carbo., 4 g fiber, 18 g pro.

Chicken, Goat Cheese, and Greens

Prep: 15 minutes   Bake: 15 minutes   Oven: 350°F

1½   pounds Swiss chard, beet greens, and/or
     mustard greens, trimmed and washed
  1   2- to 2½-pound purchased roasted chicken
  3   tablespoons olive oil
  2   tablespoons lemon juice
  2   tablespoons snipped fresh dill, oregano,
      and/or sage
  ¼   teaspoon sea salt, kosher salt, or salt
  ⅛   teaspoon cracked black pepper
  1   3- to 4-ounce log goat cheese (chèvre),
      sliced into rounds or coarsely crumbled
  ⅛   teaspoon cracked black pepper

1. Preheat oven to 350°F. Reserve one or two small leaves of chard. Tear remaining chard and place in a 3-quart rectangular baking dish. Tie chicken legs together with kitchen string. Place chicken on chard in dish. In a small bowl, combine oil and lemon juice. Drizzle oil mixture over chicken and chard. Sprinkle 1 tablespoon of the snipped herbs over the chicken and chard. Sprinkle salt and ⅛ teaspoon pepper over chard only.

2. Loosely cover baking dish with foil. Bake for 15 to 20 minutes or until chard is tender. Meanwhile, sprinkle cheese with remaining 1 tablespoon snipped herbs and ⅛ teaspoon pepper.

3. Transfer chicken to a serving platter. Place some of the goat cheese on top of chicken. Add reserved chard leaves. Toss cooked chard in dish to evenly coat with cooking liquid. Serve chard and remaining cheese with chicken. Makes 4 servings.

Per serving: 542 cal., 36 g fat (10 g sat. fat), 143 mg chol., 620 mg sodium, 7 g carbo., 3 g fiber, 48 g pro.

Chicken Salad with Orange-Balsamic Vinaigrette

Start to Finish: 25 minutes

  ⅓   cup dried cherries, cranberries,
      blueberries, or currants
  1   2- to 2½-pound purchased roasted
      chicken
  ½   cup bottled balsamic vinaigrette
      salad dressing
  2   tablespoons orange juice
  1   10-ounce package torn romaine lettuce
      or torn mixed greens (8 cups)
  ½   of an 8-ounce package sliced mushrooms

1½   cups fresh or refrigerated grapefruit
     sections, mango slices, and/or
     papaya slices, drained
  2   tablespoons dry roasted shelled
      sunflower seeds

1. In a small bowl, pour enough boiling water over cherries to cover. Let stand for 5 minutes; drain. Meanwhile, remove skin from chicken and discard. Remove chicken meat. Shred enough of the chicken meat to measure 2 cups; set aside. Reserve any remaining chicken for another use.

2. For dressing, in a screw-top jar, combine vinaigrette and orange juice. Cover and shake well.

3. To serve, arrange lettuce on four dinner plates. Top each with mushrooms and grapefruit sections. Arrange chicken in center of each salad. Sprinkle salads with cherries and sunflower seeds. Drizzle dressing over salads. Makes 4 servings.

Per serving: 326 cal., 17 g fat (3 g sat. fat), 62 mg chol., 422 mg sodium, 22 g carbo., 3 g fiber, 24 g pro.

Easy Chicken Tortilla Soup

Prep: 20 minutes   Cook: 15 minutes

  1   2- to 2¼-pound purchased roasted chicken
  2   14-ounce cans chicken broth with
      roasted garlic
  1   15-ounce can chopped tomatoes and
      green chile peppers, undrained
  1   11-ounce can whole kernel corn with sweet
      peppers, drained
  1   small fresh jalapeño chile pepper, seeded
      and finely chopped (see note, page 8)
  1   teaspoon ground cumin
  2   tablespoons snipped fresh cilantro
  1   tablespoon lime juice
      Tortilla chips with lime or regular tortilla
      chips, broken

1. Remove skin from chicken and discard. Remove chicken meat from bones. Shred enough of the chicken meat to measure 2 cups; set aside. Reserve any remaining chicken meat for another use.

2. In a large saucepan, combine broth, undrained tomatoes, corn, jalapeño pepper, and cumin. Bring to boiling; reduce heat. Simmer, covered, for 10 minutes. Stir in shredded chicken, cilantro, and lime juice. Heat through. Top each serving with tortilla chips. Makes 6 servings.

Per serving: 183 cal., 5 g fat (1 g sat. fat), 43 mg chol., 1,080 mg sodium, 18 g carbo., 2 g fiber, 16 g pro.

Spring Greens and Roasted Chicken

Start to Finish: 20 minutes

 1 2- to 2¼-pound purchased roasted chicken, chilled
 1 5-ounce package mixed spring greens salad mix (about 8 cups)
 2 cups fresh sliced strawberries or blueberries
 1 cup crumbled Gorgonzola or blue cheese
 ½ cup honey-roasted cashews or peanuts
 1 lemon, halved
 3 tablespoons olive oil

1. Remove skin from chicken and discard. Remove chicken meat from bones. Shred enough of the chicken meat to measure 3½ cups; set aside. Reserve any remaining chicken meat for another use. Place greens on a platter. Top with chicken, berries, cheese, and nuts. Drizzle with juice from lemon and oil; sprinkle with *salt* and *ground black pepper.* Makes 6 servings.

Per serving: 376 cal., 27 g fat (8 g sat. fat), 81 mg chol., 454 mg sodium, 9 g carbo., 2 g fiber, 27 g pro.

Greek-Style Quesadillas

Prep: 15 minutes   Cook: 8 minutes   Oven: 300°F

 4 7- to 8-inch whole wheat flour tortillas
    Nonstick cooking spray
 1 cup shredded purchased roasted chicken
 ½ cup crumbled feta cheese
 ¼ cup thinly sliced red onion
 ¼ cup chopped cucumber
 ¼ cup grape tomatoes, halved lengthwise
 ¼ cup Kalamata olives, halved
 2 tablespoons Italian (flat-leaf) parsley leaves
 1 tablespoon fresh oregano leaves
 ¼ cup bottled Greek vinaigrette salad dressing

1. Coat one side of each tortilla with cooking spray. Place tortillas, sprayed sides down, on a cutting board. Sprinkle with chicken, cheese, onion, cucumber, tomatoes, olives, parsley, and oregano. Drizzle with dressing. Fold tortillas in half, pressing gently.

2. Heat a large nonstick skillet over medium heat for 1 minute. Cook quesadillas, two at a time, over medium heat for 4 to 6 minutes or until light brown, turning once. Remove quesadillas from skillet; place on a baking sheet. Keep warm in a 300°F oven. Repeat with remaining quesadillas. Cut each quesadilla into three wedges. Makes 4 servings.

Per serving: 340 cal., 21 g fat (6 g sat. fat), 54 mg chol., 1,035 mg sodium, 20 g carbo., 11 g fiber, 19 g pro.

Greek-Style Quesadillas

Meatball Pizza

Prep: 15 minutes   Bake: 10 minutes   Oven: 425°F

1	14-ounce Italian bread shell (such as Boboli)
1	8-ounce can pizza sauce
8	ounces fontina cheese, shredded (2 cups)
1/2	of a 16-ounce package (16 to 18) frozen Italian-style cooked meatballs, thawed and halved
1/4	cup thinly sliced fresh basil
1/4	cup finely shredded Parmesan cheese

1. Preheat oven to 425°F. Place bread shell on an ungreased baking sheet. Spread sauce over bread shell. Sprinkle with 1 cup of the fontina cheese. Top with meatballs and basil. Sprinkle with remaining 1 cup fontina and the Parmesan cheese. Bake about 10 minutes or until heated through and cheese melts. Makes 4 servings.

Per serving: 698 cal., 38 g fat (18 g sat. fat), 110 mg chol., 1,801 mg sodium, 53 g carbo., 5 g fiber, 38 g pro.

German Meatballs with Spaetzle

Prep: 20 minutes   Cook: 15 minutes

1	10.5-ounce package dried spaetzle
1	16-ounce package frozen cooked meatballs
1	14-ounce can beef broth
1	4-ounce can (drained weight) mushroom stems and pieces, drained
1/2	cup chopped onion (1 medium)
1	8-ounce carton dairy sour cream
2	tablespoons all-purpose flour
1/2	to 1 teaspoon caraway seeds
	Snipped fresh parsley (optional)

1. Cook spaetzle according to the package directions; drain well.

2. Meanwhile, in a large saucepan, combine meatballs, beef broth, mushrooms, and onion. Bring to boiling; reduce heat. Simmer, covered, for 15 to 20 minutes or until meatballs are heated through.

3. In a small bowl, combine sour cream, flour, and caraway seeds; stir into meatball mixture. Cook and stir until mixture is thickened and bubbly. Cook and stir for 1 minute more. Spoon meatball mixture over spaetzle. If desired, sprinkle with parsley. Makes 4 to 6 servings.

Per serving: 796 cal., 38 g fat (20 g sat. fat), 122 mg chol., 2,128 mg sodium, 70 g carbo., 7 g fiber, 30 g pro.

Southwestern Meatball Soup

Start to Finish: 30 minutes

2	14-ounce cans reduced-sodium chicken broth
1	cup purchased salsa with chipotle chile peppers or regular salsa
1	cup water
1/2	of a 16-ounce package (16 to 18) frozen cooked meatballs
1/2	cup dried wagon wheel pasta
1	cup frozen whole kernel corn
2	tablespoons snipped fresh cilantro

1. In a large saucepan, combine broth, salsa, and the water. Bring to boiling. Stir in meatballs and pasta. Return to boiling; reduce heat. Simmer, covered, for 15 minutes, stirring occasionally.

2. Stir corn into broth mixture. Simmer, uncovered, for 5 minutes more. Skim off fat. Add cilantro. Makes 4 servings.

Per serving: 286 cal., 16 g fat (7 g sat. fat), 44 mg chol., 1,046 mg sodium, 23 g carbo., 3 g fiber, 14 g pro.

Italian Wedding Salad

Start to Finish: 25 minutes

6	ounces dried orzo
1	16-ounce package frozen Italian-style cooked meatballs, thawed
1/2	cup bottled Italian salad dressing
1	6-ounce package prewashed baby spinach
1	6-ounce jar marinated artichoke hearts, drained and chopped
1/4	cup chopped walnuts, toasted
	Finely shredded Parmesan or Romano cheese (optional)

1. Cook pasta according to the package directions; drain well.

2. Meanwhile, in a 4-quart Dutch oven, combine meatballs and salad dressing. Cook over medium heat until meatballs are heated through, stirring occasionally. Stir in drained pasta, spinach, artichoke hearts, and walnuts. Heat and stir just until spinach is wilted. Season with *salt* and *ground black pepper*. If desired, sprinkle with cheese. Makes 4 servings.

Per serving: 730 cal., 52 g fat (15 g sat. fat), 40 mg chol., 1,383 mg sodium, 48 g carbo., 8 g fiber, 23 g pro.

Cheesy Italian Meatball Casserole

Prep: 30 minutes   Bake: 45 minutes   Oven: 350°F

16	ounces dried ziti or penne
1	26-ounce jar tomato-base pasta sauce
1	16-ounce package frozen Italian-style cooked meatballs, thawed
1	15-ounce can Italian-style tomato sauce
1	15-ounce carton ricotta cheese
½	cup grated Parmesan cheese
2	cups shredded mozzarella cheese (8 ounces)

1. Preheat oven to 350°F. Cook pasta according to package directions; drain. Return to pan. Stir in pasta sauce, meatballs, and tomato sauce. Transfer to an ungreased 3-quart rectangular baking dish. Bake, covered, for 30 minutes.

2. Meanwhile, in a small bowl, combine ricotta cheese and Parmesan cheese. Uncover pasta mixture and spoon ricotta mixture in mounds over pasta mixture. Cover loosely; bake about 10 minutes more or until heated through. Top with mozzarella cheese and bake, uncovered, for 5 minutes more. Makes 8 to 10 servings.

Per serving: 611 cal., 28 g fat (14 g sat. fat), 86 mg chol., 1,441 mg sodium, 57 g carbo., 7 g fiber, 33 g pro.

Meatballs and Greens on Ciabatta

Start to Finish: 15 minutes

⅓	cup extra virgin olive oil
¼	cup lemon juice
1	bunch Italian (flat-leaf) parsley, large stems removed
2	cloves garlic
1	16- to 18-ounce package frozen cooked Italian-style meatballs, thawed
6	ciabatta rolls, split and toasted
½	of a small head romaine, cut up or torn

1. In a food processor or blender, combine oil, lemon juice, parsley, and garlic; cover and process until finely chopped. Add *salt* and *ground black pepper* to taste.

2. Transfer parsley mixture to a large skillet; add meatballs. Heat through, covered, over medium heat, stirring and spooning parsley mixture over meatballs occasionally.

3. Place one ciabatta roll, toasted side up, on each of six plates. Top with romaine. Using a slotted spoon, remove meatballs from skillet; place atop romaine. Drizzle warm parsley mixture over meatballs. Makes 6 servings.

Per serving: 534 cal., 31 g fat (10 g sat. fat), 49 mg chol., 1,002 mg sodium, 43 g carbo., 6 g fiber, 20 g pro.

Shredded Potatoes with Sausage and Apples

Start to Finish: 30 minutes

2	tablespoons olive oil
2	tablespoons butter
½	of a 26-ounce package frozen shredded hash brown potatoes (about 5 cups)
1	tablespoon snipped fresh thyme or 1 teaspoon dried thyme, crushed
¼	teaspoon ground black pepper
6	ounces cooked smoked sausage, coarsely chopped
1	medium apple, such as Golden Delicious, cut into thin wedges

1. In a 10-inch cast-iron or nonstick skillet, heat oil and 1 tablespoon of the butter over medium heat. Add potatoes in an even layer. Cook for 8 minutes, stirring occasionally, until light brown. Stir in half the thyme and the pepper. Using a wide metal spatula, press down firmly. Cook about 8 minutes more or until potatoes are tender.

2. Meanwhile, in a medium skillet, cook sausage and apple in remaining 1 tablespoon butter over medium heat for 10 minutes or until apple is tender, stirring occasionally. Stir in remaining thyme.

3. Unmold potatoes onto serving platter; top with apple mixture. Add salt to taste. Makes 4 servings.

Per serving: 376 cal., 27 g fat (10 g sat. fat), 45 mg chol., 866 mg sodium, 23 g carbo., 2 g fiber, 12 g pro.

Easy Beef Pot Pie

Prep: 15 minutes   Bake: 18 minutes
Stand: 10 minutes   Oven: 400°F

¹/₂ of a 15-ounce package (1 crust) folded
    refrigerated unbaked piecrust
1¹/₂ pounds lean ground beef
2   cups refrigerated loose-pack frozen diced
    hash brown potatoes with onions and
    peppers
2   cups frozen mixed vegetables
1   15-ounce can Italian-style or regular
    tomato sauce
1   14.5-ounce can Italian-style stewed
    tomatoes, undrained
2   teaspoons sesame seeds

1. Preheat oven to 400°F. Let piecrust stand at room temperature while preparing meat mixture.

2. In a large skillet, cook meat until brown. Drain off fat. Stir in potatoes, vegetables, tomato sauce, and undrained stewed tomatoes. Bring to boiling; remove from heat. Meanwhile, unfold piecrust and cut into eight wedges.

3. Spread meat mixture in a 3-quart rectangular baking dish. Place half of the pastry wedges along one long side of the dish, with points toward center, overlapping wedges slightly at the base. Repeat with remaining pastry wedges on the opposite side. Sprinkle with sesame seeds.

4. Bake for 18 to 20 minutes or until pastry is golden brown. Let stand for 10 minutes before serving. Makes 8 servings.

Per serving: 342 cal., 16 g fat (6 g sat. fat), 59 mg chol., 669 mg sodium, 32 g carbo., 3 g fiber, 19 g pro.

Meat and Potato Loaves

Prep: 25 minutes   Bake: 35 minutes   Oven: 350°F

1   egg, beaten
¹/₃ cup fine dry bread crumbs
¹/₄ cup finely chopped onion
¹/₄ cup beef broth
¹/₄ teaspoon salt
¹/₄ teaspoon ground black pepper
1   pound ground beef
1¹/₄ cups frozen shredded hash brown
    potatoes, thawed
1   cup shredded Mexican cheese blend
³/₄ cup chunky salsa

1. Preheat oven to 350°F. In a large bowl, combine egg, bread crumbs, onion, broth, salt, and pepper. Add ground beef; mix well. Divide into four portions.

2. In a medium bowl combine potatoes, ¹/₂ cup of the cheese, and ¹/₄ cup of the salsa. Set aside.

3. On foil, pat each portion of meat mixture into a 5-inch square. Place one-fourth of the potato mixture down the center of each square, leaving a 1-inch border at sides and ends. Shape meat mixture around potato mixture, pressing to seal. Place loaves seam side down in a 13×9×2-inch baking pan.

4. Bake, uncovered, for 30 minutes or until an instant-read thermometer inserted in center registers 160°F. Top with remaining salsa and cheese; bake 5 minutes more. Makes 4 servings.

Per serving: 612 cal., 45 g fat (19 g sat. fat), 166 mg chol., 863 mg sodium, 23 g carbo., 2 g fiber, 27 g pro.

Taco Hash

Start to Finish: 25 minutes

1   pound lean ground beef or pork
2   tablespoons cooking oil
3   cups frozen diced hash brown potatoes with
    onions and peppers
1   16-ounce jar chipotle salsa or desired salsa
1   11-ounce can whole kernel corn with sweet
    peppers, drained
1   cup shredded Mexican cheese blend
    (4 ounces)
2   cups shredded lettuce
1   tomato, chopped (1 cup)

1. In a large skillet, cook meat until brown; transfer to a colander to drain fat.

2. In the same skillet, heat oil over medium heat. Add hash browns, spreading in a single layer. Cook, without stirring, over medium heat for 6 minutes. Stir potatoes; spread in an even layer. Cook, without stirring, for 3 to 4 minutes more or until brown.

3. Stir in ground beef, salsa, and corn. Heat through. Sprinkle with cheese, lettuce, and tomato. Serve from skillet. Makes 4 servings.

Per serving: 588 cal., 34 g fat (13 g sat. fat), 102 mg chol., 1,303 mg sodium, 42 g carbo., 6 g fiber, 33 g pro.

Sausage and Polenta with Balsamic Vinaigrette

Start to Finish: 30 minutes   Oven: 400°F

$\frac{1}{2}$ of a 16-ounce tube refrigerated cooked polenta

1   tablespoon olive oil

4   uncooked sweet Italian sausage links (about 1 pound total), each cut into 4 pieces

$\frac{1}{2}$ cup apple juice

$\frac{1}{4}$ cup balsamic vinegar

2   tablespoons snipped dried tomatoes

1   8-ounce package mixed salad greens

$\frac{1}{4}$ cup pine nuts or slivered almonds, toasted (optional)

1. Preheat oven to 400°F. Cut polenta into $\frac{1}{4}$-inch slices; cut each slice in half. Brush polenta with oil. Arrange in a single layer in a shallow baking pan. Bake about 15 minutes or until light brown, turning once.

2. Meanwhile, in a large skillet, cook sausage over medium heat for 5 minutes, turning to brown evenly. Remove sausage from skillet. Drain off fat; wipe skillet with paper towels.

3. Return sausage to skillet; add apple juice, vinegar, and dried tomatoes. Bring to boiling; reduce heat. Simmer, covered, for 8 to 10 minutes or until sausage is no longer pink (160°F).

4. To serve, divide salad greens among four plates. Arrange polenta slices and sausage pieces next to greens. Drizzle balsamic mixture over all. If desired, sprinkle with nuts. Makes 4 servings.

Per serving: 519 cal., 39 g fat (13 g sat. fat), 86 mg chol., 1,094 mg sodium, 21 g carbo., 2 g fiber, 18 g pro.

Saucy Shrimp over Polenta

Start to Finish: 25 minutes

18 fresh or frozen peeled and deveined, cooked shrimp, tails removed (8 ounces)

1   16-ounce tube refrigerated cooked polenta, cut crosswise into 12 slices

1   tablespoon cooking oil

2   cups frozen whole kernel corn

$1\frac{1}{3}$ cups chopped roma tomatoes (4 medium)

3   tablespoons balsamic vinegar

1   teaspoon dried thyme, crushed

$\frac{1}{2}$ teaspoon ground cumin

$\frac{1}{4}$ teaspoon salt

1. Thaw shrimp, if frozen. Rinse shrimp; pat dry with paper towels. Set aside. In a large skillet, cook polenta slices in hot oil for 5 to 8 minutes or until golden brown, turning once. Transfer to a serving platter; keep warm.

2. In the same skillet, combine corn, tomatoes, balsamic vinegar, thyme, cumin, and salt. Cook and stir about 5 minutes or until heated through. Stir in shrimp. Cook and stir until heated through.

3. Using a slotted spoon, spoon shrimp mixture over polenta slices. Makes 6 servings.

Per serving: 196 cal., 3 g fat (1 g sat. fat), 74 mg chol., 483 mg sodium, 30 g carbo., 4 g fiber, 12 g pro.

Chili with Polenta

Start to Finish: 25 minutes

12 ounces lean ground beef

$\frac{1}{2}$ cup chopped onion

1   15-ounce can hot-style chili beans with chili gravy

1   15-ounce can black beans, rinsed and drained

1   8-ounce can tomato sauce

$\frac{1}{2}$ teaspoon ground cumin

1   16-ounce tube refrigerated cooked polenta, crumbled

$\frac{1}{2}$ cup shredded taco cheese (2 ounces)

    Sliced green onions (optional)

    Dairy sour cream (optional)

1. In a large skillet, cook ground beef and onion until beef is brown. Drain off fat.

2. Stir undrained chili beans, drained black beans, tomato sauce, and cumin into beef mixture in skillet. Bring to boiling. Sprinkle crumbled polenta over beef mixture. Simmer, covered, about 5 minutes or until heated through. Sprinkle with cheese. If desired, sprinkle with green onions and serve with sour cream. Makes 4 servings.

Per serving: 497 cal., 15 g fat (7 g sat. fat), 65 mg chol., 1,464 mg sodium, 58 g carbo., 14 g fiber, 34 g pro.

Creamy Macaroni and Cheese

1dish
meals

Casseroles fit the one-dish meal requirements, but that's just the beginning. Look here for stir-fries, skillet meals, and soups and stews that are entrées and side dishes in one.

Creamy Macaroni and Cheese

Prep: 20 minutes   Bake: 30 minutes
Stand: 10 minutes   Oven: 350°F

- 4 strips bacon
- 1 large sweet onion, thinly sliced
- 6 ounces dried elbow macaroni
- 8 ounces mozzarella cheese, shredded (2 cups)
- 2 to 4 ounces blue cheese, crumbled
- 1 cup half-and-half or light cream
- $\frac{1}{8}$ teaspoon ground black pepper

1. Preheat oven to 350°F. In a large skillet, cook bacon over medium heat until crisp, turning once. Drain bacon on paper towels; crumble. Reserve drippings in skillet.

2. Cook onion in reserved drippings for 5 to 8 minutes or until tender and golden brown. Set aside.

3. Cook macaroni according to package directions. Drain; place in a 1$\frac{1}{2}$-quart casserole. Add crumbled bacon, onion, 1$\frac{1}{2}$ cups of the mozzarella cheese, blue cheese, half-and-half, and pepper. Toss gently to combine.

4. Bake, uncovered, for 20 minutes. Stir gently. Top with remaining mozzarella cheese. Bake for 10 minutes more or until top of casserole is brown and bubbly. Let stand for 10 minutes. Makes 6 servings.

Per serving: 331 cal., 18 g fat (9 g sat. fat), 45 mg chol., 280 mg sodium, 26 g carbo., 1 g fiber, 16 g pro.

Tuna Italiano

Prep: 20 minutes   Cook: 8 minutes

- 1 cup dried penne pasta
- 2 fresh tuna, salmon, or swordfish steaks, cut $\frac{3}{4}$ inch thick (about 12 ounces)
- 1 teaspoon Creole seasoning
- 1 cup sliced fresh mushrooms
- $\frac{1}{3}$ cup dry white wine
- 2 tablespoons purchased basil pesto
- 1 tablespoon lemon juice
- 2 teaspoons drained capers
- 1 tablespoon olive oil or cooking oil

1. In a large saucepan, cook pasta in boiling water for 4 minutes. Drain; set aside. (Pasta will not be tender.)

2. Meanwhile, sprinkle both sides of fish steaks with Creole seasoning; set aside. In a medium bowl, combine pasta, mushrooms, wine, pesto, lemon juice, and capers; set aside.

3. In a large skillet, cook fish in hot oil over medium-high heat for 1 minute; turn and cook for 1 minute more. Reduce heat to medium. Spoon pasta mixture around fish. Bring to boiling; reduce heat. Simmer, covered, over medium heat for 6 to 9 minutes or until fish flakes easily when tested with a fork. Makes 2 servings.

Per serving: 627 cal., 30 g fat (5 g sat. fat), 109 mg chol., 352 mg sodium, 36 g carbo., 2 g fiber, 40 g pro.

No-Bake Tuna-Noodle Casserole

Start to Finish: 20 minutes

    8   ounces dried wagon wheel macaroni
        or medium shell macaroni
  $^{1}/_{4}$ to $^{1}/_{2}$ cup milk
    1   6.5-ounce container or two 4-ounce
        containers light semisoft cheese with
        cucumber and dill or garlic and herb
    1   12.25-ounce can solid white tuna,
        drained and broken into chunks
        Salt and ground black pepper

1. Cook pasta in lightly salted water according to package directions. Drain and return to pan.

2. Add $^{1}/_{4}$ cup of the milk and the cheese to pasta. Cook and stir over medium heat until cheese melts and pasta is coated, adding milk as needed to make a creamy consistency. Gently fold in tuna; heat through. Season with salt and pepper. Makes 4 servings.

Per serving: 417 cal., 10 g fat (7 g sat. fat), 66 mg chol., 552 mg sodium, 45 g carbo., 2 g fiber, 33 g pro.

Mediterranean Pizza Skillet

Prep: 20 minutes   Cook: 10 minutes

    3   medium skinless, boneless chicken
        breast halves, cut into $^{3}/_{4}$-inch pieces
    2   cloves garlic, minced
    2   tablespoons olive oil
    4   roma tomatoes, chopped
    1   14-ounce can artichoke hearts,
        drained and quartered
    1   2.25-ounce can sliced pitted
        ripe olives, drained
  $^{1}/_{2}$ teaspoon dried Italian seasoning, crushed

pasta pointers

Don't skimp on the water when cooking pasta. For 16 ounces of pasta, use 4 to 6 quarts of water in a large pot. Pasta needs to move freely in the boiling water so the pieces don't stick. Cover the pot to bring the water to boiling but cook the pasta uncovered, maintaining a rolling boil. Don't rinse pasta unless you plan to fill or layer it or are making a salad.

  $^{1}/_{4}$ teaspoon freshly ground black pepper
    2   cups romaine, chopped (2 ounces)
    1   cup crumbled feta cheese (4 ounces)
  $^{1}/_{3}$ cup fresh basil leaves, shredded or torn
        Crusty Italian or French bread, sliced

1. In a large skillet, cook and stir chicken and garlic in hot oil over medium-high heat until chicken is brown. Stir in tomatoes, artichokes, olives, seasoning, and pepper. Bring to boiling; reduce heat. Simmer, covered, for 10 minutes or until chicken is no longer pink. Top with lettuce and cheese. Cook, covered, for 1 to 2 minutes more or until lettuce starts to wilt. Sprinkle with basil and serve on or with bread. Makes 4 servings.

Per serving: 395 cal., 17 g fat (6 g sat. fat), 82 mg chol., 1,003 mg sodium, 27 g carbo., 6 g fiber, 33 g pro.

Mama's Amazing Ziti

Prep: 20 minutes   Cook: 25 minutes

    1   pound lean ground beef
    2   cups shredded carrots
    2   10.75-ounce cans reduced-fat and
        reduced-sodium condensed
        tomato soup
  $2^{1}/_{2}$ cups water
    8   ounces dried cut ziti
    2   tablespoons snipped fresh basil or
        2 teaspoons dried basil, crushed
    1   teaspoon onion powder
    1   teaspoon garlic powder
    1   cup shredded part-skim mozzarella
        cheese (4 ounces)
  $^{1}/_{4}$ cup shredded Parmesan cheese
        (1 ounce)

1. In a 4-quart Dutch oven, cook ground beef and carrots over medium heat until meat is brown. Drain off fat. Stir tomato soup, the water, uncooked ziti, dried basil (if using), onion powder, and garlic powder into meat mixture.

2. Bring mixture to boiling; reduce heat. Cook, covered, about 25 minutes or until ziti is tender, stirring occasionally. Stir in fresh basil (if using) and mozzarella cheese. Sprinkle individual servings with Parmesan cheese. Makes 6 servings.

Per serving: 420 cal., 11 g fat (4 g sat. fat), 73 mg chol., 649 mg sodium, 49 g carbo., 2 g fiber, 32 g pro.

Pasta continues to cook, even after draining. That's why it's important to complete the recipe and serve at once.

1. Preheat oven to 375°F. Lightly grease a 3-quart rectangular baking dish; set aside. Cook pasta according to package directions. Drain. In a very large bowl, combine vinaigrette and pasta; toss to coat. Stir in beans, cheese, olives, and tomatoes.

2. Sprinkle ¼ cup of the bread crumbs into prepared dish. Spoon pasta mixture into dish. In a medium bowl, stir together yogurt, milk, Parmesan cheese, and flour until smooth. Pour evenly over pasta mixture. Sprinkle top with remaining ¼ cup bread crumbs.

3. Bake, covered, for 25 minutes. Uncover and bake 10 to 15 minutes more until heated through and top is light brown. Let stand 10 minutes before serving. Makes 8 servings.

Per serving: 425 cal., 15 g fat (6 g sat. fat), 31 mg chol., 1,045 mg sodium, 57 g carbo., 6 g fiber, 19 g pro.

Lemon Chicken Lasagna

Prep: 20 minutes   Bake: 40 minutes
Stand: 20 minutes   Oven: 350°F

    Nonstick cooking spray
1 **16-ounce jar roasted garlic Alfredo sauce**
1 **tablespoon drained capers**
6 **no-boil lasagna noodles**
½ **of a 15-ounce container ricotta cheese**
6 **ounces Fontina cheese or mozzarella cheese, shredded (1½ cups)**
1½ **teaspoons finely shredded lemon peel**
¼ **cup finely shredded Parmesan cheese**
1 **9-ounce package refrigerated or frozen cooked chicken breast strips, thawed**

1. Preheat oven to 350°F. Lightly coat a 2-quart square baking dish with cooking spray; set aside. In a saucepan, combine Alfredo sauce and capers. Bring to boiling over medium heat, stirring occasionally. Spoon ⅓ cup of sauce mixture into prepared dish. Top with two lasagna noodles. In a bowl, stir together ricotta, 1 cup of the Fontina cheese, and 1 teaspoon of the lemon peel. Spoon half the cheese mixture over noodles. Sprinkle with 2 tablespoons Parmesan cheese. Top with half of the chicken. Spoon half the remaining sauce over chicken layer.

2. Top with two more noodles, remaining ricotta mixture, and remaining chicken. Add two more noodles, remaining sauce, and sprinkle with remaining Fontina and Parmesan.

3. Cover with foil. Bake for 40 minutes. Let stand, covered, on a wire rack for 20 minutes before serving. Sprinkle with remaining lemon peel. Makes 6 servings.

Per serving: 529 cal., 34 g fat (19 g sat. fat), 159 mg chol., 1,522 mg sodium, 20 g carbo., 0 g fiber, 35 g pro.

Rotini Bake

Prep: 40 minutes   Bake: 35 minutes
Stand: 10 minutes   Oven: 375°F

12 **ounces dried rotini**
½ **cup bottled balsamic vinaigrette**
1 **15-ounce can cannellini or garbanzo beans, rinsed and drained**
8 **ounces feta cheese, crumbled**
1 **cup coarsely chopped pitted Greek black olives**
1 **pound roma tomatoes, coarsely chopped**
½ **cup seasoned fine dry bread crumbs**
1 **8-ounce carton plain low-fat yogurt**
¾ **cup milk**
⅓ **cup grated Parmesan cheese**
1 **tablespoon all-purpose flour**

Baked Ratatouille-Sausage Penne

Prep: 35 minutes   Bake: 35 minutes   Oven: 350°F

 3 uncooked turkey Italian sausage links
    (12 ounces total)
 4 cloves garlic, minced
 1 teaspoon olive oil
 1 14.5-ounce can no-salt-added diced
    tomatoes, undrained
 3 tablespoons snipped fresh parsley
¼ teaspoon crushed red pepper (optional)
 1 pound eggplant, peeled and cut into
    ½-inch cubes
 6 ounces dried whole wheat penne (about
    2¼ cups)
⅓ cup finely shredded Parmesan cheese
    Snipped fresh parsley (optional)

1. Preheat oven to 350°F. Place sausage links in an unheated skillet with ½ inch of water. Bring to boiling; reduce heat. Simmer, covered, about 15 minutes or until juices run clear; drain off liquid. Cook for 2 to 4 minutes more or until brown, turning occasionally. Remove from heat. When cool enough to handle, cut sausages in half lengthwise; bias-cut into ½-inch slices. Set aside.

2. In a large skillet, cook garlic in hot oil for 1 minute. Stir in undrained tomatoes, 3 tablespoons parsley, and, if desired, crushed red pepper. Bring to boiling. Stir in eggplant. Reduce heat. Simmer, covered, for 15 minutes.

3. Meanwhile, cook pasta according to package directions, cooking it for the minimum time listed; drain. Return pasta to hot pan. Stir in eggplant mixture and sausage. Spoon into a 2-quart baking dish.

4. Bake, covered, about 30 minutes or until heated through. Sprinkle with Parmesan cheese. Uncover; bake about 5 minutes more or until cheese melts. If desired, sprinkle with additional parsley. Makes 6 servings.

Per serving: 251 cal., 8 g fat (2 g sat. fat), 39 mg chol., 559 mg sodium, 30 g carbo., 6 g fiber, 17 g pro.

Ham and Cheese Lasagna

Prep: 1 hour   Bake: 50 minutes
Stand: 20 minutes   Oven: 350°F

 1 large onion, chopped (1 cup)
 4 stalks celery, thinly sliced (2 cups)
 4 carrots, chopped (2 cups)
 2 cloves garlic, minced
 2 tablespoons olive oil
 3 cups sliced crimini mushrooms or other
    small brown mushrooms (8 ounces)
 2 cups cubed cooked ham
 2 cups whipping cream
 1 14.5-ounce can diced tomatoes with basil,
    garlic, and oregano, undrained
½ cup water
¼ cup dry red wine
    Salt and ground black pepper
 1 cup grated Parmesan cheese
1½ cups shredded Swiss cheese
    (6 ounces)
12 no-boil lasagna noodles
    (7 to 8 ounces)

1. Preheat oven to 350°F. For sauce, in a 12-inch skillet or Dutch oven, cook and stir onion, celery, carrots, and garlic in hot oil over medium heat for 10 minutes or until vegetables are just tender. Add mushrooms and ham. Cook, uncovered, for 10 minutes, stirring occasionally. Stir in cream, undrained tomatoes, the water, and wine. Bring to boiling; reduce heat. Simmer, uncovered, for 5 minutes. Season with salt and pepper.

2. Combine Parmesan and Swiss cheese. Spoon 1½ cups of the sauce into a 3-quart rectangular baking dish. Sprinkle with ⅔ cup of the cheese. Top with four lasagna noodles, overlapping as needed. Repeat twice. Spoon on remaining sauce and sprinkle with remaining cheese mixture. Cover tightly with foil. Bake about 50 minutes or until heated through and noodles are tender. Let stand, covered, for 20 minutes before serving. Makes 12 servings.

Per serving: 376 cal., 25 g fat (14 g sat. fat), 86 mg chol., 671 mg sodium, 22 g carbo., 2 g fiber, 15 g pro.

Thai-Style Veggie Pizza

Prep: 20 minutes   Bake: 5 minutes   Oven: 450°F

  1   8-inch Italian bread shell (such as Boboli)
      Nonstick cooking spray
 ½   cup sliced fresh shiitake or button
      mushrooms
 ⅓   cup fresh pea pods, cut into thin strips
  2   tablespoons coarsely shredded carrot
  2   tablespoons sliced green onion
  2   to 3 tablespoons bottled peanut sauce
  1   tablespoon chopped peanuts
      Fresh cilantro leaves

1. Preheat oven to 450°F. Place bread shell on an ungreased baking sheet. Bake for 5 to 7 minutes or until light brown and crisp. Meanwhile, lightly coat an unheated medium nonstick skillet with nonstick cooking spray. Preheat skillet over medium heat. Add mushrooms, pea pods, and carrot; cook about 2 minutes or just until tender. Stir in green onion. Remove from heat.

2. Carefully spread hot bread shell with peanut sauce. Top with hot vegetable mixture; sprinkle with peanuts and cilantro leaves. Cut in half to serve. Makes 2 servings.

Per serving: 283 cal., 10 g fat (3 g sat. fat), 0 mg chol., 634 mg sodium, 40 g carbo., 3 g fiber, 11 g pro.

Ham-Spinach Casserole

Prep: 20 minutes   Bake: 30 minutes   Stand: 5 minutes

  8   ounces dried penne or elbow macaroni
  2   medium onions, cut into thin wedges
  1   teaspoon bottled minced garlic (2 cloves)
  3   tablespoons butter
 ¼   cup all-purpose flour
 ½   teaspoon dried thyme, crushed
 ⅛   teaspoon ground black pepper
  1   14-ounce can chicken broth
1½   cups milk
1½   cups cubed cooked ham
  1   10-ounce package frozen chopped spinach,
      thawed and well drained

1. Preheat oven to 350°F. Cook pasta according to package directions; drain. Rinse with cold water; drain again. Set aside.

2. Meanwhile, in a large saucepan, cook onion and garlic in hot butter over medium heat until tender. Stir in flour, thyme, and pepper. Add chicken broth and milk all at once. Cook and stir until thickened and bubbly. Cook and stir for 1 minute more. Stir in pasta, ham, and spinach. Transfer mixture to an ungreased 2-quart casserole.

3. Bake, covered, for 30 to 35 minutes or until heated through. Let stand for 5 minutes. Stir gently before serving. Makes 6 servings.

Per serving: 340 cal., 12 g fat (6 g sat. fat), 42 mg chol., 863 mg sodium, 40 g carbo., 3 g fiber, 18 g pro.

Campanelle with Peas and Artichokes

Start to Finish: 20 minutes

  8   ounces dried campanelle, radiatore,
      or rotini
  1   cup frozen peas
 ½   cup frozen or canned artichoke hearts,
      (rinse, if canned) coarsely chopped
  2   cloves garlic, minced
 ½   cup chopped fresh tomato
 ½   cup finely shredded Pecorino Romano
      or Parmesan cheese
  1   tablespoon extra virgin olive oil
  2   tablespoons lemon juice
 ⅛   teaspoon ground black pepper
 ¼   cup cooked ham, cut into slivers
      Finely shredded Pecorino Romano or
      Parmesan cheese (optional)

1. Cook pasta according to package directions, adding frozen peas, frozen artichoke hearts (if using), and minced garlic the last 3 minutes of cooking time. Drain, reserving ¼ cup of the pasta water.

2. In a large serving bowl, toss together drained pasta mixture, the pasta water, canned artichoke hearts (if using), tomato, ½ cup Pecorino Romano cheese, olive oil, and pepper. Toss to combine. Sprinkle with ham and, if desired, additional shredded cheese. Makes 4 servings.

Per serving: 341 cal., 9 g fat (3 g sat. fat), 18 mg chol., 314 mg sodium, 50 g carbo., 5 g fiber, 15 g pro.

garlic equivalents

> To substitute bottled minced garlic in a recipe, use ½ teaspoon for each clove of garlic. Or use ⅛ teaspoon dried minced garlic or garlic powder.

Creamy Chicken and Noodles

Start to Finish: 25 minutes

 2   cups frozen stir-fry vegetables (such as
     broccoli, carrots, onion, red pepper, celery,
     water chestnuts, and mushrooms)
 1   10.75-ounce can condensed
     cheddar cheese soup
 ¾   cup milk
 ½   teaspoon dried thyme, crushed
     Several dashes bottled hot pepper sauce
 2   cups cubed cooked chicken
     Hot cooked noodles

1. In a large skillet or saucepan, cook frozen vegetables according to the package directions. Drain, if necessary; set aside.

2. In the same skillet or saucepan, stir together cheddar cheese soup, milk, thyme, and hot pepper sauce. Add chicken and cooked vegetables. Cook and stir over medium heat about 10 minutes or until heated through. Serve over hot cooked noodles. Makes 4 servings.

Per serving: 352 cal., 12 g fat (4 g sat. fat), 102 mg chol., 702 mg sodium, 35 g carbo., 2 g fiber, 29 g pro.

Chicken Thighs and Orzo

Prep: 20 minutes   Cook: 25 minutes

 1   4-ounce package pancetta, chopped, or
     4 slices bacon, chopped
     Olive oil
 6   chicken thighs (about 2¼ pounds), skinned
 2   14.5-ounce cans diced tomatoes with garlic
     and onion, undrained
 1   cup dried orzo
 2   cloves garlic, minced
 1   cup water
 ⅓   cup pitted Kalamata olives
 ¼   cup snipped fresh basil
 1   6-ounce bag prewashed baby
     spinach leaves
 3   ounces goat cheese with basil and
     roasted garlic (about ⅓ cup)

1. In a 5- to 6-quart Dutch oven, cook pancetta until brown. Remove pancetta, reserving 2 tablespoons drippings in pan (add olive oil if necessary to equal 2 tablespoons). Drain pancetta on paper towels; set aside. Cook chicken in drippings about 10 minutes or until light brown, turning to brown evenly; drain off fat. Add undrained tomatoes, orzo, garlic, and the water. Bring to boiling; reduce heat.

2. Simmer, covered, for 25 to 30 minutes or until chicken is no longer pink (180°F) and orzo is tender. If necessary, cook, uncovered, for 2 to 3 minutes or until sauce is desired consistency. Stir in pancetta, olives, and basil; heat through. Divide spinach among six plates. Top each with a thigh, some of the orzo mixture, and some of the cheese. Makes 6 servings.

Per serving: 395 cal., 18 g fat (5 g sat. fat), 77 mg chol., 1,229 mg sodium, 32 g carbo., 2 g fiber, 26 g pro.

Red Beans and Orzo

Start to Finish: 30 minutes

 1   14-ounce can chicken broth
 1   cup water
 1½ cups dried orzo
 ½   cup finely chopped onion
 1   teaspoon dried Italian seasoning,
     crushed
 1   15-ounce can red beans or pinto
     beans, rinsed and drained
 1   large tomato, peeled, seeded, and
     chopped (1 cup)
 4   slices bacon, crisp-cooked and
     crumbled, or ½ cup chopped ham
 ¼   cup snipped fresh Italian (flat-leaf)
     parsley
 ⅓   cup finely shredded Parmesan cheese

1. In a large saucepan, bring chicken broth and the water to boiling. Stir in orzo, onion, and Italian seasoning. Reduce heat. Boil gently, uncovered, for 12 to 15 minutes or until orzo is just tender and liquid is absorbed, stirring frequently.

2. Stir in beans, tomato, bacon, and parsley. Heat through. Top each serving with some of the Parmesan cheese. Makes 4 servings.

Per serving: 363 cal., 6 g fat (2 g sat. fat), 7 mg chol., 800 mg sodium, 59 g carbo., 7 g fiber, 22 g pro.

If you don't have the type of pasta your recipe calls for, you can *substitute another pasta* that's similar in size.

Sesame Orange Beef

Start to Finish: 25 minutes

8 ounces fresh green beans,
  halved crosswise
2 teaspoons sesame seeds
1/2 cup orange juice
2 tablespoons reduced-sodium soy sauce
1 tablespoon toasted sesame oil
1 teaspoon cornstarch
1/2 teaspoon finely shredded orange peel
  Nonstick cooking spray
1/2 cup bias-sliced green onions
1 tablespoon grated fresh ginger
2 cloves garlic, minced
1 teaspoon cooking oil
12 ounces boneless beef sirloin steak,
  thinly sliced
2 cups hot cooked brown rice
2 oranges, peeled and thinly sliced crosswise

1. In a medium saucepan, cook green beans, covered, in a small amount of boiling water for 6 to 8 minutes or until crisp-tender. Drain; set aside.

2. Meanwhile, in a small skillet, cook sesame seeds over medium heat for 1 to 2 minutes or until toasted, watching closely and stirring frequently. Set aside.

3. For sauce, in a small bowl, combine orange juice, soy sauce, sesame oil, cornstarch, and orange peel; set aside.

4. Coat an unheated large nonstick skillet with cooking spray. Heat over medium-high heat. Add green onions, ginger, and garlic; cook and stir for 1 minute. Add green beans; cook and stir for 2 minutes. Remove vegetables from skillet.

5. Carefully add oil to hot skillet. Add beef; cook and stir about 3 minutes or to desired doneness. Remove beef from skillet.

6. Stir sauce; add to skillet. Cook and stir until thickened and bubbly; cook and stir for 2 minutes more. Return meat and vegetables to skillet. Heat through, stirring to coat all ingredients with sauce. Serve over brown rice. Top with orange sections and sprinkle with toasted sesame seeds. Makes 4 servings.

Per serving: 348 cal., 10 g fat (2 g sat. fat), 52 mg chol., 341 mg sodium, 41 g carbo., 6 g fiber, 24 g pro.

Thai Pork Stir-Fry

Prep: 35 minutes   Cook: 9 minutes

2 tablespoons olive oil
1 tablespoon reduced-sodium soy sauce
1/2 teaspoon garlic powder
1/2 teaspoon finely chopped fresh ginger or
  1/4 teaspoon ground ginger
1/2 teaspoon ground black pepper
1/2 teaspoon ground cardamom
1/2 teaspoon chili powder
1 1/2 pounds boneless pork loin, cut into
  bite-size strips
2 cups broccoli florets
1 cup thinly sliced carrots
1 cup cauliflower florets
2 tablespoons white vinegar
1 tablespoon curry powder
2 cups hot cooked brown rice

1. In a very large skillet, combine oil, soy sauce, garlic powder, ginger, pepper, cardamom, and chili powder. Add half of the pork; cook and stir over medium-high heat for 3 minutes. Using a slotted spoon, remove pork from skillet. Repeat with the remaining pork. Return all of the pork to the skillet.

2. Add broccoli, carrots, cauliflower, vinegar, and curry powder to pork mixture. Bring to boiling; reduce heat. Simmer, covered, for 3 to 5 minutes or until vegetables are crisp-tender, stirring occasionally.

3. Serve pork and vegetables over brown rice. Makes 6 servings.

Per serving: 301 cal., 11 g fat (3 g sat. fat), 71 mg chol., 206 mg sodium, 21 g carbo., 3 g fiber, 28 g pro.

stir-frying

Have all the ingredients ready before you begin to cook—stir-frying goes fast once you begin. Heat the oil in the skillet until it's hot enough to sizzle a piece of vegetable. Avoid overloading the skillet; food should fry quickly, not simmer in its own juices. If your recipe calls for more than 12 ounces of meat or chicken, cook half at a time.

Pineapple-Chicken Stir-Fry

Start to Finish: 25 minutes

4	teaspoons cooking oil
1	medium red onion, halved lengthwise and sliced
¼	of a fresh pineapple, peeled, cored, and cut into bite-size pieces
¾	cup thin bite-size strips zucchini
¾	cup trimmed fresh pea pods
12	ounces skinless, boneless chicken breast halves, cut into thin bite-size strips
3	tablespoons bottled stir-fry sauce

1. In a wok or large skillet, heat 2 teaspoons of the oil over medium-high heat. Stir-fry red onion in hot oil for 2 minutes. Add pineapple, zucchini, and pea pods. Stir-fry for 2 minutes more. Remove mixture from wok.

2. Add the remaining 2 teaspoons oil to hot wok. Add chicken. Stir-fry for 2 to 3 minutes or until chicken is no longer pink. Return onion mixture to wok. Add stir-fry sauce. Cook and stir about 1 minute or until heated through. Makes 4 servings.

Per serving: 181 cal., 6 g fat (1 g sat. fat), 49 mg chol., 440 mg sodium, 11 g carbo., 1 g fiber, 21 g pro.

Ginger Beef Stir-Fry

Start to Finish: 25 minutes

- 8 ounces beef top round steak
- ½ cup reduced-sodium beef broth
- 3 tablespoons reduced-sodium soy sauce
- 2½ teaspoons cornstarch
- 2 to 3 teaspoons grated fresh ginger
  Nonstick cooking spray
- 1½ cups sliced fresh mushrooms
- 1 medium carrot, thinly bias-sliced
- 3 cups small broccoli florets or 1 pound
  fresh asparagus spears, trimmed
  and cut into 2-inch pieces
- 1 small red sweet pepper, seeded and
  cut into thin strips (1 cup)
- 1 tablespoon cooking oil
- 2 green onions, bias-sliced into 2-inch pieces
- 2 cups hot cooked brown rice

1. If desired, partially freeze beef for easier slicing. Trim fat from beef. Thinly slice beef across the grain into bite-size strips. Set aside. For sauce, in a small bowl, stir together beef broth, soy sauce, cornstarch, and ginger; set aside.

2. Lightly coat an unheated wok or large nonstick skillet with cooking spray. Preheat over medium-high heat. Add mushrooms and carrot; stir-fry for 2 minutes. Add broccoli and sweet pepper; stir-fry about 2 minutes more or until vegetables are crisp-tender. Remove from wok.

3. Carefully add oil to hot wok. Add beef; stir-fry for 2 to 3 minutes or to desired doneness. Push beef from center of wok. Stir sauce and add to center of wok. Cook and stir until thickened and bubbly.

4. Return vegetables to wok. Add green onions. Stir all ingredients to coat with sauce; heat through. Serve over brown rice. Makes 4 servings.

Per serving: 274 cal., 7 g fat (1 g sat. fat), 32 mg chol., 552 mg sodium, 34 g carbo., 5 g fiber, 20 g pro.

Shredded Pork Roast and Tomato Tacos

Prep: 10 minutes   Cook: 5 minutes

- 1 17-ounce package refrigerated cooked
  pork roast
- 1 10-ounce can diced tomatoes and green
  chiles, undrained
- 2 teaspoons taco seasoning
- 8 taco shells
- ½ cup shredded lettuce
- ½ cup shredded cheddar cheese (2 ounces)
  Dairy sour cream
  Purchased salsa

1. In a large skillet, combine refrigerated pork, undrained tomatoes, and taco seasoning; bring to boiling. Reduce heat; boil gently, uncovered, for 5 minutes. Remove from heat. Using two forks, carefully shred pork.

2. To serve, remove meat and tomatoes from skillet with a slotted spoon. Spoon meat mixture into taco shells. Top with shredded lettuce and cheddar cheese. Serve with sour cream and salsa. Makes 8 servings.

Per serving: 206 cal., 11 g fat (5 g sat. fat), 49 mg chol., 529 mg sodium, 12 g carbo., 2 g fiber, 16 g pro.

Vegetarian Tostadas

Start to Finish: 15 minutes

- ⅔ cup cooked brown rice
- ⅔ cup canned pinto beans, black beans,
  or red beans, rinsed and drained
- 3 cups coarsely shredded mixed greens
  or fresh spinach
- 1 cup chopped tomato
- ¼ cup chopped onion
- 2 tablespoons shredded carrot
- 2 tablespoons sliced pitted ripe olives,
  halved
- 2 tablespoons purchased salsa
- 2 tablespoons light dairy sour cream
- ¼ of a medium avocado, peeled and
  sliced (optional)

1. On each of two plates, layer rice and beans. Top with shredded greens, tomato, onion, carrot, olives, salsa, and sour cream. If desired, garnish with avocado slices. Makes 2 servings.

Per serving: 264 cal., 10 g fat (1 g sat. fat), 0 mg chol., 438 mg sodium, 38 g carbo., 9 g fiber, 10 g pro.

Chipotle Turkey-Stuffed Peppers

Prep: 35 minutes   Bake: 20 minutes + 10 minutes
Stand: 15 minutes   Oven: 425°F/375°F

4	fresh poblano chile peppers or green, red, and/or yellow sweet peppers
12	ounces ground turkey breast or lean ground beef
1$\frac{1}{3}$	cups cooked brown rice
1	cup purchased roasted tomato salsa
$\frac{1}{3}$	cup no-salt-added tomato sauce
1	canned chipotle chile pepper in adobo sauce, drained and finely chopped*
$\frac{1}{4}$	teaspoon salt
$\frac{1}{3}$	cup shredded Monterey Jack cheese with jalapeño chile peppers

1. Preheat oven to 425°F. Place whole poblano peppers on a foil-lined baking sheet. Bake for 20 to 25 minutes or until skins are blistered and dark. (Or broil 4 to 5 inches from heat for 8 to 10 minutes or until skins are blistered and dark, turning peppers occasionally.) Carefully bring the foil up and around the peppers to enclose. Let stand about 15 minutes or until cool enough to handle. Pull the skins off gently and slowly using a paring knife.* Discard skins. Reduce oven temperature to 375°F.

2. Cut a thin lengthwise slice from sides of peppers. Remove pepper stems, seeds, and membranes, keeping peppers intact. Place peppers in a 15x10x1-inch baking pan; set aside.

3. In a large skillet, cook ground turkey over medium heat until brown. Drain off fat. Stir in cooked rice, salsa, tomato sauce, chipotle pepper, and salt; heat through.

4. Divide turkey mixture among peppers, spooning as much into the cavities as possible and mounding the rest on top of and alongside the peppers. Sprinkle with cheese. Bake for 10 to 15 minutes or until cheese melts and turkey mixture is heated through. Makes 4 servings.

*Test Kitchen Tip: Because chile peppers contain volatile oils that can burn your skin and eyes, avoid direct contact with them as much as possible. When working with chile peppers, wear plastic or rubber gloves. If your bare hands do touch the peppers, wash your hands and nails well with soap and warm water.

Per serving: 340 cal., 9 g fat (3 g sat. fat), 45 mg chol., 831 mg sodium, 39 g carbo., 4 g fiber, 28 g pro.

Vegetarian Tostadas

Quick Hamburger Soup

Start to Finish: 45 minutes

8	ounces lean ground beef
8	ounces uncooked ground turkey breast
2	medium onions, finely chopped
2	carrots, coarsely shredded
2	stalks celery, sliced
2	cloves garlic, minced
6	cups reduced-sodium beef broth
2	14.5-ounce cans diced tomatoes, undrained
1	tablespoon snipped fresh sage or
	1 teaspoon dried sage, crushed
2	teaspoons snipped fresh thyme or
	1 teaspoon dried thyme, crushed
1	teaspoon snipped fresh rosemary or
	1/2 teaspoon dried rosemary, crushed
1/4	teaspoon salt
1/4	teaspoon ground black pepper
2	medium potatoes, chopped (2 cups)

1. In a Dutch oven, combine beef, turkey, onions, carrots, celery, and garlic; cook until meat is brown and onion is tender. Drain off fat. Stir beef broth, undrained tomatoes, sage, thyme, rosemary, salt, and pepper into beef mixture. Bring to boiling; stir in potatoes. Reduce heat. Simmer, covered, for 10 to 15 minutes or until vegetables are tender. Makes 12 servings.

Per serving: 103 cal., 2 g fat (1 g sat. fat), 19 mg chol., 418 mg sodium, 10 g carbo., 1 g fiber, 10 g pro.

Vegetable Pasta Soup

Start to Finish: 35 minutes

6	cloves garlic, minced
2	teaspoons olive oil
1 1/2	cups coarsely shredded carrots
1	cup chopped onion (1 large)
1	cup thinly sliced celery (2 stalks)
1	32-ounce box reduced-sodium
	chicken broth
4	cups water
1 1/2	cups dried ditalini
1/4	cup shaved Parmesan cheese
2	tablespoons snipped fresh parsley

1. In a 5- to 6-quart Dutch oven, cook garlic in hot oil over medium heat for 15 seconds. Add carrots, onion, and celery; cook for 5 to 7 minutes or until tender, stirring occasionally. Add chicken broth and the water; bring to boiling. Add pasta; cook, uncovered, for 7 to 8 minutes or until pasta is tender.

2. To serve, top individual servings with Parmesan cheese and parsley. Makes 6 servings.

Per serving: 172 cal., 4 g fat (0 g sat. fat), 2 mg chol., 454 mg sodium, 28 g carbo., 2 g fiber, 8 g pro.

Caribbean Stew with Lime Gremolata

Prep: 25 minutes   Cook: 50 minutes

	Nonstick cooking spray
1	pound lean boneless pork, cut into 1/2-inch cubes
3	medium onions, cut into wedges
1	14-ounce can reduced-sodium chicken broth
1	14.5-ounce can no-salt-added diced tomatoes, undrained
1	8-ounce can no-salt-added tomato sauce
1/4	teaspoon cayenne pepper
2	medium sweet potatoes, peeled, halved lengthwise, and cut into 1/2-inch slices
2	small green, yellow, and/or red sweet peppers, seeded and cut into bite-size strips
1	cup canned black beans, rinsed and drained
3	tablespoons lime juice
	Lime Gremolata
	Lime slices and/or wedges (optional)

1. Coat an unheated 4-quart Dutch oven with nonstick cooking spray. Preheat over medium heat. Add pork to hot Dutch oven; cook and stir until brown. Add onions, chicken broth, undrained tomatoes, tomato sauce, and cayenne pepper. Bring to boiling; reduce heat. Simmer, covered, for 30 minutes.

2. Add sweet potatoes, sweet peppers, and black beans. Return to boiling; reduce heat. Simmer, covered, about 20 minutes more or until vegetables are tender. Stir in lime juice. Top each serving with Lime Gremolata. If desired, garnish with lime slices and/or wedges. Makes 6 servings.

Lime Gremolata: In a small bowl, stir together 1/2 cup snipped fresh parsley, 1 teaspoon finely shredded lime peel, and 1 clove garlic, minced.

Per serving: 231 cal., 4 g fat (1 g sat. fat), 47 mg chol., 433 mg sodium, 29 g carbo., 7 g fiber, 22 g pro.

Seafood and Corn Chowder

Prep: 15 minutes   Cook: 20 minutes

1	**14-ounce can chicken broth**
1	**cup sliced celery (2 stalks)**
1	**cup chopped onion (1 large)**
½	**cup sliced carrot (1 medium)**
1	**14.75-ounce can cream-style corn**
1	**cup whipping cream**
½	**teaspoon snipped fresh thyme** **Few dashes bottled hot pepper sauce**
10	**to 12 ounces cooked or canned lump crabmeat and/or peeled, deveined cooked shrimp**

1. In a medium saucepan, combine broth, celery, onion, and carrot. Bring to boiling; reduce heat. Simmer, covered, about 20 minutes or until vegetables are tender. Set aside; cool slightly.

2. Transfer half of the mixture to a blender or food processor. Cover and blend or process until smooth. Repeat with remaining mixture. Return mixture to saucepan. Stir in corn, whipping cream, thyme, ⅛ teaspoon *ground black pepper,* and hot pepper sauce. Bring to boiling; reduce heat. Stir in crabmeat and/or shrimp; heat through. Makes 4 or 5 servings.

Per serving: 388 cal., 24 g fat (14 g sat. fat), 154 mg chol., 948 mg sodium, 27 g carbo., 3 g fiber, 18 g pro.

Shore Chowder

Prep: 20 minutes   Cook: 9 minutes

¹/₄   cup lime mayonnaise (see tip opposite)

2   cloves garlic, minced

1   14-ounce can reduced-sodium chicken broth

4   small carrots, peeled and cut into thin strips or 1¹/₂ cups packaged fresh carrot strips

1¹/₂   cups purchased puttanesca pasta sauce

1   cup grape tomatoes

1   pound fresh or frozen skinless fish fillets, such as cod, sole, or striped bass, thawed, if frozen, and cut into 2-inch pieces

2   cups fresh baby spinach

Sliced baguette-style French bread or French bread, toasted, if desired

1. Combine lime mayonnaise and garlic; set aside. In a 3-quart microwave-safe bowl, combine broth and carrots. Cover and microwave on 100% power (high) for 4 to 5 minutes or until carrots are crisp-tender, stirring once.

2. Uncover carrot mixture. Stir in puttanesca sauce, tomatoes, and fish. Cover and microwave on high for 3 to 4 minutes or until fish just begins to flake easily, stirring once. Stir in spinach. Ladle fish and vegetables into bowls. To serve, pass mayonnaise mixture and bread slices with chowder. Makes 4 servings.

Per serving: 380 cal., 16 g fat (2 g sat. fat), 64 mg chol., 1,168 mg sodium, 28 g carbo., 5 g fiber, 26 g pro.

Hearty Pork Stew

Prep: 25 minutes   Bake: 50 minutes   Oven: 350°F

1½   pounds lean pork stew meat,
     cut into 1-inch pieces
1   teaspoon dried sage, crushed
1   teaspoon dried mint, crushed
¼   cup butter
8   ounces fresh button mushrooms,
     halved or quartered
2   medium onions, chopped (1 cup)
4   cloves garlic, minced
1   14-ounce can chicken broth
1   bay leaf
1   pound coarsely chopped carrots
3   tablespoons all-purpose flour
1   tablespoon Worcestershire sauce
     Hot cooked noodles

1. Preheat oven to 350°F. Sprinkle pork with sage and mint. In a 12-inch ovenproof skillet, brown pork in 1 tablespoon of the butter over medium-high heat, turning often. Remove pork from skillet. Add mushrooms, onions, and garlic to skillet. Cook and stir until onion is tender. Stir in broth, bay leaf, and browned pork. Bring mixture to boiling. Remove from heat; cover. Place skillet in oven. Bake for 30 minutes. Stir in carrots; bake, covered, for 20 minutes more or until carrots are crisp-tender.

2. In a small saucepan, melt remaining 3 tablespoons butter over medium-low heat. Remove from heat. Stir in flour and Worcestershire sauce. Transfer skillet from oven to stove top; uncover. Stir in flour mixture. Bring pork mixture to boiling over medium heat, stirring occasionally. Reduce heat. Simmer, uncovered, for 2 minutes or until slightly thickened. Remove bay leaf. Serve stew over hot cooked noodles. Makes 6 servings.

Per serving: 409 cal., 16 g fat (8 g sat. fat), 118 mg chol., 504 mg sodium, 36 g carbo., 4 g fiber, 29 g pro.

lime mayonnaise

Look for lime mayonnaise, or *mayonesa con limones*, in Mexican markets. If you are unable to find it, stir ¼ teaspoon finely shredded lime peel into ¼ cup of your favorite regular mayonnaise.

Stuffed Peppers Mole

Start to Finish: 20 minutes

4   small or 2 large sweet peppers
1   8.8-ounce pouch cooked Spanish-style rice
10   to 12 ounces cooked ground beef crumbles
½   cup frozen whole kernel corn
3   tablespoons purchased mole sauce
½   cup shredded cheddar cheese (2 ounces)
2   tablespoons snipped fresh cilantro

1. Cut tops off small peppers or halve large peppers lengthwise. Remove membranes and seeds. In a 4-quart Dutch oven, cook peppers (and tops) in boiling water for 3 minutes. Remove peppers; drain, cut sides down, on paper towels.

2. For filling, in a saucepan, combine rice, beef, corn, mole sauce, and 2 tablespoons *water*. Cook, uncovered, over medium heat until heated through, stirring frequently. Remove from heat; stir in cheese. Place peppers, cut sides up, on platter. Sprinkle with *salt* and *ground black pepper*. Spoon filling into peppers. Sprinkle with cilantro. Place pepper tops on small peppers. Makes 4 servings.

Per serving: 360 cal., 15 g fat (7 g sat. fat), 75 mg chol., 732 mg sodium, 29 g carbo., 3 g fiber, 28 g pro.

Hawaiian Tacos

Start to Finish: 30 minutes

1   pound bulk hot Italian sausage
½   cup chopped onion
2   cloves garlic, minced
     Dash bottled hot pepper sauce
12   taco shells
     Hawaiian Pineapple Salsa
1   cup shredded cheddar cheese (4 ounces)

1. In a large skillet, cook sausage, onion, and garlic until sausage is brown and onion is tender, stirring to break up sausage. Drain off fat. Stir in pepper sauce. Spoon meat mixture into taco shells. Top with Hawaiian Pineapple Salsa and sprinkle with cheese. Makes 6 servings.

Hawaiian Pineapple Salsa: Combine 3 roma tomatoes, seeded and chopped; 1 cup seeded, chopped cucumber; one 8-ounce can pineapple tidbits, drained; ⅓ cup chopped onion; 1 or 2 fresh jalapeño peppers, seeded and chopped; 2 tablespoons snipped fresh cilantro; and 1 tablespoon packed brown sugar. Cover and refrigerate for up to 2 hours. Serve with a slotted spoon.

Per serving: 259 cal., 18 g fat (7 g sat. fat), 39 mg chol., 387 mg sodium, 16 g carbo., 2 g fiber, 9 g pro.

Balsamic Chicken over Greens

5ingredient recipes

Looking for a win-win mealtime situation? Here's your answer. These recipes bring you *shorter* grocery lists, *quicker* preparation, *easier* cleanup, plus *great-tasting* dishes your family will love.

Balsamic Chicken over Greens

Prep: 15 minutes   Marinate: 1 to 4 hours
Grill: 12 minutes

    4   skinless, boneless chicken breast halves
    3/4 cup bottled balsamic vinaigrette salad
        dressing
    3   cloves garlic, minced
    1/4 teaspoon crushed red pepper
    1   8-ounce package torn mixed greens
        (8 cups)

1. Place chicken breast halves in a resealable plastic bag set in a shallow dish. For the marinade, stir together 1/2 cup of the vinaigrette, the garlic, and crushed red pepper. Pour marinade over chicken. Seal bag; turn to coat chicken. Marinate in the refrigerator for 1 to 4 hours, turning bag occasionally.

2. Drain chicken, reserving marinade. Grill chicken on the rack of an uncovered grill directly over medium coals for 12 to 15 minutes or until chicken is no longer pink (170°F), turning once and brushing with the reserved marinade halfway through grilling time. Discard any remaining marinade.

3. Arrange greens on four dinner plates. Cut grilled chicken into strips. Arrange chicken on top of greens. Serve with remaining vinaigrette. Makes 4 servings.

Broiler method: Place chicken on the unheated rack of a broiler pan. Broil 4 to 5 inches from the heat for 12 to 15 minutes or until chicken is no longer pink (170°F), turning once and brushing with the reserved marinade halfway through broiling time. Discard any remaining marinade.

Per serving: 304 cal., 15 g fat (2 g sat. fat), 82 mg chol., 609 mg sodium, 7 g carbo., 1 g fiber, 34 g pro.

Apple-Dijon Chicken

Start to Finish: 30 minutes

 4 large skinless, boneless chicken breast
   halves
   Salt and black ground black pepper
 2 tablespoons butter
 1 medium tart cooking apple
   (such as Granny Smith), thinly sliced
 1/3 cup whipping cream
 2 tablespoons Dijon-style mustard

1. Butterfly each chicken breast half by cutting horizontally from one long side of the breast almost to, but not through, the opposite side. Lay the breast open. Sprinkle both sides of chicken breasts with salt and pepper.

2. In a large skillet, cook chicken breasts, half at a time, in 1 tablespoon of the butter over medium-high heat for 2 to 3 minutes per side or until no longer pink (170F°), turning to brown evenly. Remove from skillet; cover and keep warm.

3. Add remaining 1 tablespoon butter to skillet. Add apple slices; cook and stir for 3 minutes or until tender. Add whipping cream and mustard to skillet. Cook and stir until heated through and thickened slightly. Season with additional salt and pepper. Serve sauce and apples over chicken. Makes 4 servings.

Per serving: 342 cal., 16 g fat (9 g sat. fat), 142 mg chol., 407 mg sodium, 6 g carbo., 1 g fiber, 40 g pro.

Warm Chicken and Wilted Greens

Start to Finish: 25 minutes

 2 cups frozen pepper stir-fry vegetables
 1 9-ounce package frozen chopped,
   cooked chicken breast, thawed
 1/4 cup bottled sesame salad dressing
 6 cups fresh baby spinach and/or
   torn leaf lettuce

1. In a 12-inch skillet, prepare frozen stir-fry vegetables according to package directions. Stir in chicken and salad dressing; heat through. Add spinach. Toss mixture in skillet for 30 to 60 seconds or until spinach is just wilted. Makes 4 servings.

Per serving: 153 cal., 6 g fat (1 g sat. fat), 34 mg chol., 309 mg sodium, 8 g carbo., 2 g fiber, 17 g pro.

Sweet Pepper and Peach Chicken

Start to Finish: 30 minutes

 4 skinless, boneless chicken breast halves
 1 1/2 teaspoons fajita seasoning
 2 tablespoons olive oil or butter
 1 1/2 cups red, yellow, and/or green sweet
   pepper strips
 1 cup frozen peach slices, thawed

1. Sprinkle both sides of chicken breast halves with fajita seasoning. In a large skillet, cook chicken in 1 tablespoon hot oil over medium heat for 8 to 10 minutes or until chicken is no longer pink (170°F), turning occasionally to brown evenly. Remove chicken from skillet; cover and keep warm.

2. Add remaining oil to skillet; add sweet pepper strips. Cook and stir about 3 minutes or until pepper strips are crisp-tender. Gently stir in peach slices. Cook and stir for 1 to 2 minutes more or until heated through. Spoon over chicken. Makes 4 servings.

Per serving: 243 cal., 9 g fat (1 g sat. fat), 82 mg chol., 150 mg sodium, 7 g carbo., 2 g fiber, 33 g pro.

Smoky-Lime Chicken Succotash Skillet

Prep: 20 minutes   Cook: 15 minutes

 1 16-ounce package frozen whole kernel corn
 1 12-ounce package frozen sweet soybeans
   (edamame) or one 16-ounce package frozen
   baby lima beans
 1 3/4 cups water
   Finely shredded peel and juice of 1 lime
 1 2-pound purchased roasted chicken, cut into
   6 to 8 pieces
 1 16-ounce jar chipotle salsa
   Lime wedges (optional)

1. In a very large skillet, combine corn and sweet soybeans; add the water. Bring to boiling; reduce heat. Simmer, uncovered, for 5 to 6 minutes or until edamame is just tender. Add lime peel and lime juice to skillet. Stir until combined. Place chicken pieces atop corn mixture. Pour salsa over all. Cook, covered, over medium heat for 10 minutes or until heated through. If desired, serve with lime wedges. Makes 4 to 6 servings.

Per serving: 621 cal., 28 g fat (7 g sat. fat), 134 mg chol., 823 mg sodium, 41 g carbo., 8 g fiber, 58 g pro.

Turkey Tenderloin with Bean and Corn Salsa

Start to Finish: 25 minutes

2 turkey breast tenderloins, halved
   horizontally (1 pound total)
   Salt and ground black pepper
¼ cup red jalapeño jelly
1¼ cups purchased black bean and corn salsa
2 tablespoons snipped fresh cilantro

1. Preheat broiler. Place turkey on the unheated rack of a broiler pan. Season with salt and pepper. Broil 4 to 5 inches from heat for 5 minutes.

2. Meanwhile, in a small saucepan, melt jelly. Remove 2 tablespoons of the jelly. Turn turkey and brush with the 2 tablespoons jelly. Broil 4 to 6 minutes more or until no longer pink (170°F). Transfer turkey to a serving plate. Spoon remaining jelly over turkey; cover and keep warm.

3. In a small saucepan, heat salsa. Spoon salsa over turkey. Sprinkle with cilantro. Makes 4 servings.

Per serving: 196 cal., 2 g fat (1 g sat. fat), 66 mg chol., 377 mg sodium, 16 g carbo., 1 g fiber, 27 g pro.

Chicken Breasts with Caper Vinaigrette

Prep: 15 minutes   Grill: 12 minutes

¼ cup oil-packed dried tomato strips
4 skinless, boneless chicken breast halves
¼ cup bottled Italian salad dressing
2 tablespoons capers, drained
¼ teaspoon ground black pepper
1 clove garlic, minced

1. Drain tomato strips, reserving oil. Set tomato strips aside. Brush chicken with some of the reserved oil.

2. For a charcoal grill, grill chicken on the rack of an uncovered grill directly over medium coals for 12 to 15 minutes or until chicken is no longer pink (170°F), turning once and brushing with remaining reserved oil halfway through grilling. (For a gas grill, preheat grill. Reduce heat to medium. Place chicken on grill rack over heat. Cover and grill as above.)

3. Meanwhile, for vinaigrette, in a small bowl, whisk together salad dressing, capers, pepper, and garlic.

4. Diagonally slice chicken breasts. Spoon vinaigrette over chicken. Top with tomato strips. Makes 4 servings.

Per serving: 218 cal., 4 g fat (1 g sat. fat), 99 mg chol., 447 mg sodium, 3 g carbo., 1 g fiber, 40 g pro.

speedy burger options

Cranberry-Blue Cheese Burgers

Start to Finish: 15 minutes

6 4-ounce frozen ground beef patties
1 8-ounce carton dairy sour cream
   blue cheese-flavor dip
½ cup dried cranberries
6 kaiser rolls or hamburger buns, split and
   toasted
   Lettuce leaves, tomato slices, onion slices
   (optional)

1. Cook patties according to package directions. Meanwhile stir together dip and dried cranberries.

2. Place each patty on the bottom of a bun. Top with dip mixture, and if desired, lettuce, tomato, and/or onion slices. Cover with bun tops. Makes 6 burgers.

Per burger: 698 cal., 49 g total fat (20 g sat. fat), 95 mg chol., 702 mg sodium, 39 g carbo., 1 g fiber, 24 g pro.

Mexican-Style Burgers: Prepare as directed above, except substitute Mexican-style dip for the blue cheese-flavor dip and 2 to 3 tablespoons chopped, sliced pickled jalapeños for the dried cranberries.

Per burger: 554 cal., 36 g total fat (20 g sat. fat), 103 mg chol., 644 mg sodium, 33 g carbo., 1 g fiber, 23 g pro.

Broccoli Slaw Burgers: Prepare as directed above, except substitute chive-style or chive and onion-style dip for the blue cheese-flavor dip and ½ cup packaged shredded broccoli (broccoli slaw mix) for the dried cranberries.

Per burger: 568 cal., 36 g total fat (20 g sat. fat), 103 mg chol., 552 mg sodium, 33 g carbo., 1 g fiber, 24 g pro.

Double Onion Burgers: Prepare as directed above, except substitute French onion dip for the blue cheese-flavor dip and ½ cup sliced green onions for the dried cranberries.

Per burger: 560 cal., 35 g total fat (20 g sat. fat), 76 mg chol., 632 mg sodium, 34 g carbo., 2 g fiber, 24 g pro.

Ham and Cheese Calzones
Prep: 15 minutes   Bake: 15 minutes
Stand: 5 minutes   Oven: 400°F

1   13.8-ounce package refrigerated pizza
    dough (for 1 crust)
1/4 cup coarse-grain mustard
6   ounces sliced Swiss or provolone cheese
1 1/2 cups cubed cooked ham (8 ounces)
1/2 teaspoon caraway seeds

1. Preheat oven to 400°F. Line a baking sheet with foil; lightly grease foil. Set aside.

2. Unroll pizza dough. On a lightly floured surface, roll or pat dough into a 15x10-inch rectangle. Cut dough in half crosswise and lengthwise to make four rectangles. Spread mustard over rectangles. Divide half of the cheese among rectangles, placing cheese on half of each rectangle and cutting or tearing to fit as necessary. Top with ham and sprinkle with caraway seeds. Top with remaining cheese. Brush edges with water. For each calzone, fold dough over filling to opposite edge, stretching slightly if necessary. Seal edges with the tines of a fork. Place calzones on prepared baking sheet. Prick tops to allow steam to escape.

3. Bake about 15 minutes or until golden. Let stand for 5 minutes before serving. Makes 4 servings.

Per serving: 421 cal., 21 g fat (10 g sat. fat), 72 mg chol., 1,390 mg sodium, 28 g carbo., 1 g fiber, 30 g pro.

Lamb Chops with Cranberry Relish
Prep: 15 minutes   Broil: 10 minutes

1/2 cup purchased cranberry-orange relish
1/4 cup chopped pecans, toasted
2   tablespoons orange juice
2   teaspoons snipped fresh rosemary or
    1/2 teaspoon dried rosemary, crushed
8   lamb loin chops, cut 3/4 inch thick
    Salt and black ground black pepper

1. Preheat broiler. In a small bowl, combine cranberry-orange relish, pecans, orange juice, and rosemary. Set aside. Trim fat from chops. Place chops on the unheated rack of a broiler pan. Season generously with salt and pepper. Broil chops 3 to 4 inches from the heat for 9 to 11 minutes for medium doneness (160°F), turning once. Spread relish mixture over chops. Broil for 1 minute more. Makes 4 servings.

Per serving: 325 cal., 13 g fat (3 g sat. fat), 100 mg chol., 245 mg sodium, 18 g carbo., 1 g fiber, 33 g pro.

Taco Pizza
Prep: 15 minutes   Bake: 20 minutes   Oven: 400°F

8   ounces lean ground beef and/or
    bulk pork sausage
1   medium sweet pepper, chopped (3/4 cup)
1   11.5-ounce package refrigerated
    corn bread twists
1/2 cup purchased salsa
3   cups shredded taco cheese (12 ounces)

1. Preheat oven to 400°F. In a skillet, cook beef and sweet pepper over medium heat until meat is brown, stirring frequently. Drain off fat. Set meat mixture aside.

2. Unroll corn bread dough (do not separate into strips). Press dough into the bottom and up the edges of a greased 12-inch pizza pan. Spread salsa on top of dough. Sprinkle with meat mixture and cheese. Bake about 20 minutes or until the bottom of the crust is golden brown. Cut into wedges. Makes 6 servings.

Per slice: 465 cal., 30 g fat (15 g sat. fat), 73 mg chol., 870 mg sodium, 27 g carbo., 1 g fiber, 22 g pro.

Scalloped Potatoes and Ham
Prep: 15 minutes   Bake: 45 minutes
Stand: 10 minutes   Oven: 400°F

1   10.75-ounce can condensed cream of onion
    or cream of celery soup
1/2 cup milk
1/8 teaspoon ground black pepper
1   pound cooked ham, cubed
1   20-ounce package refrigerated diced
    potatoes with onion
3/4 cup shredded Swiss or cheddar cheese
    (3 ounces)

1. Preheat oven to 350°F. In a large bowl, stir together soup, milk, and pepper. Stir in ham and potatoes. Transfer to an ungreased 2-quart rectangular baking dish.

2. Bake, covered, for 40 minutes. Stir mixture; sprinkle with cheese. Bake, uncovered, for 5 to 10 minutes more or until heated through and cheese melts. Let stand for 10 minutes before serving. Makes 6 to 8 servings.

Per serving: 332 cal., 14 g fat (6 g sat. fat), 64 mg chol., 1,613 mg sodium, 29 g carbo., 2 g fiber, 21 g pro.

Cheese-Topped Steaks
Prep: 20 minutes   Grill: 15 minutes

  2   ounces Gorgonzola cheese or other blue
      cheese, crumbled (½ cup)
 ¼   cup cooked bacon pieces
 ¼   cup pine nuts or slivered almonds, toasted
  2   tablespoons fresh thyme leaves
  2   cloves garlic, minced
 ¼   teaspoon freshly ground black pepper
  4   boneless beef top loin steaks, cut 1 inch
      thick

1. In a small bowl, combine cheese, bacon, nuts, thyme, garlic, and pepper; set aside.

2. Sprinkle steaks lightly with salt. For a charcoal grill, grill steaks on rack of an uncovered grill directly over medium heat to desired doneness, turning once halfway through grilling. Allow 10 to 12 minutes for medium-rare (145°F) or 12 to 15 minutes for medium (160°F). (For a gas grill, preheat grill. Reduce heat to medium. Place steaks on grill rack over heat. Cover and grill as above.)

3. To serve, top steaks with cheese mixture. Grill 1 to 2 minutes or until cheese is soft. Makes 4 servings.

Per serving: 640 cal., 30 g fat (11 g sat. fat), 181 mg chol., 616 mg sodium, 3 g carbo., 0 g fiber, 86 g pro.

Herbed Steaks with Horseradish
Start to Finish: 20 minutes

    2   12- to 14-ounce beef top loin steaks,
        cut 1 inch thick
        Salt and ground black pepper
    2   tablespoons prepared horseradish
    1   tablespoon Dijon-style mustard
    2   teaspoons snipped fresh Italian
        (flat-leaf) parsley
    1   teaspoon snipped fresh thyme
        Broiled cherry tomatoes (optional)
        Broiled sweet pepper strips (optional)
        Herbed mayonnaise (optional)

1. Preheat broiler; season steaks with salt and pepper. Place steaks on the unheated rack of a broiler pan. Broil 4 inches from heat for 7 minutes. Meanwhile, combine horseradish, mustard, parsley, and thyme.

2. Turn steaks. Broil 8 to 9 minutes more for medium (160°F). Spread with horseradish mixture the last 1 minute of broiling, If desired, serve with tomatoes, peppers, and mayonnaise. Makes 4 servings.

Per serving: 284 cal., 15 g fat (6 g sat. fat), 84 mg chol., 351 mg sodium, 1 g carbo., 0 g fiber, 33 g pro.

Upside-Down Pizza Casserole
Prep: 20 minutes   Bake: 15 minutes   Oven: 400°F

 1½   pounds lean ground beef
    1   15-ounce can Italian-style tomato sauce
 1½   cups shredded mozzarella cheese
        (6 ounces)
    1   10-ounce package refrigerated biscuits

1. Preheat oven to 400°F. In a large skillet, cook ground beef until brown, stirring frequently. Drain off fat. Stir in tomato sauce; heat through. Transfer mixture to a 2-quart rectangular baking dish. Sprinkle with cheese.

2. Flatten each biscuit with your hands; arrange the biscuits on top of the cheese. Bake about 15 minutes or until biscuits are golden. Makes 5 servings.

Per serving: 642 cal., 41 g fat (16 g sat. fat), 116 mg chol., 1,103 mg sodium, 30 g carbo., 2 g fiber, 38 g pro.

Salsa Beef
Start to Finish: 30 minutes

 1½   pounds ground beef
    1   16-ounce jar bottled salsa
    3   to 4 teaspoons mild curry powder
    6   tablespoons snipped fresh mint
        or cilantro
        Hot cooked basmati rice (optional)
  ½   cup plain low-fat yogurt

1. In a very large skillet, cook ground beef over medium heat until brown, breaking up beef with the back of a spoon. Drain off fat.

2. Stir salsa, curry powder, and 3 tablespoons of the mint into beef. Cook, uncovered, over medium-low heat for 10 minutes, stirring occasionally.

3. If desired, serve with hot cooked basmati rice. Top with yogurt. Sprinkle with remaining 3 tablespoons mint. Makes 4 servings.

Per serving: 390 cal., 22 g fat (9 g sat. fat), 109 mg chol., 981 mg sodium, 15 g carbo., 0 g fiber, 34 g pro.

Stroganoff-Sauced Beef Roast
Prep: 15 minutes   Cook: 15 minutes

    1   16-ounce package cooked beef
        pot roast with gravy
    2   cups shiitake, crimini, or button
        mushrooms
  ½   cup dairy sour cream French onion dip
    2   cups hot cooked noodles

1. Transfer beef with gravy to a large skillet (leave meat whole). Remove stems from shiitake mushrooms; halve or quarter mushrooms.

2. Add mushrooms to skillet. Cook, covered, over medium-low heat for 15 minutes or until heated through, stirring mushrooms once and turning roast over halfway through cooking time.

3. Use a wooden spoon to break meat into bite-size pieces. Stir onion dip into meat mixture; heat through (do not boil). Stir in cooked noodles. Makes 3 to 4 servings.

Per serving: 542 cal., 7 g fat (11 g sat. fat), 99 mg chol., 787 mg sodium, 46 g carbo., 4 g fiber, 8 g pro.

Ham and Slaw Stuffed Peppers

Start to Finish: 20 minutes

3   cups packaged shredded broccoli (broccoli slaw mix) (about $1/2$ of a 16-ounce package)
1   cup cubed cooked ham (about 6 ounces)
$1/4$ cup bottled Parmesan ranch or peppercorn ranch salad dressing
4   small yellow, orange, red and/or green sweet peppers
2   tablespoons sunflower kernels

1. In a Dutch oven bring water to boiling. Meanwhile, in a large mixing bowl combine shredded broccoli, ham, and salad dressing; set aside.

2. Meanwhile, cut tops off peppers; remove seeds and membranes and discard. Place the pepper bottoms and tops in the boiling water. Reduce heat; cover and simmer for 3 minutes. Drain. Rinse with cold running water until cooled; drain again.

3. Place pepper halves, cut-side-up, on plates. Mound salad into pepper halves, allowing any extra to overflow onto plate. Sprinkle with sunflower kernels. Replace pepper tops. Makes 4 servings.

Per serving: 190 cal., 13 g fat (3 g sat. fat), 24 mg chol., 597 mg sodium, 13 g carbo., 4 g fiber, 9 g pro.

Southwest Pork Chops

Start to Finish: 30 minutes

6   pork rib chops, cut $3/4$ inch thick
    Nonstick cooking spray
1   15-ounce can Mexican-style or Tex-Mex-style chili beans
1   cup bottled salsa
1   cup frozen whole kernel corn
3   cups hot cooked rice
    Snipped fresh cilantro (optional)

1. Trim fat from chops. Coat a 12-inch nonstick skillet with nonstick cooking spray. Heat skillet over medium-high heat. Add chops, half at a time if necessary, to skillet; cook about 2 minutes per side or until brown. Remove chops from skillet.

2. Add chili beans, salsa, and corn to skillet; stir to combine. Place chops on top of bean mixture. Bring to boiling; reduce heat. Simmer, covered, for 15 to 20 minutes or until chops are done (160°F). Serve over hot cooked rice. If desired, sprinkle with cilantro. Makes 6 servings.

Per serving: 379 cal., 10 g fat (3 g sat. fat), 71 mg chol., 490 mg sodium, 38 g carbo., 5 g fiber, 33 g pro.

Roast Beef and Mashed Potato Stacks

Start to Finish: 15 minutes

1   17-ounce package refrigerated cooked beef tips with gravy
$1/2$ cup onion-flavor beef broth
1   20-ounce package refrigerated mashed potatoes
2   tablespoons butter
$1/8$ teaspoon ground black pepper
4   thick slices white bread

1. In a large skillet, combine beef tips with gravy and beef broth. Cook and stir over medium heat until heated through.

2. Meanwhile, prepare mashed potatoes according to package directions, adding the butter and pepper.

3. To serve, place bread slices on four dinner plates. Divide mashed potatoes among bread slices. Ladle beef mixture over potatoes and bread. Makes 4 servings.

Cherry-Stuffed Ham

Prep: 35 minutes   Bake: 2 hours 10 minutes
Stand: 15 minutes   Oven: 325°F

1   cup dried tart cherries, chopped
$1/2$ cup cherry juice or orange juice
1   3- to 4-pound cooked boneless ham
1   18-ounce jar peach preserves
2   tablespoons lemon juice

1. Preheat oven to 325°F. In a small saucepan, combine $1/2$ cup of the cherries and cherry juice; bring just to boiling. Remove from heat; let stand for 15 minutes. Drain cherries; discard juice.

2. With a sharp knife, cut three or four $1^1/2$- to 2-inch-deep slits in ham, making cuts at a right angle to the direction ham will be sliced. As each slit is made, press in some of the soaked cherries. Place ham on a rack in a shallow roasting pan. Cover with foil. Bake for 2 hours or until a meat thermometer registers 140°F.

3. Transfer preserves to a bowl; snip any large pieces of fruit. Add remaining dried cherries and lemon juice. Spoon $1/2$ cup of the preserves mixture over ham. Bake, uncovered, for 10 minutes. In a saucepan, heat remaining preserves; pass with ham. Makes 4 servings.

Per serving: 413 cal., 12 g fat (4 g sat. fat), 78 mg chol., 1,795 mg sodium, 52 g carbo., 3 g fiber, 23 g pro.

Curried Coconut Shrimp

Start to Finish: 30 minutes

1 **pound fresh or frozen large shrimp in shells, thawed (14 to 16 count)**
1 **cup uncooked jasmine rice**
1 **15.25-ounce can tropical fruit salad or pineapple chunks**
1 **teaspoon red curry paste**
1 **cup unsweetened coconut milk**

1. Thaw shrimp, if frozen. Prepare rice according to package directions; set aside. Meanwhile, peel and devein shrimp. Rinse shrimp; pat dry with paper towels; set aside. Drain liquid from fruit, reserving $\frac{1}{2}$ cup. Set liquid and fruit aside.

2. In a large nonstick skillet, stir-fry shrimp and curry paste over medium-high heat for 3 to 4 minutes or until shrimp are opaque. Remove shrimp from skillet; set aside. Add coconut milk and reserved liquid from fruit to skillet. Bring to boiling; reduce heat. Simmer, uncovered, for 5 to 7 minutes until mixture is slightly thickened and reduced to about 1 cup.

3. Divide hot cooked rice among four shallow bowls. Arrange shrimp on top of rice; spoon sauce over shrimp and rice. Top each serving with $\frac{1}{4}$ cup drained fruit. Makes 4 servings.

Per serving: 463 cal., 17 g fat (13 g sat. fat), 151 mg chol., 263 mg sodium, 55 g carbo., 2 g fiber, 24 g pro.

Salmon with Wilted Greens

Prep: 15 minutes   Broil: 6 minutes

1 **pound fresh or frozen salmon fillets**
1 **tablespoon bottled Asian salad dressing, such as sesame ginger**
6 **cups torn mixed salad greens**
1 **medium orange, peeled and sectioned**
$\frac{1}{2}$ **cup bottled Asian salad dressing, such as sesame ginger**

1. Thaw salmon, if frozen. Rinse salmon; pat dry. Cut into four pieces. On the greased unheated rack of a broiler pan, broil salmon 4 inches from the heat for 6 to 9 minutes or until salmon flakes easily when tested with a fork. Brush with 1 tablespoon dressing halfway through broiling. Cover; keep warm.

2. In a salad bowl, combine greens and orange sections. In a large skillet bring $\frac{1}{2}$ cup dressing to boiling. Boil gently, uncovered, for 1 minute. Pour over greens; toss.

3. Divide greens among four plates. Serve immediately. Makes 4 servings.

Per serving: 397 cal., 25 g fat (5 g sat. fat), 67 mg chol., 623 mg sodium, 20 g carbo., 3 g fiber, 24 g pro.

Orange Roughy with Dill

Prep: 15 minutes   Grill: 6 minutes

4 **5- to 6-ounce fresh or frozen orange roughy or sea bass fillets, $\frac{3}{4}$ inch thick**
2 **tablespoons olive oil**
2 **tablespoons snipped fresh dill**
$\frac{1}{4}$ **teaspoon salt**
$\frac{1}{4}$ **teaspoon ground white pepper**
5 **large oranges**
  Fresh dill sprigs (optional)

1. Thaw fish, if frozen. Rinse fish; pat dry with paper towels. Combine oil, 2 tablespoons dill, salt, and white pepper. Brush dill mixture over both sides of fish.

2. Cut four oranges into $\frac{1}{4}$-inch slices. For a charcoal grill, arrange a bed of orange slices on a greased grill rack. Arrange the fish on the orange slices. Grill orange slices and fish on the rack of an uncovered grill directly over medium coals for 6 to 9 minutes or until fish flakes easily when tested with a fork. (For a gas grill, preheat grill. Reduce heat to medium. Arrange orange slices and fish on greased grill rack over heat. Cover and grill as above.)

3. To serve, use a spatula to transfer fish and grilled orange slices to a serving platter. Cut remaining orange into wedges; squeeze the juice from the wedges over the fish. If desired, garnish with fresh dill sprigs. Makes 4 servings.

Per serving: 268 cal., 10 g fat (2 g sat. fat), 58 mg chol., 242 mg sodium, 18 g carbo., 3 g fiber, 28 g pro.

Shrimp Quesadillas
Start to Finish: 20 minutes

    Nonstick cooking spray
4 8-inch vegetable tortillas
$^1/_2$ of a 7-ounce carton garlic or spicy three-pepper hummus ($^1/_3$ cup)
6 ounces peeled, deveined, cooked shrimp
1 6-ounce jar marinated artichoke hearts or $^1/_2$ of a 16-ounce jar pickled mixed vegetables, drained and coarsely chopped
1 4-ounce package crumbled feta cheese

1. Coat one side of each tortilla with nonstick cooking spray. Place tortillas, sprayed side down, on a work surface; spread with hummus. Top half of each tortilla with shrimp, artichokes, and cheese. Fold tortillas in half, pressing gently.

2. Heat a large nonstick skillet or griddle over medium heat for 1 minute. Cook quesadillas, two at a time, for 4 to 6 minutes or until brown and heated through, turning once. Makes 4 servings.

Per serving: 430 cal., 20 g fat (7 g sat. fat), 108 mg chol., 1,099 mg sodium, 42 g carbo., 4 g fiber, 21 g pro.

Parmesan Baked Fish
Start to Finish: 22 minutes   Oven: 450°F

4 4- to 5-ounce fresh or frozen skinless salmon or other firm fish fillets, $^3/_4$ to 1 inch thick
$^1/_4$ cup mayonnaise or salad dressing
2 tablespoons grated Parmesan cheese
1 tablespoon snipped fresh chives
1 teaspoon Worcestershire sauce for chicken

1. Thaw fish, if frozen. Preheat oven to 450°F. Rinse fish; pat dry with paper towels. Place fish in a greased 2-quart baking dish, tucking under any thin edges to make fish uniform thickness. Set aside.

2. In a small bowl, stir together mayonnaise, Parmesan cheese, chives, and Worcestershire sauce. Spread mixture evenly over fish. Bake, uncovered, for 12 to 15 minutes or until fish begins to flake when tested with a fork. Makes 4 servings.

Per serving: 302 cal., 22 g fat (4 g sat. fat), 77 mg chol., 185 mg sodium, 0 g carbo., 0 g fiber, 25 g pro.

Salmon with Dijon-Cream Sauce
Start to Finish: 25 minutes

$1^1/_4$ pounds fresh or frozen skinless salmon fillets
1 tablespoon butter
$^1/_3$ cup reduced-sodium chicken broth
$^1/_3$ cup half-and-half or light cream
2 tablespoons Dijon-style mustard
$^1/_4$ teaspoon coarsely ground black pepper

1. Thaw fish, if frozen. Rinse fish; pat dry with paper towels. Cut fillets crosswise into $^1/_2$-inch slices. In a large skillet, cook salmon slices, half at a time, in hot butter over medium-high heat about 2 minutes or until fish begins to flake when tested with a fork, turning once. Remove from skillet; keep warm.

2. For sauce, add chicken broth to drippings in skillet. Bring to boiling; reduce heat. Simmer, uncovered, for 1 minute. Whisk together half-and-half and mustard; stir into skillet. Return to boiling; reduce heat. Simmer, uncovered, for 2 to 3 minutes more or until sauce is slightly thickened. Spoon sauce over salmon; sprinkle with pepper. Makes 4 servings.

Per serving: 318 cal., 20 g fat (6 g sat. fat), 95 mg chol., 343 mg sodium, 1 g carbo., 0 g fiber, 29 g pro.

Thaw *frozen fish* in the refrigerator, never at room temperature. Allow a 1-pound package to thaw overnight.

Thai Chicken Pasta

Start to Finish: 20 minutes

8   ounces dried angel hair pasta
3   cups cooked chicken cut into strips
1   14-ounce can unsweetened coconut milk
1   teaspoon Thai seasoning
¼   cup roasted peanuts

1. Cook pasta according to package directions; drain well. Return pasta to pan; keep warm.

2. Meanwhile, in a large skillet, combine chicken, coconut milk, and Thai seasoning. Cook and gently stir over medium heat until mixture is heated through. Pour hot chicken mixture over cooked pasta in pan. Toss gently to coat. Transfer to a serving platter or bowl. Sprinkle with peanuts. Makes 4 servings.

Per serving: 644 cal., 31 g fat (19 g sat. fat), 93 mg chol., 236 mg sodium, 47 g carbo., 2 g fiber, 42 g pro.

Asian Noodle Bowl

Start to Finish: 25 minutes

8   ounces dried buckwheat soba, udon, or vermicelli noodles
2   cups vegetable broth
½   cup bottled peanut sauce
2   cups Chinese-style frozen stir-fry vegetables
½   cup dry-roasted peanuts, chopped

1. Cook noodles according to package directions. Drain but do not rinse. Set aside. In the same pan, combine broth and peanut sauce. Bring to boiling. Stir in frozen vegetables and cooked noodles. Return to boiling; reduce heat to medium low. Simmer, uncovered, for 2 to 3 minutes or until vegetables are heated through. Divide noodles and broth among four bowls. Sprinkle with peanuts. Makes 4 servings.

Per serving: 403 cal., 15 g fat (2 g sat. fat), 0 mg chol., 1,326 mg sodium, 59 g carbo., 4 g fiber, 15 g pro.

Tortellini Alfredo with Roasted Peppers

Start to Finish: 15 minutes

1   9-ounce package refrigerated meat- or cheese-filled tortellini
1   4-ounce jar roasted red sweet peppers, drained and cut into ½-inch strips
⅓   cup refrigerated light Alfredo sauce
½   cup shredded fresh basil
    Coarsely ground black pepper

1. Cook tortellini according to package directions. Drain and return pasta to pan. Stir in roasted peppers and Alfredo sauce. Cook and stir over medium-low heat until heated through. Stir in half of the basil. Sprinkle with remaining basil and black pepper. Makes 2 to 3 servings.

Per serving: 384 cal., 12 g fat (6 g sat. fat), 50 mg chol., 919 mg sodium, 52 g carbo., 3 g fiber, 15 g pro.

Ravioli with Spinach Pesto

Start to Finish: 20 minutes

1   9-ounce package refrigerated four-cheese ravioli or tortellini
12   ounces baby pattypan squash, halved, or yellow summer squash, halved lengthwise and sliced ½ inch thick
3½   cups fresh baby spinach
½   cup torn fresh basil
¼   cup bottled Caesar Parmesan vinaigrette salad dressing
2   tablespoons water
     Shredded Parmesan cheese (optional)

1. Cook ravioli according to package directions, adding squash the last 2 minutes of cooking. Drain.

2. Meanwhile, for pesto, in a blender, combine spinach, basil, salad dressing, and the water. Cover and process until smooth, stopping to scrape down blender as needed.

3. Toss ravioli mixture with pesto. If desired, sprinkle with cheese. Makes 4 servings.

Per serving: 218 cal., 6 g fat (2 g sat. fat), 27 mg chol., 525 mg sodium, 31 g carbo., 3 g fiber, 11 g pro.

For a pasta and vegetable dish, save a pan by cooking the veggie with the pasta for the last few minutes.

20-Minute Marinara Sauce

Start to Finish: 20 minutes

1 28-ounce can whole tomatoes, undrained
3 tablespoons snipped fresh basil
1 teaspoon bottled minced garlic
2 tablespoons olive oil
¼ teaspoon salt
¼ teaspoon ground black pepper
8 to 12 ounces dried pasta, cooked and drained
  Snipped fresh basil (optional)

1. In a food processor or blender, puree undrained tomatoes. Add 3 tablespoons snipped basil. In a medium skillet, cook garlic in hot olive oil over medium heat until garlic is light brown. Remove garlic. Add salt and pepper to oil. Add pureed tomatoes. Bring to boiling; reduce heat. Simmer, uncovered, for 10 minutes. Remove from heat. Serve over hot pasta. If desired, top each serving with additional basil. Makes 4 to 6 servings.

Per serving: 310 cal., 8 g fat (1 g sat. fat), 0 mg chol., 441 mg sodium, 51 g carbo., 4 g fiber, 9 g pro.

Polenta and Black Beans

Start to Finish: 20 minutes

1 cup yellow cornmeal
½ teaspoon salt
1 15-ounce can black beans,
  rinsed and drained
1 14.5-ounce can diced tomatoes, undrained
1 cup bottled salsa with cilantro or other salsa
¾ cup shredded Mexican cheese blend
  (3 ounces)

1. For polenta, in a large saucepan, bring 3 cups *water* to boiling. In a medium bowl, combine cornmeal, 1 cup *water*, and salt. Stir cornmeal mixture slowly into boiling water. Cook and stir until mixture comes to boiling. Reduce heat to low. Cook for 5 to 10 minutes or until mixture is thick, stirring occasionally. (If mixture is too thick, stir in additional water.)
2. Meanwhile, in a large skillet, combine beans, undrained tomatoes, and salsa. Bring to boiling; reduce heat. Simmer, uncovered, for 10 minutes, stirring frequently. Stir ½ cup of the cheese into the polenta. Divide polenta among four bowls. Top with bean mixture; sprinkle with remaining cheese. Makes 4 servings.

Per serving: 311 cal., 8 g fat (4 g sat. fat), 19 mg chol., 751 mg sodium, 49 g carbo., 8 g fiber, 15 g pro.

Polenta and Black Beans

Hot and Saucy Tortellini

Start to Finish: 25 minutes

7 to 8 ounces dried cheese-filled tortellini (about 1¾ cups)
8 ounces bulk Italian sausage
1 13- to 14-ounce jar tomato-base pasta sauce
1 16-ounce jar salsa
2 tablespoons snipped fresh cilantro

1. Cook tortellini according to package directions; drain well. Keep pasta warm. Meanwhile, in a large skillet, cook sausage until no longer pink; drain off fat. Stir in pasta sauce and salsa. Bring to boiling; reduce heat. Simmer, covered, for 5 minutes. Stir pasta and 1 tablespoon of the cilantro into sauce mixture; heat through. Transfer to a serving bowl or platter. Sprinkle with the remaining 1 tablespoon cilantro. Makes 4 servings.

Per serving: 450 cal., 20 g fat (5 g sat. fat), 38 mg chol., 1,848 mg sodium, 42 g carbo., 3 g fiber, 21 g pro.

Spicy Pasta and Broccoli

Start to Finish: 25 minutes

12 ounces dried orecchiette or medium shell pasta (about 4 cups)
2 tablespoons extra virgin olive oil
3 cups chopped broccolini or broccoli florets
1 cup chicken with Italian herbs broth
¼ to ½ teaspoon crushed red pepper

1. Cook pasta according to package directions; drain. Return pasta to pan. Drizzle 1 tablespoon of the olive oil over pasta; toss to coat. Cover and keep warm.
2. Meanwhile, in a large skillet, cook and stir broccolini in remaining 1 tablespoon oil over medium-high heat for 3 minutes. Add broth and red pepper. Bring to boiling; reduce heat. Simmer, covered, for 2 to 3 minutes more until broccolini is crisp-tender. Combine pasta and broccolini mixture; toss to mix. Makes 4 servings.

Per serving: 404 cal., 9 g fat (1 g sat. fat), 0 mg chol., 214 mg sodium, 67 g carbo., 4 g fiber, 14 g pro.

Pasta with Sausage-Tomato Sauce

Start to Finish: 30 minutes

8 ounces dried penne, fettuccine, linguine, or rotelle
1 pound sweet or hot Italian sausage links
1½ cups water
2 medium fennel bulbs, cut into thin wedges (about 2 cups)
1 26-ounce jar tomato-base pasta sauce
⅓ cup water

1. Cook pasta according to package directions; drain.
2. Meanwhile, cut sausage into 1-inch pieces. In a large skillet, combine sausage and the 1½ cups water. Heat to boiling. Cook, uncovered, on high for 10 minutes; drain off fat and return sausage to skillet. Add fennel and cook for 3 to 4 minutes until sausage is brown and fennel is crisp-tender. Add pasta sauce and the ⅓ cup water. Heat to boiling; reduce heat. Simmer, covered, for 5 minutes. Serve with pasta. Makes 4 servings.

Per serving: 714 cal., 38 g fat (13 g sat. fat), 86 mg chol., 1,474 mg sodium, 65 g carbo., 8 g fiber, 28 g pro.

Sweet Beans and Noodles

Start to Finish: 30 minutes

8 ounces dried linguine
1½ cups frozen sweet soybeans (shelled edamane)
1 cup purchased shredded carrot
1 10-ounce container purchased Alfredo sauce
2 teaspoons snipped fresh rosemary

1. Cook pasta according to package directions, adding soybeans and carrot the last 10 minutes of cooking. Drain and return mixture to pan. Add Alfredo sauce and rosemary; toss to combine. Heat through. Makes 4 servings.

Per serving: 544 cal., 27 g fat (1 g sat. fat), 35 mg chol., 280 mg sodium, 57 g carbo., 5 g fiber, 20 g pro.

Hearty Ham Stew
Start to Finish: 20 minutes

2 16-ounce cans pork and beans in tomato sauce
1 16-ounce package frozen mixed vegetables, thawed
1 8-ounce ham slice, cut into ½-inch cubes
1 tablespoon dried minced onion
1 cup broken corn chips (optional)

1. In a 10-inch skillet, stir together pork and beans, vegetables, ham, and minced onion. Cook over medium heat until bubbly, stirring occasionally. If desired, top each serving with corn chips. Makes 6 to 8 servings.

Per serving: 255 cal., 5 g fat (2 g sat. fat), 32 mg chol., 1,189 mg sodium, 41 g carbo., 10 g fiber, 17 g pro.

Pesto Meatball Soup
Start to Finish: 20 minutes

½ of a 16-ounce package frozen cooked Italian-style meatballs (16), thawed
2 14.5-ounce cans diced tomatoes with Italian herbs, undrained
1 15- to 19-ounce can cannellini beans (white kidney beans), rinsed and drained
½ cup water
¼ cup purchased basil pesto
½ cup finely shredded Parmesan cheese (2 ounces)

1. In a 4-quart Dutch oven, combine meatballs, undrained tomatoes, beans, the water, and pesto. Bring to boiling; reduce heat. Simmer, covered, for 10 minutes or until meatballs are heated through. Sprinkle each serving with Parmesan cheese. Makes 4 servings .

Per serving: 459 cal., 26 g fat (8 g sat. fat), 46 mg chol., 1,925 mg sodium, 89 g carbo., 8 g fiber, 24 g pro.

Spinach-Pesto Meatball Soup: Prepare as directed above, except stir 2 cups fresh baby spinach leaves into the soup before serving.

Italian Meatball Stew
Start to Finish: 25 minutes

1 16-ounce package frozen cooked Italian-style meatballs
2 14.5-ounce cans Italian-style stewed tomatoes, undrained and cut up
1 15- to 19-ounce can cannellini (white kidney beans), rinsed and drained
¾ cup water
¼ cup purchased basil pesto

1. In a large saucepan, combine meatballs, undrained tomatoes, drained beans, the water, and pesto. Bring to boiling; reduce heat. Simmer, covered, for 15 minutes. Makes 6 servings.

Per serving: 391 cal., 25 g fat (8 g sat. fat), 50 mg chol., 1,031 mg sodium, 25 g carbo., 7 g fiber, 19 g pro.   ·

Tomato-Tortellini Soup
Start to Finish: 15 minutes

2 14-ounce cans reduced-sodium chicken broth or vegetable broth
1 9-ounce package refrigerated tortellini
½ of an 8-ounce tub cream cheese spread with chive and onion
1 10.75- or 11-ounce can condensed tomato or tomato bisque soup
   Snipped fresh chives (optional)

1. In a medium saucepan, bring broth to boiling. Add tortellini; reduce heat. Simmer, uncovered, for 5 minutes. In a bowl, whisk ⅓ cup of the hot broth into the cream cheese spread until smooth. Return all to saucepan along with tomato soup; heat through. If desired, sprinkle with chives. Makes 4 servings.

Per serving: 363 cal., 14 g fat (8 g sat. fat), 57 mg chol., 1,264 mg sodium, 44 g carbo., 1 g fiber, 14 g pro.

sandwiches
& wraps

Satisfying, versatile sandwiches and wraps are an appealing solution to the "what's for dinner" puzzle. Served hot or cold, they go together in minutes.

Chicken-Veggie Wraps

Start to Finish: 15 minutes

1/2 cup mayonnaise or salad dressing

3 to 4 tablespoons purchased dried tomato pesto

12 6-inch corn tortillas or eight 7- to 8-inch flour tortillas

2 6-ounce packages refrigerated grilled chicken breast strips

2 small yellow summer squash or zucchini (8 ounces total), cut into thin strips

1 medium sweet pepper, cut into strips
Fresh cilantro sprigs (optional)

1. Stir together mayonnaise and pesto; divide into four small bowls. Place tortillas on a microwave-safe plate, cover with a paper towel. Microwave on 100% power (high) for 30 to 45 seconds or until warm.

2. Divide chicken, squash and pepper strips, and warm tortillas among four shallow bowls. If desired, top with cilantro. Serve with pesto mixture. Makes 4 servings.

Per serving: 481 cal., 30 g fat (6 g sat. fat), 66 mg chol., 1,021 mg sodium, 30 g carbo., 5 g fiber, 24 g pro.

White Beans and Goat Cheese Wraps

Start to Finish: 20 minutes

1 19-ounce can cannellini beans (white kidney beans), rinsed and drained

1 4-ounce package soft goat cheese (chèvre)

1 tablespoon snipped fresh oregano or 1/2 teaspoon dried oregano, crushed

1 tablespoon snipped fresh Italian (flat-leaf) parsley

6 8-inch whole wheat flour tortillas, warmed, if desired

6 cups fresh baby spinach leaves

1 12-ounce jar roasted red sweet peppers, drained and cut into thin strips

1. In a medium bowl, mash beans lightly with a fork. Add goat cheese, oregano, and parsley; stir until well mixed. Divide bean mixture among tortillas, spreading evenly to the edges. Top bean mixture with spinach and roasted peppers. Roll up tortillas; cut in half to serve. Makes 6 servings.

Per serving: 248 cal., 8 g fat (4 g sat. fat), 9 mg chol., 552 mg sodium, 31 g carbo., 16 g fiber, 18 g pro.

Asian Tuna Wraps

Start to Finish: 10 minutes

1   12-ounce can solid white tuna (water pack), drained and broken into chunks
1/3 cup bottled Asian sesame-ginger salad dressing
4   7- to 8-inch flour tortillas
1   small red or green sweet pepper, seeded and cut into thin strips

1. In a medium bowl, stir together tuna and dressing. Divide mixture among tortillas. Top with pepper strips and roll up. Makes 4 servings.

Per serving: 208 cal., 9 g fat (2 g sat. fat), 17 mg chol., 543 mg sodium, 21 g carbo., 1 g fiber, 11 g pro.

Asian Chicken Wraps: Prepare as above except omit the tuna. Use one 10-ounce can chunk-style chicken, drained, in place of tuna.

Turkey-Avocado Wraps

Start to Finish: 25 minutes

1/2 cup mayonnaise or salad dressing
1   to 2 canned chipotle peppers in adobo sauce, drained and finely chopped
6   10-inch flour tortillas or flat-bread wraps
    Black Bean-Corn Salsa
12 ounces sliced cooked turkey or chicken
1   avocado, halved, seeded, peeled and sliced

1. In a small bowl, combine mayonnaise and chipotle peppers. Spread mixture evenly on tortillas. Spoon Black Bean-Corn Salsa over mayonnaise mixture. Top with turkey and avocado slices. Roll up tortillas. Serve immediately or cover and chill for up to 4 hours. Makes 6 servings.

Black Bean-Corn Salsa: In a large bowl, combine one 15-ounce can black beans, rinsed and drained; 1 cup chopped, seeded tomatoes; 1/2 cup frozen whole kernel corn, thawed; 2 tablespoons thinly sliced green onion; 2 tablespoons snipped fresh cilantro; 1 tablespoon cooking oil; 1 tablespoon lime juice; 1/4 teaspoon salt; 1/4 teaspoon ground cumin; and 1/4 teaspoon ground black pepper. Cover and chill for up to 24 hours. Makes about 3 cups.

Per serving: 496 cal., 28 g fat (5 g sat. fat), 50 mg chol., 608 mg sodium, 39 g carbo., 7 g fiber, 25 g pro.

Five-Spice Steak Wraps

Start to Finish: 25 minutes

12 ounces boneless beef round steak
2   cups packaged coleslaw mix
1/4 cup red and/or green sweet pepper cut into thin bite-size strips
1/4 cup carrot cut into thin bite-size strips
1/4 cup snipped fresh chives
2   tablespoons rice vinegar
1/2 teaspoon toasted sesame oil
1/2 teaspoon five-spice powder
1/4 teaspoon salt
    Nonstick cooking spray
1/4 cup plain low-fat yogurt or light dairy sour cream
4   8-inch flour tortillas

1. If desired, partially freeze steak for easier slicing. In a medium bowl, combine coleslaw mix, sweet pepper, carrot, and chives. In a small bowl, combine vinegar and sesame oil. Pour vinegar mixture over coleslaw mixture; toss to coat. Set aside.

2. Trim fat from steak. Thinly slice steak across the grain into bite-size strips. Sprinkle strips with five-spice powder and salt. Lightly coat an unheated large nonstick skillet with nonstick cooking spray. Preheat over medium-high heat. Add steak strips; stir-fry for 3 to 4 minutes or until brown.

3. Spread 1 tablespoon of the yogurt down the center of each tortilla. Top with steak strips. Stir coleslaw mixture; spoon over steak. Fold in sides of tortillas. If desired, secure with wooden toothpicks. Makes 4 servings.

Per serving: 237 cal., 7 g fat (2 g sat. fat), 51 mg chol., 329 mg sodium, 20 g carbo., 2 g fiber, 22 g pro.

Salmon and Asparagus Wraps
Start to Finish: 25 minutes

- 12 thin fresh asparagus spears (about 4 ounces)
- ½ cup tub-style cream cheese spread with chive and onion
- 2 teaspoons finely shredded lemon peel
- 2 tablespoons lemon juice
- ⅛ teaspoon cayenne pepper
- 6 ounces smoked salmon, flaked, with skin and bones removed
- 4 6- to 7-inch whole wheat flour tortillas
- 2 tablespoons snipped fresh basil or 1 teaspoon dried basil, crushed
- ½ of a medium red sweet pepper, seeded and cut into thin bite-size strips

1. Snap off and discard woody bases from asparagus. In a covered medium saucepan, cook asparagus spears in a small amount of boiling lightly salted water for 2 to 3 minutes or until crisp-tender. Drain; plunge into ice water to cool. Drain again; pat dry with paper towels.

2. In a medium bowl, stir together cream cheese, lemon peel, lemon juice, and cayenne pepper. Fold in flaked salmon. Spread on tortillas. Arrange spinach, three asparagus spears, and one-fourth of the sweet pepper strips over salmon mixture on each tortilla. Roll up tortillas. If necessary, secure with toothpicks. Serve immediately or wrap in plastic wrap and chill for up to 6 hours. Makes 4 servings.

Per serving: 223 cal., 14 g fat (1 g sat. fat), 40 mg chol., 650 mg sodium, 16 g carbo., 9 g fiber, 15 g pro.

For wraps, *flour tortillas* usually work better than corn tortillas because they are more flexible.

Beef and Cabbage Wraps
Start to Finish: 20 minutes   Oven: 350°F

  8   8-inch flour tortillas
 12   ounces lean ground beef
 $^1/_2$ cup chopped onion (1 medium)
  1   clove garlic, minced
  1   cup whole kernel corn
 $^1/_2$ to $^2/_3$ cup bottled barbecue sauce
  2   cups packaged coleslaw mix

1. Wrap tortillas in foil; place on a baking sheet. Heat in a 350°F oven for 10 minutes or until heated through.

2. Meanwhile, in a large skillet, cook beef, onion, and garlic over medium heat until beef is brown and onion is tender. Drain off fat. Stir in corn and $^1/_3$ cup of the barbecue sauce. Cook and stir until heated through.

3. To serve, spread one side of each tortilla with some of the remaining barbecue sauce. Spoon about $^1/_2$ cup filling on each tortilla. Top with some of the coleslaw mix. Roll up. Makes 4 servings.

Per serving: 391 cal., 14 g fat (4 g sat. fat), 54 mg chol., 535 mg sodium, 46 g carbo., 3 g fiber, 21 g pro.

Crunchy Curried Chicken Salad Wraps

Start to Finish: 20 minutes

- 4   10-inch flour tortillas
- 1   9-ounce package frozen cooked chicken breast strips, thawed
- 1/3 cup mayonnaise or salad dressing
- 1 1/2 teaspoons curry powder
- 1/8 teaspoon ground black pepper
- 1 1/2 cups packaged coleslaw mix
- 1   medium apple, cored and chopped
- 1/2 cup pine nuts or slivered almonds, toasted (optional)
- 1/3 cup fresh mint leaves, finely shredded

1. Place tortillas on a flat surface; divide chicken among tortillas, placing near edge.

2. In a large bowl, combine mayonnaise, curry powder, and pepper. Add coleslaw mix, apple, pine nuts, if desired, and mint. Stir until well mixed. Spoon over chicken. Roll tortillas around filling; secure with wooden toothpicks, if necessary. Serve immediately or, if desired, wrap and chill for up to 24 hours. Makes 4 servings.

Per wrap: 366 cal., 19 g fat (4 g sat. fat), 44 mg chol., 329 mg sodium, 29 g carbo., 2 g fiber, 18 g pro.

Southwestern Chicken Wraps

Start to Finish: 15 minutes

- 1/2 cup dairy sour cream
- 2   tablespoons purchased guacamole
- 4   10-inch dried tomato, spinach, and/or plain flour tortillas
- 2   5.5-ounce packages Southwestern-flavor refrigerated cooked chicken breast strips
- 2   roma tomatoes, sliced
- 2   cups shredded lettuce

1. In a small bowl, stir together sour cream and guacamole. Spread mixture over one side of each tortilla. Divide chicken, tomato, and lettuce among tortillas. Roll up; cut in half to serve. Makes 4 servings.

Per serving: 395 cal., 13 g fat (4 g sat. fat), 49 mg chol., 1,015 mg sodium, 45 g carbo., 2 g fiber, 25 g pro.

Chicken in Pitas

Start to Finish: 5 minutes

- 4   8-inch white or whole wheat pita bread rounds
- 2   cups chopped cooked deli-roasted turkey breast
- 2   cups deli coleslaw
- 1/4 cup snipped and drained oil-packed dried tomatoes

1. Cut pita bread rounds in half crosswise; gently open halves. Fill with turkey, coleslaw, and dried tomato. Makes 4 servings.

Per serving: 298 cal., 3 g fat (0 g sat. fat), 35 mg chol., 1,284 mg sodium, 44 g carbo., 3 g fiber, 23 g pro.

Middle Eastern Pitas

Start to Finish: 15 minutes

- 1   7- or 8-ounce container roasted-garlic-flavor hummus
- 4   pita rounds, halved crosswise
- 12   ounces thinly sliced deli roast beef
- 1/2 cup plain yogurt
- 1/2 cup chopped cucumber

1. Spread hummus in the pita halves. Add beef to pitas. In a small bowl, stir together yogurt and cucumber; spoon over beef in pitas. Makes 4 servings.

Per serving: 463 cal., 18 g fat (5 g sat. fat), 70 mg chol., 735 mg sodium, 44 g carbo., 3 g fiber, 34 g pro.

Deli Roast Beef Sandwiches

Start to Finish: 10 minutes

- 8   ounces thinly sliced deli roast beef
- 4   slices pumpernickel, rye, or whole wheat bread
- 1/2 cup purchased coleslaw
      Herb pepper seasoning

1. Arrange roast beef on two of the bread slices. Spread coleslaw over beef; sprinkle with herb pepper seasoning. Top with the remaining two bread slices. Makes 2 sandwiches.

Per sandwich: 369 cal., 8 g fat (2 g sat. fat), 80 mg chol., 507 mg sodium, 34 g carbo., 5 g fiber, 39 g pro.

Shrimp-Avocado Hoagies
Start to Finish: 20 minutes

1 10- to 12-ounce package frozen peeled, cooked shrimp, thawed and chopped
2 large avocados, pitted, peeled, and chopped
1/2 cup packaged shredded carrots
1/3 cup bottled coleslaw salad dressing
4 hoagie buns
Lemon wedges (optional)

1. In a large bowl, combine shrimp, avocados, carrots, and salad dressing.

2. Halve hoagie buns. Using a spoon, slightly hollow bottoms and tops of hoagie buns, leaving a 1/2-inch shell. Discard excess bread. Toast buns.

3. Spoon shrimp mixture into hoagie buns. If desired, serve with lemon wedges. Makes 4 servings.

Per serving: 560 cal., 24 g fat (4 g sat. fat), 144 mg chol., 825 mg sodium, 63 g carbo., 8 g fiber, 25 g pro.

Island Reubens
Prep: 10 minutes Broil: 5 minutes

8 slices dark rye bread, toasted
1/2 cup bottled Thousand Island salad dressing
6 ounces sliced cooked turkey
6 ounces sliced cooked ham
4 slices Swiss cheese
1 cup canned sauerkraut, well drained
1/2 cup canned crushed pineapple, well drained
4 slices sharp cheddar cheese
4 slices red onion

1. Place bread slices on an extra-large baking sheet. Spread one side of each slice with salad dressing. Top half of the bread slices with turkey, ham, and Swiss cheese. Top remaining bread slices with sauerkraut, crushed pineapple, cheese, and onion.

2. Broil 5 inches from the heat for 5 minutes or until cheese melts. Carefully top turkey-topped bread slices with sauerkraut-topped slices, onion side down. Makes 4 servings.

Per serving: 677 cal., 36 g fat (15 g sat. fat), 120 mg chol., 2,948 mg sodium, 44 g carbo., 9 g fiber, 40 g pro.

Beef Sandwiches with Onion and Horseradish
Start to Finish: 20 minutes

1 large red onion, thinly sliced
1 tablespoon olive oil
3 tablespoons white wine vinegar
1 teaspoon honey
1/4 cup dairy sour cream
2 tablespoons prepared horseradish
1 tablespoon white wine vinegar
1/4 teaspoon salt
1/4 teaspoon ground black pepper
12 slices dark rye bread, toasted
1/4 cup creamy Dijon-style mustard blend
16 ounces thinly sliced cooked roast beef

1. In a large skillet, cook onion in hot oil, covered, over medium heat for 5 to 10 minutes or until nearly tender, stirring occasionally. Add 3 tablespoons vinegar and honey. Bring to boiling; cook, uncovered, for 5 to 10 minutes or until liquid has evaporated.

2. Meanwhile, in a small bowl, stir together sour cream, horseradish, 1 tablespoon vinegar, salt, and pepper; set aside.

3. To assemble, spread one side of six of the bread slices with mustard blend. Top with roast beef and onion mixture. Spoon sour cream mixture over all. Add remaining bread slices. Cut in half to serve. Makes 6 servings.

Per serving: 417 cal., 17 g fat (5 g sat. fat), 63 mg chol., 735 mg sodium, 39 g carbo., 4 g fiber, 26 g pro.

Salsa Beef Sandwiches
Prep: 10 minutes Cook: 10 minutes

1 pound lean ground beef
1 cup bottled chunky salsa
1/4 cup water
1 1/2 teaspoons chili powder
6 hamburger buns, split and toasted

1. In a large skillet, cook meat until brown. Drain off fat. Stir in salsa, the water, and chili powder. Bring to boiling. Reduce heat. Simmer, uncovered, for 5 to 10 minutes or until desired consistency. Spoon mixture into hamburger buns. Makes 6 servings.

Per serving: 257 cal., 9 g fat (3 g sat. fat), 48 mg chol., 466 mg sodium, 24 g carbo., 1 g fiber, 18 g pro.

Open-Face Chicken and Basil Sandwiches

Start to Finish: 30 minutes

1	8-ounce container whipped cream cheese
1/2	cup snipped fresh basil
3	tablespoons bottled ranch salad dressing
2	6-ounce packages refrigerated chopped cooked chicken
1	cup diced roma tomatoes
2	tablespoons snipped fresh basil
8	1/2-inch-thick slices French or Italian bread, toasted
1/2	cup finely shredded Parmesan cheese

1. In a small bowl, combine cream cheese, 1/2 cup basil, and salad dressing. Stir well to combine; set aside. In a medium bowl, combine chicken, tomatoes, and 2 tablespoons basil.

2. Spread one side of each bread slice with cream cheese mixture. Top with chicken mixture; sprinkle with Parmesan. Broil 3 to 4 inches from heat for 1 to 2 minutes or until Parmesan melts. Makes 8 servings.

Per serving: 268 cal., 15 g fat (7 g sat. fat), 62 mg chol., 795 mg sodium, 17 g carbo., 1 g fiber, 17 g pro.

Chicken Focaccia Sandwiches

Start to Finish: 15 minutes

1	8- to 10-inch tomato or onion Italian flatbread (focaccia) or 1 loaf sourdough bread
1/3	cup light mayonnaise dressing or salad dressing
1	cup lightly packed fresh basil
1 1/2	cups sliced or shredded cooked chicken
1/2	of a 7-ounce jar roasted red sweet peppers, drained and cut into strips (about 1/2 cup)

1. Using a long serrated knife, cut bread in half horizontally. Spread cut sides of bread halves with mayonnaise dressing. On bottom half of bread, layer basil leaves, chicken, and roasted sweet peppers. Cover with top half of bread. Cut into quarters. Makes 4 servings.

Per serving: 314 cal., 10 g fat (1 g sat. fat), 40 mg chol., 597 mg sodium, 40 g carbo., 1 g fiber, 19 g pro.

Mariachi Turkey Sandwiches

Start to Finish: 25 minutes

4	hoagie buns, split
3	tablespoons cooking oil
1 1/2	teaspoons chili powder
12	ounces thinly sliced cooked turkey
1	8-ounce container refrigerated guacamole
1/4	cup snipped fresh cilantro
1/4	to 1/2 teaspoon chipotle-flavor bottled hot pepper sauce or bottled hot pepper sauce
2	medium roma tomatoes, thinly sliced
1	cup shredded Mexican cheese blend (4 ounces)

1. Preheat broiler. Place buns, cut sides up, on one very large or two large baking sheets. In a small bowl, combine oil and chili powder; lightly brush mixture on cut sides of buns. Broil, one sheet at a time if necessary, 3 to 4 inches from the heat for 2 to 3 minutes or until toasted.

2. Meanwhile, in a medium bowl, combine guacamole, cilantro, and bottled hot pepper sauce; set aside.

3. Divide turkey among bottom halves of toasted buns. Top with tomatoes and cheese. If desired, broil 3 to 4 inches from heat for 1 to 2 minutes or until cheese melts. Top with guacamole and bun tops. Makes 4 servings.

Per serving: 851 cal., 39 g fat (11 g sat. fat), 90 mg chol., 1,141 mg sodium, 79 g carbo., 9 g fiber, 44 g pro.

from the freezer

With a selection of specialty breads in the freezer, you'll be able to have a family-pleasing sandwich supper ready in a matter of minutes. Italian flat bread (focaccia), ciabatta, kaiser rolls, French bread rolls, and artisanal breads elevate even ordinary fillings to the special category. Place purchased breads in freezer bags and store in the freezer for up to 3 months. Thaw frozen breads and rolls at room temperature.

Stuffed Focaccia

Start to Finish: 20 minutes

1/2 of a 9- to 10-inch garlic, onion, or plain Italian flat bread (focaccia), split horizontally

1/2 of an 8-ounce container mascarpone cheese

1 6-ounce jar marinated artichoke hearts, drained and chopped

1 tablespoon capers, drained (optional)

4 ounces thinly sliced Genoa salami

1 cup arugula leaves

1. Spread cut sides of focaccia with mascarpone cheese. Sprinkle bottom half of focaccia with artichoke hearts and, if desired, capers. Top with salami and arugula leaves. Cover with top of focaccia, spread side down.

2. Cut sandwich into thirds. Serve immediately or wrap and chill for up to 4 hours. Makes 3 servings.

Per serving: 545 cal., 36 g fat (16 g sat. fat), 83 mg chol., 970 mg sodium, 43 g carbo., 3 g fiber, 23 g pro.

Cheesy Grilled Ham Sandwiches

Start to Finish: 15 minutes

- 2 to 3 teaspoons Dijon-style mustard
- 4 slices firm whole wheat, white, or sourdough bread
- 2 ounces thinly sliced cooked ham
- 2 slices Swiss cheese (2 ounces)
- $^1/_4$ cup milk
- 1 egg white
  Nonstick cooking spray

1. Spread mustard on two of the bread slices. Top with ham and cheese. Place remaining bread slices on top of ham and cheese. In a shallow bowl or pie plate, beat together milk and egg white.

2. Coat an unheated nonstick griddle or large skillet with nonstick cooking spray. Heat over medium heat. Dip each sandwich in milk mixture, turning to coat. Place on griddle or in skillet; cook for 1 to 2 minutes on each side or until golden and cheese melts. Makes 2 servings.

Per serving: 317 cal., 13 g fat (6 g sat. fat), 43 mg chol., 855 mg sodium, 31 g carbo., 0 g fiber, 20 g pro.

Italian-Style Sloppy Joes
Prep: 30 minutes   Bake: 20 minutes   Oven: 400°F

```
12   ounces lean ground beef
 1   8-ounce can tomato sauce
 1   tablespoon dried minced onion
1/4  teaspoon dried oregano, crushed
1/4  teaspoon dried basil, crushed
 8   3-inch hard rolls
 1   cup shredded mozzarella cheese (4 ounces)
1/4  cup grated Parmesan cheese
```

1. In a large skillet, cook ground beef until brown. Drain off fat. Stir in tomato sauce, onion, oregano, and basil. Bring mixture to boiling; reduce heat. Simmer, covered, for 15 minutes.

2. Meanwhile, preheat oven to 400°F. Cut a thin slice from the top of each roll; set tops of rolls aside. Scoop out insides of rolls, leaving 1/2-inch-thick shells. Set shells aside. Reserve scooped-out bread for another use.

3. Spoon beef mixture into bread shells. Top with mozzarella and Parmesan cheeses. Cover with roll tops. Wrap each roll in foil. Place on a large baking sheet. Bake about 20 minutes or until heated through. Makes 8 servings.

Per serving: 291 cal., 9 g fat (4 g sat. fat), 38 mg chol., 580 mg sodium, 32 g carbo., 2 g fiber, 18 g pro.

Super Subs
Start to Finish: 15 minutes

```
 1   16-ounce loaf French bread, sliced in half
     lengthwise and crosswise
 8   ounces thinly sliced assorted deli turkey,
     ham, roast beef, and/or salami
 8   ounces thinly sliced cheddar, mozzarella,
     Swiss, or provolone cheese
 2   medium tomatoes, sliced
1/2  of a 16-ounce package torn mixed salad
     greens
 2   tablespoons bottled Italian salad dressing
```

1. Use a spoon or fork to remove bread from center of each portion of loaf, leaving a 1/2-inch-thick shell. Reserve scooped-out bread for another use.

2. Layer meat, cheese, tomatoes, and greens on bottom portions of bread. Drizzle layers with dressing and top with remaining bread portions. Cut each sandwich into four pieces. Makes 8 servings.

Per serving: 360 cal., 16 g fat (8 g sat. fat), 50 mg chol., 817 mg sodium, 33 g carbo., 1 g fiber, 18 g pro.

Catfish Po'Boys
Start to Finish: 20 minutes

```
 1   to 1 1/4 pounds farm-raised catfish fillets
     Salt and ground black pepper
1/2  cup fine dry bread crumbs
 2   tablespoons olive oil
 4   hoagie buns, split and toasted, if desired
 2   medium red and/or yellow sweet peppers,
     cored and sliced in rings
 4   ounces Monterey Jack cheese with
     jalapeño peppers, shredded (1 cup)
 1   cup purchased deli coleslaw
     Bottled hot pepper sauce (optional)
     Small hot peppers (optional)
```

1. Cut catfish fillets into 3-inch pieces. Season catfish lightly with salt and pepper. Coat with bread crumbs. In a very large skillet, cook catfish in hot oil for 6 to 8 minutes, turning once, until golden brown and fish flakes easily when tested with a fork.

2. Place catfish in buns; top fish with sweet pepper rings, cheese, and coleslaw. If desired, pass hot pepper sauce and serve with hot peppers. Makes 4 servings.

Per serving: 675 cal., 30 g fat (10 g sat. fat), 86 mg chol., 1,004 mg sodium, 67 g carbo., 4 g fiber, 35 g pro.

Tall Turkey Sandwich
Start to Finish: 10 minutes

```
 1   tablespoon low-fat plain yogurt
 2   teaspoons Dijon-style mustard
 2   slices multigrain bread, toasted
 3   to 4 leaves lettuce, such as leaf or Bibb
 2   to 3 ounces sliced cooked fat-free turkey
     breast
 2   slices tomato
 1   slice yellow sweet pepper
1/4  cup snow pea pods, cut lengthwise into
     thin pieces (optional)
```

1. In a small bowl, stir together yogurt and mustard; spread mixture on one toasted bread slice. Layer lettuce, turkey, tomato, and sweet pepper on top of bread. Add the pea pods, if desired, and second toasted bread slice. Makes 1 serving.

Per serving: 225 cal., 2 g fat (1 g sat. fat), 21 mg chol., 1,211 mg sodium, 34 g carbo., 4 g fiber, 17 g pro.

slow-cooker
meals

Slow-Cooker
Pot Roast Stew

Despite cooking times measured in hours, *we love slow cooking because it's super easy.* No wonder many cooks would part with anything in their kitchens before giving up their slow cookers.

Slow-Cooker Pot Roast Stew

Prep: 20 minutes
Cook: 6 hours (low) or 3 hours (high) plus 1½ hours (high)

- 2 large onions, cut into ½-inch wedges
- 1 3- to 3½-pound boneless beef chuck pot roast, cut into 1-inch cubes
- ¾ cup dry red wine or lower-sodium beef broth
- ¼ cup tomato paste
- 3 tablespoons balsamic vinegar or cider vinegar
- 2 3-inch cinnamon sticks
- 1 teaspoon dried rosemary, crushed
- 1 teaspoon ground allspice
- ¾ teaspoon salt
- ¼ to ½ teaspoon crushed red pepper
- 1 2-pound butternut squash, peeled, seeded, and cut into 1½-inch pieces
- 2 large firm cooking apples (such as Granny Smith, Fuji, or Gala), cut into ½-inch wedges
- 4 cups hot cooked couscous

1. Place onions in a 5- to 6-quart slow cooker. Place beef on top of onions. In a bowl, combine wine, tomato paste, vinegar, cinnamon, rosemary, allspice, salt, and crushed red pepper. Pour over beef.

2. Cover; cook on low-heat setting for 6 hours or on high-heat setting for 3 hours. Adjust low-heat setting to high-heat setting. Stir in squash. Cook, covered, for 1 hour. Add apples. Cook, covered, for 30 minutes more or until squash is tender. Remove and discard cinnamon. Serve stew with couscous and juices. Makes 8 servings.

Per serving: 339 cal., 8 g fat (2 g sat. fat), 100 mg chol., 347 mg sodium, 35 g carbo., 4 g fiber, 41 g pro.

Saturday Night Beef Vegetable Soup

Prep: 25 minutes
Cook: 8 to 10 hours (low) or 4 to 5 hours (high)

- 1 **pound boneless beef chuck roast, cut into 1-inch pieces**
- 1 **tablespoon cooking oil**
- 2 **14.5-ounce cans diced tomatoes, undrained**
- 3 **medium carrots, sliced**
- 2 **small potatoes, peeled, if desired, and cut into $1/2$-inch cubes**
- 1 **large onion, chopped (1 cup)**
- 1 **cup water**
- 1 **teaspoon salt**
- $1/2$ **teaspoon dried thyme, crushed**
- $1/2$ **cup frozen loose-pack peas, thawed**

1. In a large skillet, brown beef on all sides in hot oil over medium-high heat. Place meat in a $3 1/2$- to $4 1/2$-quart slow cooker. Add undrained tomatoes, carrots, potatoes, onion, the water, salt, and thyme.

2. Cover; cook on low-heat setting for 8 to 10 hours or on high-heat setting for 4 to 5 hours. Stir in peas. Ladle into bowls to serve. Makes 4 to 5 servings.

Per serving: 335 cal., 8 g fat (2 g sat. fat), 67 mg chol., 1,054 mg sodium, 35 g carbo., 5 g fiber, 29 g pro.

Italian Beef Sandwiches

Prep: 10 minutes
Cook: 10 to 12 hours (low) or 5 to 6 hours (high)

- 1 **4-pound beef sirloin or rump roast, cut into 2- to 3-inch pieces**
- $1/2$ **cup water**
- 1 **0.7-ounce package dry Italian salad dressing mix**
- 2 **teaspoons dried Italian seasoning, crushed**
- $1/2$ **to 1 teaspoon crushed red pepper**
- $1/2$ **teaspoon garlic powder**
- 12 **kaiser rolls or other sandwich rolls, split**

1. Place beef in a $3 1/2$- to 5-quart slow cooker. In a bowl, combine the water, salad dressing mix, Italian seasoning, crushed red pepper, and garlic powder; pour over beef.

2. Cover; cook on low-heat setting for 10 to 12 hours or on high-heat setting for 5 to 6 hours.

3. Use a slotted spoon to transfer beef to a cutting board. Shred beef using two forks to pull the meat apart. To serve, spoon shredded beef onto half of each roll;

drizzle with some of the cooking liquid to moisten. Cover with roll tops. Makes 12 servings.

Per serving: 361 cal., 8 g fat (2 g sat. fat), 91 mg chol., 598 mg sodium, 31 g carbo., 10 g fiber, 38 g pro.

Oriental Beef Brisket

Prep: 20 minutes
Cook: 10 to 11 hours (low) or 5 to $5 1/2$ hours (high)

- 1 **pound baking potatoes, peeled and cut into 1-inch cubes**
- 1 **pound sweet potatoes, peeled and cut into 1-inch cubes**
- 1 **3- to $3 1/2$-pound fresh beef brisket, fat trimmed**
- $1/2$ **cup hoisin sauce**
- $1/2$ **cup bottled salsa**
- 2 **tablespoons quick-cooking tapioca**
- 2 **cloves garlic, minced**

1. In a 5- to 6-quart slow cooker, place baking potatoes and sweet potatoes. Top with beef brisket. In a small bowl, combine hoisin sauce, salsa, tapioca, and garlic. Pour sauce mixture over meat; spread evenly.

2. Cover; cook on low-heat setting for 10 to 11 hours or on high-heat setting for 5 to $5 1/2$ hours. Transfer meat to a cutting board. Cut across the grain into slices. Serve cooking liquid and potatoes with beef. Makes 8 servings.

Per serving: 344 cal., 11 g fat (3 g sat. fat), 103 mg chol., 382 mg sodium, 22 g carbo., 2 g fiber, 38 g pro.

golden oldies

Do you have a favorite recipe that you want to try fixing in the slow cooker? Many stews, pot roasts, and similar dishes do well in the slow cooker. Start with a less-tender meat cut, such as beef chuck or pork shoulder roast. Look for a recipe similar to yours and use it as guide for quantities, piece sizes, liquid amounts, and cooking time. Cut the vegetables into uniform, bite-size pieces. If using large pieces of meat, place the meat on top of the vegetables to ensure the vegetables will be tender when the meat is done. Because there's no evaporation in a slow cooker, you can reduce the liquid in your recipe by half.

Beef Burgundy

Beef Burgundy

Prep: 20 minutes
Cook: 7 to 9 hours (low) or 3½ to 4½ hours (high)

    Nonstick cooking spray
2   pounds beef stew meat, cut into 2-inch cubes
1   16-ounce package frozen stew vegetables
1   10.75-ounce can condensed golden mushroom soup
⅔   cup Burgundy wine
⅓   cup water
1   tablespoon quick-cooking tapioca
    Snipped fresh parsley

1. Lightly coat a large skillet with cooking spray. Heat over medium heat. In skillet, brown beef, half at a time, over medium heat; drain off fat. Place frozen vegetables in a 3½- or 4-quart slow cooker. Place beef on vegetables. In a medium bowl, stir together soup, wine, the water, and tapioca. Pour over meat and vegetables in cooker.

3. Cover and cook on low-heat setting for 7 to 9 hours or on high-heat setting for 3½ to 4½ hours. Sprinkle with snipped parsley. Makes 6 servings.

Per serving: 291 cal., 8 g fat (3 g sat. fat), 91 mg chol., 535 mg sodium, 14 g carbo., 1 g fiber, 34 g pro.

Round Steak with Mushroom-Onion Sauce

Prep: 20 minutes
Cook: 8 to 10 hours (low) or 4 to 5 hours (high)

2   pounds boneless beef round steak, cut ¾ inch thick
1   tablespoon cooking oil
2   medium onions, sliced
3   cups sliced fresh mushrooms
1   12-ounce jar beef gravy
1   1.1-ounce envelope mushroom gravy mix

1. Trim fat from meat. Cut meat into 8 serving-size pieces. In a large skillet, brown meat, half at a time, in hot oil over medium heat. Drain off fat. Set aside.

2. Place onions in a 3½- or 4-quart slow cooker. Add meat and mushrooms. In a small bowl, stir together gravy and gravy mix. Pour over mixture in cooker.

3. Cover; cook on low-heat setting for 8 to 10 hours or on high-heat setting for 4 to 5 hours. Makes 8 servings.

Per serving: 194 cal., 7 g fat (2 g sat. fat), 57 mg chol., 479 mg sodium, 7 g carbo., 1 g fiber, 24 g pro.

Round Steak with Mushroom-Onion Sauce

Pennsylvania Pot Roast

Prep: 30 minutes
Cook: 7 to 9 hours (low) or 3½ to 4½ hours (high)

1   2½- to 3-pound boneless pork shoulder roast
1   tablespoon cooking oil
6   small parsnips, peeled and quartered
2   small sweet potatoes, peeled and
      quartered
1   small onion, sliced
1   cup beef broth
½   cup apple cider or apple juice
1   teaspoon dried basil, crushed
1   teaspoon dried marjoram, crushed
½   teaspoon salt
¼   teaspoon ground black pepper
2   small cooking apples, cored and
      cut into wedges
½   cup cold water
¼   cup all-purpose flour
      Salt and ground black pepper

1. Trim fat from meat. In a large skillet, brown meat in hot oil over medium heat, turning to brown on all sides. In a 4½- to 6-quart slow cooker, combine parsnips, sweet potatoes, and onion. Place meat on vegetables. In a medium bowl, combine broth, apple cider, basil, marjoram, the ½ teaspoon salt, and the ¼ teaspoon pepper. Pour over meat.

2. Cover; cook on low-heat setting for 7 to 9 hours or on high-heat setting for 3½ to 4½ hours, adding apple wedges the last 30 minutes of cooking. Remove meat, vegetables, and apples to a serving platter; keep warm.

3. For gravy, skim fat from cooking liquid; strain liquid through a fine mesh sieve. Measure 1¾ cups of the cooking liquid; pour into a medium saucepan. In a small bowl, stir the cold water into the flour; stir into cooking liquid in saucepan. Cook and stir until thickened and bubbly. Cook and stir for 1 minute more. Season with additional salt and pepper. Pass gravy with meat. Makes 6 servings.

Per serving: 485 cal., 16 g fat (5 g sat. fat), 126 mg chol., 492 mg sodium, 45 g carbo., 8 g fiber, 40 g pro.

loving leftovers

With a large-capacity slow cooker, you can cook food for two or three family dinners at one time. Immediately after dinner, transfer the leftover food to freezer-safe containers. Label, then freeze for up to 6 months. Always thaw frozen cooked food in the refrigerator. Heat it in a saucepan, never in the slow cooker.

For smaller amounts of leftovers, immediately after dinner, transfer the food to storage containers. Cover and refrigerate. Don't leave food in the cooker to cool or put food into the refrigerator while in the cooker.

Game-Day Chili

Prep: 30 minutes
Cook: 10 to 12 hours (low) or 5 to 6 hours (high)

2   pounds boneless beef round steak
      or pork shoulder roast, trimmed and
      cut into ½-inch cubes
2   large onions, chopped (2 cups)
2   large yellow, red, and/or green sweet
      peppers, chopped
2   15-ounce cans chili beans in chili gravy
2   14.5-ounce cans Mexican-style stewed
      tomatoes, undrained and cut up
1   15-ounce can red kidney beans or pinto
      beans, rinsed and drained
1   cup beer or beef broth
1   to 2 tablespoons chopped canned
      chipotle pepper in adobo sauce
2   teaspoons garlic salt
2   teaspoons ground cumin
1   teaspoon dried oregano, crushed
      Dairy sour cream, lime wedges, and/or
      snipped fresh cilantro (optional)

1. In a 5½- or 6-quart slow cooker, combine meat, onions, sweet peppers, undrained chili beans, undrained tomatoes, undrained kidney beans, beer, chipotle pepper, garlic salt, cumin, and oregano.

2. Cover; cook on low-heat setting for 10 to 12 hours or on high-heat setting for 5 to 6 hours. Spoon off fat.

3. If desired, serve chili with sour cream, lime wedges, and/or cilantro. Makes 10 to 12 servings.

Per serving: 294 cal., 5 g fat (1 g sat. fat), 52 mg chol., 823 mg sodium, 32 g carbo., 8 g fiber, 29 g pro.

Don't peek! Every time you lift your slow cooker lid, you release heat, adding 30 minutes to the cooking time.

> Canned soups and gravies make *good slow-cooker sauces;* they don't become thin during long cooking.

Meatball-Vegetable Stew

Prep: 10 minutes
Cook: 6 to 8 hours (low) or 3 to 4 hours (high)

- 1   16- to 18-ounce package frozen cooked meatballs
- ½   of a 16-ounce package (about 2 cups) frozen mixed vegetables
- 1   14.5-ounce can diced tomatoes with onion and garlic, or stewed tomatoes, undrained
- 1   12-ounce jar mushroom gravy
- 1½   teaspoons dried basil, crushed

1. In a 3½- or 4-quart slow cooker, combine meatballs and mixed vegetables. In a large bowl, stir together undrained tomatoes, gravy, ⅓ cup *water,* and basil; pour over meatballs and vegetables.

2. Cover; cook on low-heat setting for 6 to 8 hours or on high-heat setting for 3 to 4 hours. Makes 4 servings.

Per serving: 472 cal., 32 g fat (14 g sat. fat), 87 mg chol., 1,883 mg sodium, 26 g carbo., 6 g fiber, 21 g pro.

Fireside Beef Stew

Prep: 25 minutes Cook: 8 to 10 hours (low) or
4 to 5 hours (high); plus 15 minutes (high)

- 1½   pounds boneless beef chuck pot roast
- 1   pound butternut squash, peeled, seeded, and cut into 1-inch pieces (about 2½ cups)
- 2   small onions, cut into wedges
- 2   cloves garlic, minced
- 1   14-ounce can reduced-sodium beef broth
- 1   8-ounce can tomato sauce
- 2   tablespoons Worcestershire sauce
- 1   teaspoon dry mustard
- ¼   teaspoon ground black pepper

- ⅛   teaspoon ground allspice
- 2   tablespoons cold water
- 4   teaspoons cornstarch
- 1   9-ounce package frozen Italian green beans

1. Trim fat from meat. Cut meat into 1-inch pieces. Place meat in a 3½- to 4½-quart slow cooker. Add squash, onions, and garlic. Stir in beef broth, tomato sauce, Worcestershire sauce, dry mustard, pepper, and allspice.

2. Cover; cook on low-heat setting for 8 to 10 hours or on high-heat setting for 4 to 5 hours.

3. If using low-heat setting, turn to high-heat setting. In a small bowl, combine the cold water and cornstarch. Stir cornstarch mixture and green beans into mixture in slow cooker. Cover and cook about 15 minutes more or until thickened. Makes 6 servings.

Per serving: 206 cal., 4 g fat (1 g sat. fat), 67 mg chol., 440 mg sodium, 15 g carbo., 3 g fiber, 27 g pro.

Italian Steak Rolls

Prep: 35 minutes
Cook: 8 to 10 hours (low) or 4 to 5 hours (high)

- ½   cup grated carrot
- ⅓   cup chopped zucchini
- ⅓   cup chopped red or green sweet pepper
- ¼   cup sliced green onions
- 2   tablespoons grated Parmesan cheese
- 1   tablespoon snipped fresh parsley
- 1   clove garlic, minced
- ¼   teaspoon ground black pepper
- 6   tenderized beef round steaks (about 2 pounds total)
- 1   14-ounce jar meatless pasta sauce
     Hot cooked pasta (optional)

1. For the vegetable filling, in a small bowl, combine carrot, zucchini, sweet pepper, green onions, Parmesan cheese, parsley, garlic, and black pepper. Spoon ¼ cup of the vegetable filling on each piece of meat. Roll up meat around the filling; tie each roll with string or secure with wooden toothpicks.

3. Place meat rolls in a 3½- or 4-quart slow cooker. Pour pasta sauce over the meat rolls.

4. Cover; cook on low-heat setting for 8 to 10 hours or on high-heat setting for 4 to 5 hours. Discard string or toothpicks. Serve meat rolls with sauce and, if desired, pasta. Makes 6 servings.

Per serving: 261 cal., 9 g fat (3 g sat. fat), 73 mg chol., 523 mg sodium, 7 g carbo., 2 g fiber, 33 g pro.

Classic Beef Stroganoff

Prep: 30 minutes   Cook: 8 to 10 hours (low) or
4 to 5 hours (high); plus 30 minutes (high)

1½	pounds beef stew meat
1	tablespoon cooking oil
2	cups sliced fresh mushrooms
½	cup sliced green onions or 1 medium onion, chopped
1	bay leaf
1	teaspoon bottled minced garlic
½	teaspoon dried oregano, crushed
¼	teaspoon salt
¼	teaspoon dried thyme, crushed
¼	teaspoon ground black pepper
1½	cups beef broth
⅓	cup dry sherry
1	8-ounce carton dairy sour cream
⅓	cup all-purpose flour
¼	cup cold water

1. Cut up any large pieces of meat. In large skillet, brown meat, half at a time, in hot oil. Drain off fat.

2. In 3½- or 4-quart slow cooker, combine mushrooms, green onions, bay leaf, garlic, oregano, salt, thyme, and pepper. Add meat. Pour broth and sherry over meat.

3. Cover; cook on low-heat setting for 8 to 10 hours or on high-heat setting for 4 to 5 hours. Discard bay leaf. If using low-heat setting, turn to high-heat setting.

4. In a medium bowl, whisk together sour cream, flour, and the water. Stir about 1 cup of the hot liquid into sour cream mixture. Return all to slow cooker; stir to combine. Cover; cook about 30 minutes more or until thickened and bubbly. Makes 6 servings.

Per serving: 302 cal., 15 g fat (7 g sat. fat), 84 mg chol., 402 mg sodium, 10 g carbo., 1 g fiber, 28 g pro.

Ham and Broccoli Potatoes

Prep: 15 minutes   Cook: 1½ hours

2	cups shredded smoked Gouda cheese (8 ounces)
1	10.75-ounce can condensed cream of celery or cream of chicken soup
1	10-ounce package frozen chopped broccoli, thawed
8	ounces diced cooked ham
6	medium baking potatoes, baked and split*
1	tablespoon snipped fresh chives

Ham and Broccoli Potatoes

1. In a 1½-quart slow cooker combine Gouda cheese, soup, broccoli, and ham.

2. Cover; cook for 1½ to 2½ hours. Stir before serving. Spoon ham mixture over baked potatoes. Sprinkle with chives. Makes 6 servings.

***Note:** To bake potatoes, scrub potatoes and pat dry. Prick potatoes with a fork. (For soft skins, rub potatoes with shortening or wrap each potato in foil.) Bake in a 425°F oven for 40 to 60 minutes or until tender. Roll each potato gently under your hand. Using a knife, cut an X in each top. Press in and up on ends of each potato.

Tip: To double recipe; prepare in a 3½- or 4-quart slow cooker. Cover; cook on low-heat setting for 3½ to 4 hours.

Per serving: 339 cal., 15 g fat (9 g sat. fat), 53 mg chol., 1,469 mg sodium, 34 g carbo., 5 g fiber, 18 g pro.

Mushroom-Sauced Pork Chops tip

To make 6 servings of this recipe, use 6 pork loin chops and leave the remaining ingredient amounts the same. Prepare the chops in a 5- to 6-quart slow cooker.

Mushroom-Sauced Pork Chops

Prep: 15 minutes
Cook: 8 to 9 hours (low) or 4 to 4$\frac{1}{2}$ hours (high)

- 4   pork loin chops, cut $\frac{3}{4}$ inch thick (about 2 pounds)
- 1   tablespoon cooking oil
- 1   small onion, thinly sliced
- 2   tablespoons quick-cooking tapioca
- 1   10.75-ounce can reduced-fat and reduced-sodium condensed cream of mushroom soup
- $\frac{1}{2}$ cup apple juice or apple cider
- 1$\frac{1}{2}$ teaspoons Worcestershire sauce
- 2   teaspoons snipped fresh thyme or $\frac{3}{4}$ teaspoon dried thyme, crushed
- $\frac{1}{4}$ teaspoon garlic powder
- 1$\frac{1}{2}$ cups sliced fresh mushrooms
   Fresh thyme sprigs (optional)

1. Trim fat from chops. In a large skillet, brown chops in hot oil over medium heat, turning to brown evenly. Drain off fat. Place onion in a 3$\frac{1}{2}$- or 4-quart slow cooker. Add chops. Using a mortar and pestle, crush tapioca. In a medium bowl, combine tapioca, soup, apple juice, Worcestershire sauce, thyme, and garlic powder; stir in mushrooms. Pour over chops in slow cooker.

2. Cover; cook on low-heat setting for 8 to 9 hours or on high-heat setting for 4 to 4$\frac{1}{2}$ hours. If desired, garnish with thyme sprigs. Makes 4 servings.

Per serving: 314 cal., 12 g fat (4 g sat. fat), 74 mg chol., 356 mg sodium, 17 g carbo., 1 g fiber, 30 g pro.

Ham-Bean Stew

Prep: 25 minutes Stand: 1 hour
Cook: 8 to 10 hours (low) or 4 to 5 hours (high)

 2 cups dry navy beans
 4 cups cold water
 2 pounds cooked ham, cut into $\frac{1}{2}$-inch cubes
 5 cups water
 4 stalks celery, sliced
 4 medium carrots, sliced
 1 medium onion, chopped
 $\frac{1}{2}$ teaspoon dried thyme, crushed
 $\frac{1}{2}$ teaspoon liquid smoke (optional)
 $\frac{1}{4}$ cup snipped fresh parsley

1. Rinse beans; place in a large saucepan. Add the 4 cups cold water. Bring to boiling; reduce heat. Simmer, uncovered, for 10 minutes. Remove from heat. Cover; let stand for 1 hour. Drain and rinse beans.

2. In a 4- to 6-quart slow cooker, combine beans, ham, the 5 cups water, celery, carrots, onion, thyme, and, if desired, liquid smoke. Cover; cook on low-heat setting for 8 to 10 hours or on high-heat setting for 4 to 5 hours. Stir in parsley. Makes 8 servings.

Per serving: 393 cal., 11 g fat (4 g sat. fat), 67 mg chol., 1,751 mg sodium, 36 g carbo., 14 g fiber, 38 g pro.

Jerk Pork Wraps with Lime Mayo

Prep: 30 minutes
Cook: 8 to 10 hours (low) or 4 to 5 hours (high)

 1 $1\frac{1}{2}$- to 2-pound boneless pork shoulder roast
 1 tablespoon Jamaican jerk seasoning
 $\frac{1}{4}$ teaspoon dried thyme, crushed
 1 cup water
 1 tablespoon lime juice
 6 to 8 9- or 10-inch flour tortillas
 6 to 8 lettuce leaves (optional)
 1 medium red or green sweet pepper, chopped (optional)
 1 medium mango, peeled, seeded, and chopped (optional)
    Lime Mayo

1. Trim fat from pork. Sprinkle jerk seasoning evenly over pork; rub in with your fingers. Place pork in a $3\frac{1}{2}$- or 4-quart slow cooker. Sprinkle with thyme. Pour the water over pork. Cover; cook on low-heat setting for 8 to 10 hours or on high-heat setting for 4 to 5 hours.

2. Remove pork from cooker, reserving cooking juices. Using two forks, shred pork, discarding any fat. Place pork in a shallow bowl. Skim fat from cooking juices. Add enough of the cooking juices to pork to moisten it (about $\frac{1}{2}$ cup). Stir lime juice into pork.

3. If desired, line tortillas with lettuce leaves. Use a slotted spoon to place pork mixture onto center of each tortilla. If desired, top with sweet pepper and mango. Spoon some of the Lime Mayo onto pork on each tortilla. Fold up one side of each tortilla; fold in side edges. Roll up to serve. Makes 6 to 8 servings.

Lime Mayo: In a small bowl, stir together $\frac{1}{2}$ cup light mayonnaise dressing or regular mayonnaise, $\frac{1}{4}$ cup finely chopped red onion, $\frac{1}{4}$ teaspoon finely shredded lime peel, 1 tablespoon lime juice, and 1 clove garlic, minced. Cover; chill in refrigerator until ready to serve or up to 1 week.

Per serving: 360 cal., 17 g fat (4 g sat. fat), 80 mg chol., 543 mg sodium, 26 g carbo., 1 g fiber, 25 g pro.

Italian Sausage Basil Lasagna

Prep: 20 minutes Cook: 4 to 6 hours (low) or 2 to 3 hours (high) Stand: 15 minutes

    Nonstick cooking spray
 1 pound bulk sweet Italian sausage
 1 26-ounce jar chunky tomato, basil, and cheese pasta sauce
 $\frac{3}{4}$ cup water
 12 no-boil lasagna noodles
 1 15-ounce container ricotta cheese
 1 8-ounce package shredded Italian blend cheese

1. Lightly coat a $3\frac{1}{2}$- or 4-quart slow cooker with cooking spray. Cook sausage in a large skillet until brown. Drain off fat. Stir in pasta sauce and the water.

2. Place $\frac{1}{2}$ cup of the meat mixture in the bottom of the slow cooker. Place four of the noodles on top of the meat mixture (break noodles to fit, if necessary). Top with one-third each of the ricotta cheese, remaining meat mixture, and shredded cheese. Repeat layers two more times starting with noodles and ending with meat mixture. Cover and refrigerate the remaining shredded cheese.

3. Cover; cook on low-heat setting for 4 to 6 hours or on high-heat setting for 2 to 3 hours.

4. Turn off slow cooker. Sprinkle the reserved shredded cheese on the lasagna. Cover; let stand about 15 minutes. Makes 8 to 10 servings.

Per serving: 497 cal., 30 g fat (14 g sat. fat), 87 mg chol., 909 mg sodium, 26 g carbo., 1 g fiber, 26 g pro.

Pork Lo Mein

Prep: 20 minutes   Cook: 6¹/₂ to 7 hours (low) or
3¹/₂ to 4 hours (high); plus 10 to 15 minutes (high)

1¹/₂	pounds boneless pork shoulder
2	medium onions, cut into wedges
2	cups frozen sliced carrots
1	12-ounce jar teriyaki glaze
1	cup thinly bias-sliced celery
1	8-ounce can sliced water chestnuts, drained
1	5-ounce can sliced bamboo shoots, drained
1	teaspoon grated fresh ginger
1	6-ounce package frozen snow peas
1	cup broccoli florets
9	ounces dried curly thin egg noodles
¹/₄	cup cashews

1. Trim fat from pork. Cut pork into ³/₄-inch pieces. In a 3¹/₂- or 4-quart slow cooker, combine pork, onions, frozen carrots, teriyaki glaze, celery, water chestnuts, bamboo shoots, and ginger. Cover; cook on low-heat setting for 6¹/₂ to 7 hours or on high-heat setting for 3¹/₂ to 4 hours. If using low-heat setting, turn to high-heat setting. Stir in frozen snow peas and broccoli. Cover; cook for 10 to 15 minutes or until pea pods are crisp-tender.

4. Meanwhile, cook noodles according to package directions; drain. Serve pork mixture over noodles. Sprinkle with cashews. Makes 6 servings.

Per serving: 509 cal., 12 g fat (3 g sat. fat), 73 mg chol., 2,274 mg sodium, 66 g carbo., 6 g fiber, 33 g pro.

Corn-Sausage Chowder

Prep: 15 minutes
Cook: 8 to 10 hours (low) or 4 to 5 hours (high)

1	pound cooked smoked turkey sausage, halved lengthwise and cut into ¹/₂-inch slices
3	cups loose-pack frozen diced hash brown potatoes with onion and peppers
2	medium carrots, coarsely chopped
1	15- to 16.5-ounce can cream-style corn
1	10.75-ounce can condensed golden mushroom soup
2¹/₂	cups water

1. In a 3¹/₂- to 5-quart slow cooker, layer sausage, frozen potatoes, and carrots. In a medium bowl, stir together corn, soup, and the water. Add to slow cooker.

2. Cover; cook on low-heat setting for 8 to 10 hours or on high-heat setting for 4 to 5 hours. Makes 6 servings.

Per serving: 238 cal., 8 g fat (2 g sat. fat), 53 mg chol., 1,280 mg sodium, 28 g carbo., 2 g fiber, 15 g pro.

Fruited Pork Chops

Prep: 15 minutes
Cook: 4 to 4¹/₂ hours (low) or 2 to 2¹/₂ hours (high)

6	boneless pork loin chops, cut 1 inch thick
1	teaspoon dried thyme, crushed
2	7-ounce packages mixed dried fruit
1	medium red sweet pepper, chopped
1	cup bottled barbecue sauce

1. Trim fat from pork chops. Place chops in a 3¹/₂- or 4-quart slow cooker. Sprinkle with thyme. Add dried fruit and sweet pepper. Pour barbecue sauce over all.

2. Cover; cook on low-heat setting for 4 to 4¹/₂ hours or on high-heat setting for 2 to 2¹/₂ hours. Transfer chops to a platter. Skim fat from sauce. Spoon some of the sauce over chops; pass remaining sauce. Makes 6 servings.

Per serving: 450 cal., 11 g fat (4 g sat. fat), 92 mg chol., 421 mg sodium, 49 g carbo., 3 g fiber, 40 g pro.

Chipotle Country-Style Ribs

Prep: 15 minutes   Cook: 10 to 12 hours (low) or
5 to 6 hours (high); plus 15 minutes (high)

2¹/₂	to 3 pounds boneless pork country-style ribs
1	12-ounce bottle barbecue sauce
2	canned chipotle chiles in adobo sauce, finely chopped
2	tablespoons cornstarch

1. Place ribs in a 4- to 5-quart slow cooker. Combine barbecue sauce and chipotle chiles. Pour over ribs. Cover; cook on low-heat setting for 10 to 12 hours or on high-heat setting for 5 to 6 hours. Transfer ribs to a serving platter, reserving cooking liquid. Cover ribs to keep warm. If using low-heat setting, turn to high-heat setting. In a small bowl combine cornstarch and 2 tablespoons *water*. Stir into liquid in cooker. Cover and cook about 15 minutes more or until thickened. Serve ribs with sauce. Makes 8 servings.

Per serving: 260 cal., 12 g fat (4 g sat. fat), 90 mg chol., 459 mg sodium, 8 g carbo., 1 g fiber, 28 g pro.

Cranberry Chicken

Prep: 15 minutes
Cook: 5 to 6 hours (low) or 2½ to 3 hours (high)

2½   to 3 pounds chicken thighs and/or
     drumsticks, skinned
1   16-ounce can whole cranberry sauce
2   tablespoons dry onion soup mix
2   tablespoons quick-cooking tapioca
3   cups hot cooked rice

1. Place chicken pieces in a 3½- or 4-quart slow cooker. In a small bowl, stir together cranberry sauce, soup mix, and tapioca. Pour over chicken pieces.

2. Cover; cook on low-heat setting for 5 to 6 hours or on high-heat setting for 2½ to 3 hours. Serve chicken and sauce over hot cooked rice. Makes 6 servings.

Per serving: 357 cal., 4 g fat (1 g sat. fat), 89 mg chol., 268 mg sodium, 55 g carbo., 1 g fiber, 23 g pro.

Chicken-Shrimp Jambalaya

Prep: 20 minutes   Cook: 5 to 6 hours (low) or 2½ to 3 hours (high)   Stand: 10 to 15 minutes

1   cup sliced celery
1   large onion, chopped
1   14.5-ounce can low-sodium tomatoes,
     undrained and cut up
1   14.5-ounce can reduced-sodium
     chicken broth
½   of a 6-ounce can (⅓ cup) tomato paste
1   tablespoon Worcestershire sauce
1½   teaspoons Cajun seasoning
1   pound skinless, boneless chicken breast
     halves or thighs, cut into ¾-inch pieces
1½   cups instant rice
8   ounces cooked peeled, deveined shrimp
¾   cup chopped green sweet pepper

1. In a 3½- or 4-quart slow cooker, combine celery, onion, undrained tomatoes, broth, tomato paste, Worcestershire sauce, and Cajun seasoning. Stir in chicken.

2. Cover; cook on low-heat setting for 5 to 6 hours or on high-heat setting for 2½ to 3 hours. Stir in rice, shrimp, and sweet pepper. Cover and let stand for 10 to 15 minutes or until most of the liquid is absorbed and rice is tender. Makes 6 servings.

Per serving: 261 cal., 2 g fat (0 g sat. fat), 118 mg chol., 391 mg sodium, 30 g carbo., 2 g fiber, 30 g pro.

Chicken and Mushrooms

Prep: 25 minutes
Cook: 8 to 9 hours (low) or 4 to 4½ hours (high)

2   cups sliced fresh mushrooms
1   14.5-ounce can diced tomatoes with
     basil, garlic, and oregano, undrained
1   medium red sweet pepper, cut into bite-
     size strips
1   medium onion, thinly sliced
¼   cup dry red wine or canned beef broth
2   tablespoons quick-cooking tapioca
2   tablespoons balsamic vinegar
3   cloves garlic, minced
2   to 2½ pounds meaty chicken pieces
     (breasts, thighs, and/or drumsticks),
     skinned
¼   teaspoon salt
¼   teaspoon paprika
¼   teaspoon ground black pepper
     Hot cooked pasta

1. In a 5- to 6-quart slow cooker, combine mushrooms, undrained tomatoes, sweet pepper, onion, wine, tapioca, balsamic vinegar, and garlic. Place chicken pieces on top. In a small bowl, combine salt, paprika, and black pepper; sprinkle over chicken.

2. Cover; cook on low-heat setting for 8 to 9 hours or on high-heat setting for 4 to 4½ hours.

3. Serve chicken in shallow bowls with sauce and cooked pasta. Makes 4 servings.

Per serving: 307 cal., 8 g fat (2 g sat. fat), 92 mg chol., 764 mg sodium, 23 g carbo., 2 g fiber, 33 g pro.

To be food-safe, always thaw frozen meat and poultry completely before adding it to the slow cooker.

Rosemary Chicken

Prep: 25 minutes   Cook: 6 to 7 hours (low) or
3 to 3½ hours (high); plus 15 minutes (high)

    Nonstick cooking spray
1½ **pounds skinless, boneless chicken breast**
    halves or thighs
1 **8- or 9-ounce package frozen**
    artichoke hearts
12 **cloves garlic, minced**
½ **cup chopped onion**
½ **cup reduced-sodium chicken broth**
2 **teaspoons dried rosemary, crushed**
1 **teaspoon finely shredded lemon peel**
½ **teaspoon ground black pepper**
1 **tablespoon cornstarch**
1 **tablespoon cold water**

1. Coat an unheated large nonstick skillet with nonstick cooking spray. Heat over medium heat. Brown chicken, half at a time, in hot skillet. In a 3½- or 4-quart slow cooker, combine frozen artichoke hearts, garlic, and onion. In a small bowl, combine broth, rosemary, lemon peel, and pepper. Pour over vegetables in slow cooker. Add chicken; spoon some of the garlic mixture over chicken.

2. Cover; cook on low-heat setting for 6 to 7 hours or on high-heat setting for 3 to 3½ hours.

3. Transfer chicken and artichokes to a serving platter, reserving cooking liquid. Cover chicken and artichokes with foil to keep warm.

4. If using low-heat setting, turn to high-heat setting. In a small bowl, combine cornstarch and the cold water. Stir into liquid in slow cooker. Cover and cook about 15 minutes more or until slightly thickened. Spoon sauce over chicken and artichokes. Makes 6 servings.

Per serving: 161 cal., 2 g fat (0 g sat. fat), 66 mg chol., 126 mg sodium, 8 g carbo., 2 g fiber, 28 g pro.

Chicken with Creamy Chive Sauce

Prep: 15 minutes   Cook: 4 to 5 hours (low)

6 **skinless, boneless chicken breast halves**
    (about 2 pounds total)
¼ **cup butter**
1 **0.7-ounce package Italian salad**
    dressing mix
1 **10.75-ounce can condensed golden**
    mushroom soup
½ **cup dry white wine or chicken broth**
½ **of an 8-ounce tub cream cheese with chive**
    and onion

1. Place chicken in a 3½- or 4-quart slow cooker. In a medium saucepan, melt butter over medium heat. Stir in Italian salad dressing mix. Stir in soup, white wine, and cream cheese. Pour over chicken. Cover; cook on low-heat setting for 4 to 5 hours. Makes 6 servings.

Per serving: 310 cal., 17 g fat (9 g sat. fat), 110 mg chol., 1,043 mg sodium, 6 g carbo., 0 g fiber, 28 g pro.

Spinach, Turkey, and Wild Rice Soup

Prep: 15 minutes
Cook: 7 to 8 hours (low) or 3½ to 4 hours (high)

3 **cups water**
1 **14-ounce can chicken broth**
1 **10.75-ounce can condensed cream of**
    chicken soup
¾ **cup wild rice, rinsed and drained**
½ **teaspoon dried thyme, crushed**
¼ **teaspoon ground black pepper**
3 **cups chopped cooked turkey or**
    chicken (about 1 pound)
2 **cups shredded fresh spinach**

1. In a 3½- or 4-quart slow cooker, combine the water, chicken broth, cream of chicken soup, uncooked wild rice, thyme, and pepper.

2. Cover; cook on low-heat setting for 7 to 8 hours or on high-heat setting for 3½ to 4 hours. Just before serving, stir in turkey and spinach. Makes 6 servings.

Per serving: 263 cal., 9 g fat (3 g sat. fat), 66 mg chol., 741 mg sodium, 19 g carbo., 2 g fiber, 25 g pro.

Spinach, Turkey, and Wild Rice Soup

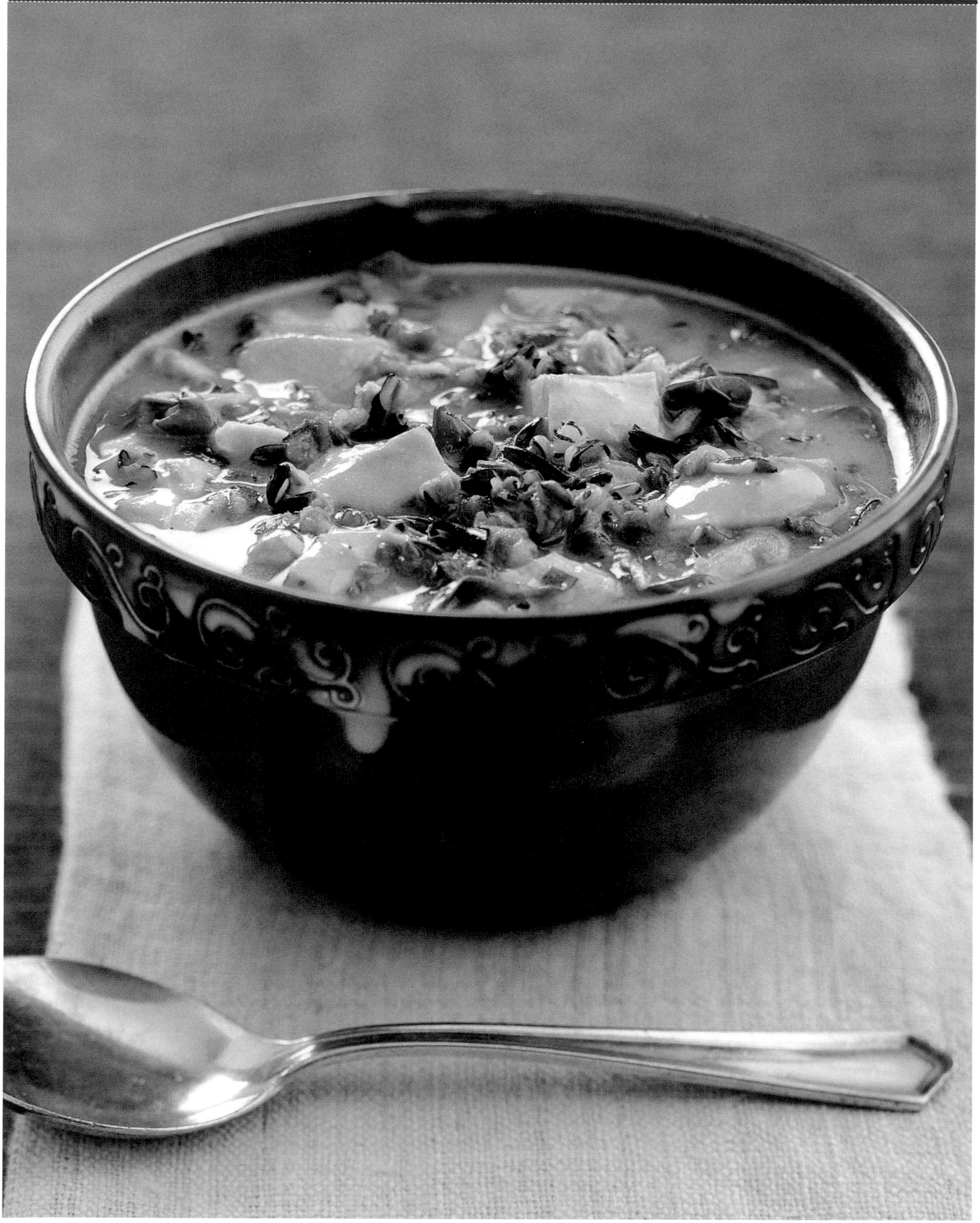

Chicken with Olives and Capers

Prep: 20 minutes
Cook: 6 to 7 hours (low) or 3 to 3½ hours (high)

2½	pounds meaty chicken pieces (breast halves, thighs, and drumsticks), skinned
¼	teaspoon salt
⅛	teaspoon ground black pepper
1	26-ounce jar pasta sauce with olives
2	tablespoons drained capers
1	teaspoon finely shredded lemon peel
3	cups hot cooked orzo

1. Place chicken pieces in a 3½- or 4-quart slow cooker. Lightly sprinkle with salt and pepper. In a medium bowl, stir together pasta sauce, capers, and lemon peel. Pour over chicken.

2. Cover; cook on low-heat setting for 6 to 7 hours or on high-heat setting for 3 to 3½ hours. Serve chicken and sauce over hot cooked orzo. Makes 6 servings.

Per serving: 315 cal., 8 g fat (2 g sat. fat), 77 mg chol., 678 mg sodium, 30 g carbo., 3 g fiber, 30 g pro.

Lamb Shanks with Barley

Prep: 25 minutes   Cook: 7 to 9 hours (low)

3	to 3½ pounds lamb shanks or beef shank crosscuts
1	tablespoon cooking oil
1	cup regular barley
1	medium onion, chopped
4	carrots, cut into ½-inch slices
3	stalks celery, cut into ½-inch slices
1	14-ounce can chicken broth
1	14.5-ounce can diced tomatoes, undrained
⅓	cup water
½	teaspoon ground black pepper
2	tablespoons balsamic vinegar (optional)

1. In a large skillet, brown the lamb shanks in hot oil over medium heat. Drain off fat.

2. In a 5- to 6-quart slow cooker, combine barley, onion, carrots, celery, broth, undrained tomatoes, the water, and pepper. Add lamb shanks.

3. Cover; cook on low-heat setting for 7 to 9 hours or until lamb pulls easily from bones and barley is tender. Transfer lamb shanks to a serving platter. Skim off fat from vegetable-barley mixture. If desired, stir in balsamic vinegar. Serve with lamb. Makes 6 to 8 servings.

Per serving: 370 cal., 8 g fat (2 g sat. fat), 99 mg chol., 529 mg sodium, 36 g carbo., 7 g fiber, 37 g pro.

For best results, be sure your slow cooker is at *least half full* but no more than two-thirds full when it's in use.

Braised Lamb with Dill Sauce

Prep: 40 minutes
Cook: 7 to 8 hours (low) or 3½ to 4 hours (high)

12	ounces tiny new potatoes
3	medium carrots, cut into 1-inch pieces
6	lamb rib chops, cut 1 inch thick (about 2½ pounds)
2	teaspoons cooking oil
¾	cup water
2	teaspoons snipped fresh dill or ½ teaspoon dried dillweed
½	teaspoon salt
¼	teaspoon ground black pepper
½	cup plain low-fat yogurt
4	teaspoons all-purpose flour

1. Remove a narrow strip of peel from the center of each potato. Place potatoes and carrots in a 3½- or 4-quart slow cooker. In a large skillet, brown both sides of chops, a few at a time, in hot oil over medium heat. Drain off fat. Place chops on vegetables. Add the water; sprinkle with half of the dill, salt, and pepper.

2. Cover; cook on low-heat setting for 7 to 8 hours or high-heat setting for 3½ to 4 hours.

3. Transfer chops and vegetables to a serving platter. Cover to keep warm.

4. For sauce, strain cooking liquid into a glass measuring cup; skim off fat. Measure ½ cup liquid. In a small saucepan, combine yogurt and flour. Stir in cooking liquid and remaining dill. Cook and stir over medium heat until thickened and bubbly. Cook and stir for 1 minute more. Season with additional salt and pepper. Serve chops and vegetables with sauce. Makes 6 servings.

Per serving: 288 cal., 10 g fat (3 g sat. fat), 54 mg chol., 510 mg sodium, 29 g carbo., 3 g fiber, 21 g pro.

Bean-and-Rice-Stuffed Peppers

Prep: 15 minutes
Cook: 6 to 6½ hours (low) or 3 to 3½ hours (high)

- **4 medium green, red, or yellow sweet peppers**
- **1 15-ounce can chili beans with chili gravy**
- **1 cup cooked converted rice**
- **4 ounces Monterey Jack cheese, shredded (1 cup)**
- **1 15-ounce can chunky tomato sauce with onion, celery, and green pepper**

1. Remove tops, membranes, and seeds from sweet peppers. In a medium bowl, stir together chili beans with chili gravy, rice, and ½ cup of the cheese; spoon into peppers. Pour tomato sauce into a 5- or 6-quart slow cooker. Place peppers, filled side up, in cooker.

2. Cover; cook on low-heat setting for 6 to 6½ hours or on high heat setting for 3 to 3½ hours. Transfer peppers to a serving plate. Spoon tomato sauce over peppers and sprinkle with remaining cheese. Makes 4 servings.

Per serving: 332 cal., 12 g fat (5 g sat. fat), 25 mg chol., 918 mg sodium, 42 g carbo., 10 g fiber, 16 g pro.

Red Beans over Spanish Rice

Prep: 25 minutes   Cook: 10 to 11 hours (low) or
5 to 5½ hours (high)   Stand: 1 hour

- **2 cups dry red beans or dry red kidney beans**
- **12 ounces boneless pork shoulder, cut into 1-inch pieces**
- **1 tablespoon cooking oil**
- **Nonstick cooking spray**
- **2½ cups chopped onions**
- **1 tablespoon bottled minced garlic or 6 cloves garlic, minced**
- **1 tablespoon ground cumin**
- **1 6.75-ounce package Spanish rice mix**

1. Rinse beans; drain. In a large saucepan, combine beans and 5 cups *cold water*. Bring to boiling; reduce heat. Simmer, uncovered, for 10 minutes. Remove from heat. Cover; let stand for 1 hour. (Or omit simmering; soak beans in 5 cups cold water for 6 to 8 hours or overnight in covered saucepan.) Rinse and drain the beans.

2. In a large skillet, brown pork, half at a time, in hot oil over medium heat. Drain off fat. Lightly coat a 3½- or 4-quart slow cooker with nonstick cooking spray. In the slow cooker, combine beans, pork, onions, garlic, and cumin. Stir in 4 cups *water*.

3. Cover; cook on low-heat setting for 10 to 11 hours or on high-heat setting for 5 to 5½ hours.

4. Prepare rice mix according to package directions. Use a slotted spoon to remove beans from cooker. Serve beans over cooked rice. Spoon some of the cooking liquid from the cooker over each serving, if desired. Makes 6 to 8 servings.

Per serving: 344 cal., 1 g fat (0 g sat. fat), 0 mg chol., 450 mg sodium, 68 g carbo., 17 g fiber, 19 g pro.

Pesto Beans and Pasta

Prep: 20 minutes
Cook: 7 to 9 hours (low) or 3½ to 4½ hours (high)

- **2 19-ounce cans cannellini beans (white kidney beans), rinsed and drained**
- **1 14.5-ounce can Italian-style stewed tomatoes, undrained**
- **1 medium green sweet pepper, chopped**
- **1 medium red sweet pepper, chopped**
- **1 medium onion, cut into thin wedges**
- **2 teaspoons dried Italian seasoning, crushed**
- **¼ teaspoon cracked black pepper**
- **4 cloves garlic, minced**
- **½ cup vegetable broth**
- **½ cup dry white wine or vegetable broth**
- **1 7-ounce container refrigerated basil pesto**
- **12 ounces dried penne pasta**
- **½ cup finely shredded Parmesan or Romano cheese**

1. In a 3½- or 4-quart slow cooker, combine beans, undrained tomatoes, sweet peppers, onion, Italian seasoning, black pepper, and garlic. Pour vegetable broth and wine over all.

2. Cover; cook on low-heat setting for 7 to 9 hours or on high-heat setting for 3½ to 4½ hours. Use a slotted spoon to transfer bean mixture to a large serving bowl; reserve cooking liquid. Stir pesto into bean mixture.

3. Meanwhile, cook pasta according to package directions; drain. Add pasta to bean mixture; gently toss to combine, adding enough of the liquid to make mixture of desired consistency. To serve, spoon pasta into pasta bowls; sprinkle with cheese. Makes 4 servings.

Per serving: 580 cal., 20 g fat (2 g sat. fat), 10 mg chol., 843 mg sodium, 80 g carbo., 11 g fiber, 25 g pro.

Proscuitto-Basil
Cheese Ball

Appetizers are lighthearted foods, designed for fun and friends. Whether you're hosting a casual party or need a snack for a potluck, you'll find lots of tasty finger foods here.

Prosciutto-Basil Cheese Ball

Prep: 35 minutes   Chill: 4 hours   Stand: 15 minutes

- 1   8-ounce package cream cheese
- 4   ounces Fontina cheese, finely shredded (1 cup)
- ¼   cup butter
- 1   tablespoon milk
- ½   teaspoon Worcestershire sauce for chicken
- 2   ounces prosciutto, chopped
- 2   tablespoons thinly sliced green onion
- 2   tablespoons snipped fresh basil
- ½   cup chopped toasted pine nuts
  Apples, assorted crackers, and/or flatbreads

1. In a large mixing bowl, let cream cheese, shredded cheese, and butter stand at room temperature for 30 minutes. Add milk and Worcestershire sauce. Beat with an electric mixer on medium speed until light and fluffy. Stir in prosciutto, green onion, and basil. Cover and chill for 4 to 24 hours.

2. Before serving, shape mixture into a ball. Roll ball in pine nuts and let stand for 15 minutes. Serve with apples, crackers, and/ or flatbread. Makes about 2 cups.

Make-Ahead directions: Prepare as directed in Step 1. Wrap cheese ball in moisture- and vapor-proof plastic wrap. Freeze for up to 1 month. To serve, thaw in refrigerator overnight. Unwrap and roll in nuts. Let stand for 15 minutes at room temperature before serving.

To make logs: Divide mixture into four portions. Shape into 5-inch-long logs before rolling in nuts.

Per tablespoon spread: 63 cal., 6 g fat (3 g sat. fat), 16 mg chol., 62 mg sodium, 1 g carbo., 0 g fiber, 2 g pro.

Black Bean Nachos

Prep: 20 minutes   Bake: 23 minutes   Oven: 350°F

- 6   7- or 8-inch flour tortillas
  Nonstick cooking spray
- 2   teaspoons taco seasoning mix
- 2   cups shredded Monterey Jack cheese or Colby and Monterey Jack cheese or Monterey Jack cheese with jalapeño chile peppers (8 ounces)
- ¾   cup canned black beans, rinsed and drained
- ¾   cup bottled thick and chunky salsa
- ½   cup loose-pack frozen whole kernel corn
  Dairy sour cream (optional)
  Snipped fresh cilantro (optional)

1. Preheat oven to 350°F. Cut each tortilla into eight wedges. Place half of the tortilla wedges in a single layer on a large baking sheet. Lightly coat with nonstick cooking spray; sprinkle with half of the taco seasoning mix. Bake for 8 to 10 minutes or until dry and crisp; cool. Repeat with remaining tortilla wedges and taco seasoning mix.

2. Mound chips on an 11- or 12-inch ovenproof platter or large baking sheet. Sprinkle with cheese. Bake for 5 to 7 minutes more or until cheese melts.

3. Meanwhile, in a small saucepan, combine beans, salsa, and corn. Cook over medium heat until heated through, stirring occasionally.

4. To serve, spoon bean mixture over the cheese-topped chips. If desired, top with sour cream and sprinkle with cilantro. Makes 12 servings.

Per serving: 137 cal., 7 g fat (4 g sat. fat), 17 mg chol., 338 mg sodium, 12 g carbo., 1 g fiber, 7 g pro.

Appetizer Sampler with Lime-Chive Dip

Prep: 10 minutes (dip)   Chill: up to 24 hours

1 lime
2 8-ounce containers dairy sour cream chive-flavor dip
  Assorted dippers, such as whole wheat pita bread wedges; cherry tomatoes; baby carrots; broccoli florets; assorted crackers; sesame breadsticks; small cooked and deveined shrimp; thick-sliced salami, pepperoni, or summer sausage; and/or thick-sliced cheddar, provolone, or Monterey Jack cheese

1. For dip, finely shred $1/2$ teaspoon peel from lime; set aside. Cut lime in half; squeeze juice from lime. Place 1 tablespoon juice in a medium bowl. Stir in sour cream dip and lime peel. Cover and chil until serving time or up to 24 hours.

2. To serve, transfer dip to a small serving bowl. Serve with assorted dippers. Makes 10 servings.

Per serving (dip only): 98 cal., 8 g fat (5 g sat. fat), 32 mg chol., 211 mg sodium, 3 g carbo., 0 g fiber, 0 g pro.

Sweet-and-Salty Party Mix

Prep: 10 minutes

2 8.6- to 8.75-ounce packages party snack mix (original flavor)
2 cups honey and nut bite-size shredded wheat cereal
1 cup plain or honey roasted mixed nuts
1 cup plain candy-coated milk-chocolate pieces
$1/2$ cup peanuts in crunchy sugar coating (French burnt peanuts)
$1/2$ cup dried banana chips

1. In a very large bowl, combine packaged snack mix, shredded wheat cereal, mixed nuts, candy-coated milk-chocolate pieces, peanut candy, and banana chips. Toss gently until well combined. Store, covered, in an airtight container at room temperature for up to 2 weeks. Makes 28 ($1/2$-cup) servings.

Per serving: 174 cal., 7 g fat (2 g sat. fat), 1 mg chol., 265 mg sodium, 32 g carbo., 2 g fiber, 3 g pro.

Asian Dip
Start to Finish: 15 minutes

1   cup chopped, peeled, seeded cucumber
¼   cup hoisin sauce
¼   cup seasoned rice vinegar
1   tablespoon snipped fresh cilantro
1   teaspoon grated fresh ginger
1   clove garlic, minced
¼   teaspoon crushed red pepper
     Sesame seeds, toasted* (optional)
     Black sesame seeds (optional)
     Sugar snap pea pods, sweet pepper strips,
        diagonal carrot slices, trimmed whole
        green onions, daikon sticks, blanched
        broccoli, and/or blanched green beans

1. In a blender or food processor, combine cucumber, hoisin sauce, vinegar, cilantro, ginger, garlic, and crushed red pepper. Cover and blend or process until smooth. Place in a shallow dish or small bowl. If desired, sprinkle toasted sesame seeds and black sesame seeds over the mixture in concentric circles or alternating rows. Serve with desired dippers. Makes about 1¼ cups.

Make-Ahead Directions: Cover and chill dip for up to 6 hours before serving. If desired, sprinkle with sesame seeds as directed.

*Test Kitchen Tip: To toast sesame seeds, spread seeds in a single layer in a shallow baking pan. Bake in a preheated 350°F oven about 5 minutes or until golden brown, stirring once or twice and checking to make sure seeds don't become too brown. If they start to burn, they go quickly and generally can't be salvaged.

Per 2 tablespoons dip: 37 cal., 1 g fat (0 g sat. fat), 0 mg chol., 98 mg sodium, 7 g carbo., 1 g fiber, 1 g pro.

Artichoke-and-Mushroom-Topped Camembert
Start to Finish: 20 minutes

1   4½-ounce package Camembert or Brie cheese
1   6-ounce jar marinated artichokes
2   cups crimini or button mushrooms, quartered
¼   cup bottled roasted red pepper, chopped
¼   cup finely shredded Parmesan cheese
12   ¼-inch-thick baguette slices, toasted*

1. Cut cheese into six wedges. Place one wedge on each of six small plates; set aside.

2. Drain artichoke hearts, reserving liquid. Cut artichokes into thin slivers; set aside. In a large skillet, heat reserved liquid. Add mushrooms; cook until tender. Stir in artichokes and roasted red pepper. Heat through.

3. Spoon mixture atop cheese wedges. Sprinkle with Parmesan cheese. Add two baguette slices to each plate. Serve at once. Makes 6 servings.

*To toast baguette slices: Preheat broiler. Place baguette slices on a baking sheet. Broil 2 to 3 inches from heat for 2 to 3 minutes or until light brown, turning once.

Per serving: 142 cal., 8 g fat (4 g sat. fat), 18 mg chol., 401 mg sodium, 11 g carbo., 1 g fiber, 8 g pro.

Layered Fiesta Shrimp Dip
Start to Finish: 20 minutes

2   8-ounce packages cream cheese, softened
2   tablespoons mayonnaise or salad dressing
1   fresh jalapeño pepper, seeded and finely chopped*
2   cloves garlic, minced
1   cup bottled lime and garlic salsa or habanero lime salsa
12   ounces fresh or frozen peeled, cooked shrimp, halved lengthwise
1   cup chopped mango
1   cup chopped, seeded roma tomatoes
¼   cup sliced green onions
2   tablespoons snipped fresh cilantro
     Tortilla chips

1. In a medium mixing bowl, beat cream cheese, mayonnaise, jalapeño, and garlic with an electric mixer on medium to high speed until creamy. Spread mixture on a 12-inch serving platter. Spread salsa over cream cheese layer to cover. Top with shrimp.

2. In a medium bowl, combine mango, tomato, green onion, and cilantro. Sprinkle mango mixture over shrimp. Serve immediately or cover and refrigerate for up to 4 hours. Serve with tortilla chips. Makes about 4 cups.

*Note: Because chile peppers contain oils that can burn skin and eyes, avoid direct contact with them as much as possible. When working with chile peppers, wear plastic or rubber gloves. If your bare hands do touch the peppers, wash them well with soap and warm water.

Per serving dip with chips: 221 cal., 15 g fat (7 g sat. fat), 64 mg chol., 301 mg sodium, 14 g carbo., 1 g fiber, 8 g pro.

Marinated Shrimp Scampi

Prep: 35 minutes   Marinate: 1 hour   Broil: 4 minutes

- 2 **pounds fresh or frozen extra-jumbo shrimp in shells (30 to 40)**
- ¼ **cup olive oil**
- ¼ **cup dry white wine**
- 6 **cloves garlic, minced (1 tablespoon)**
- 2 **teaspoons finely shredded lemon peel**
- ½ **teaspoon crushed red pepper**
- ½ **teaspoon salt**
- 2 **tablespoons snipped fresh Italian (flat-leaf) parsley**

1. Thaw shrimp, if frozen. Peel and devein shrimp, leaving tails intact. Rinse shrimp; pat dry. Place shrimp in a large resealable plastic bag set in a shallow bowl.

2. Combine olive oil, wine, garlic, lemon peel, crushed red pepper, and salt. Pour over shrimp. Seal bag; toss gently to coat. Marinate in refrigerator for 1 hour.

3. Remove shrimp from marinade, reserving marinade. Arrange shrimp on unheated rack of a broiler pan. Broil 4 to 5 inches from heat for 2 minutes. Turn shrimp and brush with reserved marinade; broil 2 to 4 minutes more or until shrimp are opaque. To serve, mound shrimp on platter; sprinkle with parsley. Makes 10 to 12 servings.

Per serving: 126 cal., 4 g fat (1 g sat. fat), 138 mg chol., 193 mg sodium, 2 g carbo., 1 g fiber, 19 g pro.

parsley pointers

Italian or flat-leaf parsley has a slightly stronger flavor than the more familiar curly-leaf type. To store either type, place the bunch of herb upright with the stems in a glass of water. Slip glass and all into a plastic bag and refrigerate.

Garbanzo Bean Dip

Start to Finish: 10 minutes

- 1   15-ounce can garbanzo beans (chickpeas), rinsed and drained
- ½   cup plain low-fat yogurt
- ¼   cup bottled buttermilk salad dressing
- 2   tablespoons seasoned fine dry bread crumbs
- 2   teaspoons lemon juice
- ½   teaspoon crushed red pepper
- 2   tablespoons chopped pitted ripe olives
-      Assorted crackers and/or vegetable dippers, such as zucchini or yellow summer squash strips, pea pods, and/or broccoli florets

1. In a food processor or blender, combine garbanzo beans, yogurt, salad dressing, bread crumbs, lemon juice, and crushed red pepper. Cover and process or blend until smooth. Stir in olives. Serve with crackers and/or vegetable dippers. Makes about 1¾ cups.

Make-Ahead Directions: Prepare as directed in Step 1. Cover; chill for up to 24 hours. Serve as directed.

Per 2 tablespoons dip: 82 cal., 3 g fat (1 g sat. fat), 2 mg chol., 198 mg sodium, 10 g carbo., 2 g fiber, 2 g pro.

Artichoke-Water Chestnut Spread

Start to Finish: 15 minutes   Chill: 1 hour

- 1   13¾-ounce can artichoke bottoms, drained and cut up
- 1   8-ounce can sliced water chestnuts, drained
- 2   cloves garlic, minced
- ½   cup mayonnaise
- ¼   cup tahini (sesame seed paste)
- ¼   teaspoon salt
- 2   tablespoons thinly sliced green onion
-      Sesame seed crackers and/or assorted vegetable dippers

1. In a food processor, combine artichoke bottoms and water chestnuts. Process with on/off turns until finely chopped. Add garlic, mayonnaise, tahini, and salt; process until combined. Cover and chill for 1 to 24 hours.

2. Sprinkle with green onions. Serve with crackers and/or vegetable dippers. Makes 2¼ cups.

Per 2 tablespoons spread: 88 cal., 7 g fat (1 g sat. fat), 2 mg chol., 142 mg sodium, 5 g carbo., 1 g fiber, 1 g pro.

Hot Crab Spread

Start to Finish: 15 minutes

- ½   of an 8-ounce tub cream cheese with garden vegetables
- 1   6- to 6½-ounce can crabmeat, drained, flaked, and cartilage removed
- 2   tablespoons sliced green onion
- 1   teaspoon lemon juice
- ½   teaspoon dried dill
-      Several dashes bottled hot pepper sauce
-      Assorted crackers

1. In a small saucepan, heat cream cheese over medium-low heat until softened. Stir in crabmeat, green onion, lemon juice, dill, and hot pepper sauce. Cook and stir for 3 to 4 minutes more or until heated through. Serve warm with crackers. Makes about 1 cup.

Per 2 tablespoons spread: 72 cal., 5 g fat (3 g sat. fat), 31 mg chol., 151 mg sodium, 1 g carbo., 0 g fiber, 5 g pro.

Muffaletta Spread

Start to Finish: 20 minutes

- 1¼   cups pimiento-stuffed green olives
- 1¼   cups pitted Kalamata olives
- 3   cloves garlic
- ⅓   cup olive oil
- 2   tablespoons red wine vinegar
- ½   cup finely chopped salami (2 ounces)
- ½   cup finely chopped capocolla or cooked ham (2 ounces)
- ½   cup shredded Provolone cheese (2 ounces)
- 2   tablespoons snipped fresh parsley
- 1   teaspoon dried Italian seasoning, crushed
- ¼   teaspoon ground black pepper
-      Assorted crackers or toasted baguette-style French bread slices

1. In a food processor, combine olives and garlic. Cover and process with three or four on-off turns or until finely chopped. With food processor running, slowly add olive oil and vinegar until nearly smooth. Transfer mixture to a medium bowl. Stir in salami, capocolla, cheese, parsley, Italian seasoning, and pepper. Serve with crackers or toasted baguette slices. Serve immediately or cover and chill up to 24 hours. Makes about 2¼ cups.

Per 2 tablespoons spread: 100 cal., 10 g fat (2 g sat. fat), 8 mg chol., 392 mg sodium, 2 g carbo., 1 g fiber, 2 g pro.

Blue Cheese-Pecan Phyllo Bites

Start to Finish: 30 minutes

  1 **8-ounce package cream cheese, softened**
  2 **2.1-ounce packages baked miniature phyllo dough shells (30 total)**
  4 **ounces blue cheese, crumbled**
 $^{1}/_{3}$ **cup dried tart cherries, snipped**
    Sugared Pecans

1. In a small bowl, stir cream cheese until smooth. Spoon into dough shells. Top with blue cheese and cherries. Sprinkle with Sugared Pecans. Makes 30.

Sugared Pecans: In a medium skillet, spread $^{1}/_{3}$ cup chopped pecans. Sprinkle with 1 tablespoon sugar and $^{1}/_{4}$ teaspoon salt. Heat, without stirring, over medium heat. When sugar begins to melt, turn heat to medium-low. Gently stir pecans until all sugar melts and pecans are lightly coated. Transfer pecans to a foil-lined baking sheet; cool. Break apart. Store in a tightly covered container in the refrigerator for up to 24 hours.

Per appetizer: 77 cal., 6 g fat (2 g sat. fat), 11 mg chol., 104 mg sodium, 4 g carbo., 0 g fiber, 2 g pro.

Turkey Salad Tartlets
Start to Finish: 25 minutes

1¼ cups chopped cooked turkey breast
  3 slices packaged ready-to-serve cooked
     bacon, chopped, or 3 slices bacon, crisp-
     cooked, drained, and crumbled
  2 tablespoons finely chopped onion
  2 tablespoons mayonnaise
  2 tablespoons dairy sour cream
  2 teaspoons lime juice
  1 teaspoon Dijon-style mustard
     Salt and ground black pepper
  1 avocado, halved, seeded, peeled, and
     chopped
  2 2.1-ounce packages baked miniature
     phyllo dough shells (30 shells)
  8 grape tomatoes, quartered lengthwise

1. In a medium bowl, combine turkey, bacon, and onion. Set aside.

2. Stir together mayonnaise, sour cream, lime juice, mustard, and salt and pepper to taste. Add mayonnaise mixture to turkey mixture, stirring to combine.

3. Add avocado to turkey salad, gently tossing to combine. Spoon turkey salad into phyllo shells. Garnish tartlets with tomato wedges. Makes 30.

Make-Ahead Directions: Prepare turkey salad through Step 2. Cover and chill for up to 24 hours. Just before serving, stir in avocado and spoon salad into tart shells.

Per tartlet: 52 cal., 3 g fat (0 g sat. fat), 6 mg chol., 38 mg sodium, 3 g carbo., 0 g fiber, 3 g pro.

Ham Bites with Cilantro-Corn Cream
Start to Finish: 25 minutes

  ¾ cup frozen whole kernel corn, thawed
  1 8-ounce carton dairy sour cream
  ⅓ cup snipped fresh cilantro
  1 teaspoon bottled minced garlic
  1 teaspoon Dijon-style mustard
  ¼ teaspoon salt
  ⅛ teaspoon cayenne pepper
  4 to 6 ounces thinly sliced cooked ham
 36 ¼-inch thick diagonally sliced baguette
     slices, toasted

1. Drain corn; pat dry with paper towels. In a medium bowl, combine corn, sour cream, cilantro, garlic, mustard, salt, and cayenne pepper. Use immediately or cover and chill for up to 6 hours.

2. Cut ham slices to fit baguette slices. Place ham on baguette slices; top with sour cream mixture. Serve immediately. Makes 36.

Per serving: 39 cal., 2 g fat (1 g sat. fat), 5 mg chol., 102 mg sodium, 4 g carbo., 0 g fiber, 1 g pro.

Horseradish Bacon Dip
Start to Finish: 15 minutes

1¼ cups finely shredded cheddar cheese
  ½ cup dairy sour cream
  1 3-ounce package cream cheese, softened
  3 to 4 teaspoons prepared horseradish
  ¼ cup cooked bacon pieces
  1 tablespoon snipped fresh chives
     Assorted crackers

1. In a medium mixing bowl, beat together 1 cup of the shredded cheese, sour cream, cream cheese, and horseradish with an electric mixer until nearly smooth. Spread mixture in a microwave-safe 9-inch pie plate. Microwave, uncovered, on 100% power (high) for 1 minute; stir mixture and spread in an even layer. Sprinkle with the remaining ¼ cup cheese and bacon. Cook for 1 to 2 minutes or until cheese melts, turning once. Sprinkle with chives. Serve with crackers. Makes 10 servings.

Per serving: 118 cal., 10 g fat (6 g sat. fat), 30 mg chol., 211 mg sodium, 1 g carbo., 0 g fiber, 6 g pro.

Cheater's Guacamole
Start to Finish: 15 minutes

  ½ of a 16-ounce package (1 pouch)
     refrigerated guacamole (about 1 cup)
  1 coarsely chopped, peeled ripe avocado
1½ teaspoons chipotle pepper in adobo sauce
  ¼ teaspoon ground cumin
     Quartered grape tomatoes
     Sliced ripe olives
     Snipped fresh cilantro
     Tortilla chips

1. In a bowl, combine guacamole, avocado, chipotle pepper in adobo sauce, and cumin. Top with tomatoes, olives, and cilantro. Serve immediately with tortilla chips. Makes 10 servings.

Per serving: 80 cal., 6 g fat (1 g sat. fat), 0 mg chol., 77 mg sodium, 5 g carbo., 4 g fiber, 2 g pro.

To keep *appetizer meatballs warm* on a buffet table, place them in a slow cooker on the warm setting.

Sweet and Sassy Meatballs
Start to Finish: 30 minutes

- 2   1-pound packages frozen cooked meatballs, thawed
- 1   16-ounce can jellied cranberry sauce
- 1   18-ounce bottle barbecue sauce

1. For sauce, in a large skillet, stir together cranberry sauce and barbecue sauce. Cook over medium heat until cranberry sauce melts, stirring occasionally.

2. Add meatballs to sauce. Cook, uncovered, for 10 minutes or until meatballs are heated through, stirring occasionally. Makes 64 meatballs.

Chipotle Sauce: Prepare sauce as directed except substitute one 12-ounce bottle chili sauce for the barbecue sauce and stir in 3 to 4 tablespoons finely chopped canned chipotle pepper in adobo sauce.

Hawaiian Sauce: Prepare sauce as directed except substitute one 8-ounce can crushed pineapple for the cranberry sauce.

Make-ahead directions: Prepare as directed in Step 1. Stir in meatballs. Cover and chill for up to 24 hours. Heat meatballs and sauce in a large skillet over medium heat until heated through, stirring occasionally.

Per 4 meatballs: 60 cal., 4 g fat (2 g sat. fat), 5 mg chol., 177 mg sodium, 5 g carbo., 1 g fiber, 2 g pro.

Maple-Mustard Cocktail Sausages

Prep: 10 minutes   Cook: 4 to 5 hours (low) or
2 to 2½ hours (high)

- ½ cup bottled chili sauce
- ⅓ cup pure maple syrup or maple-flavor syrup
- 2 tablespoons Dijon-style mustard
- 1 tablespoon packed brown sugar
- 1 teaspoon cider vinegar
- 2 16-ounce packages small, cooked smoked sausage links

1. For sauce, in a large bowl stir together chili sauce, maple syrup, mustard, brown sugar, and vinegar until combined. Add sausages, stirring to coat. Transfer sausage mixture to a 1½- or 2-quart slow cooker.

2. Cover; cook on low-heat setting for 4 to 5 hours or on high-heat setting for 2 to 2½ hours. If no heat setting is available, cook for 3 hours. Serve immediately or keep warm, covered, on warm setting or low-heat setting (if available) for up to 2 hours. Serve with a slotted spoon or decorative toothpicks. Makes 32 servings.

Per serving: 102 cal., 8 g fat (3 g sat. fat), 18 mg chol., 433 mg sodium, 4 g carbo., 0 g fiber, 4 g pro.

Sensational Portobellos

Prep: 20 minutes   Broil: 5 minutes

- 6 medium portobello mushrooms (about 4½ inches in diameter)
- ¼ cup purchased basil pesto
- ¾ cup bottled roasted red sweet peppers, cut into strips
- 1½ ounces sliced pepperoni, coarsely chopped
- ⅓ cup walnuts, toasted and chopped
- ⅛ to ¼ teaspoon crushed red pepper
- 1 cup shredded Italian cheese blend (4 ounces)

1. Preheat broiler. If desired, remove stems and gills from mushrooms. Place mushrooms, gills sides up, in a 15x10x1-inch baking pan. Broil 3 to 4 inches from the heat for 4 minutes.

2. Meanwhile, in a medium bowl, combine pesto, roasted red pepper, pepperoni, walnuts, and crushed red pepper. Divide among mushrooms; sprinkle with cheese.

3. Broil for 1 to 2 minutes or until heated through and cheese is bubbly. Halve to serve. Makes 12 servings.

Per serving: 132 cal., 11 g fat (2 g sat. fat), 12 mg chol., 166 mg sodium, 5 g carbo., 1 g fiber, 7 g pro.

Spicy Spinach-Stuffed Mushrooms

Prep: 30 minutes   Bake: 10 minutes   Oven: 425°F

- 24 large fresh button mushrooms (1½ to 2 inches in diameter)
- 2 tablespoons olive oil
  Salt and ground black pepper
- 8 ounces spicy bulk Italian sausage
- ¼ cup finely chopped onion
- ¼ cup finely chopped red sweet pepper
- 1 clove garlic, minced
- 1 cup fresh spinach, chopped
- ¼ cup finely shredded Parmesan cheese
- ¼ cup fine dry bread crumbs

1. Preheat oven to 425°F. Rinse and drain mushrooms. Remove stems; set aside. Brush mushroom caps with olive oil. Sprinkle with salt and pepper. Set aside.

2. In a large skillet, cook chopped stems, sausage, onion, sweet pepper, and garlic over medium heat until sausage is brown. Stir in spinach until wilted. Stir in Parmesan cheese and bread crumbs. Remove from heat. Spoon sausage mixture into mushroom caps. Place on a greased baking sheet.

3. Bake about 10 minutes or until stuffing is brown and mushrooms are tender. Makes 24.

Per appetizer: 57 cal., 5 g fat (1 g sat. fat), 8 mg chol., 127 mg sodium, 2 g carbo., 0 g fiber, 2 g pro.

Mojito

Mojito
Start to Finish: 10 minutes

    Crushed ice
3   tablespoons light rum
1   teaspoon sugar
4   fresh mint leaves
¼   cup lemon-lime carbonated beverage
1   lime slice
    Fresh mint sprig (optional)

1. Fill a cocktail shaker with crushed ice. Add rum, sugar, and mint leaves. Cover and shake vigorously. Strain mixture into an 8-ounce glass. Pour carbonated beverage into glass; stir gently. Fill glass with additional crushed ice. Garnish with lime slice and, if desired, mint. Makes 1 serving.

Per serving: 138 cal., 0 g fat (0 g sat. fat), 0 mg chol., 14 mg sodium, 11 g carbo., 0 g fiber, 0 g pro.

Sangria Sparklers
Prep: 10 minutes. Chill: 2 hours

1   750-milliliter bottle dry red wine
1   cup orange juice
¼   cup sugar
¼   cup brandy or cognac
¼   cup orange liqueur
1   medium orange, sliced
1   medium blood orange or orange, sliced
1   medium lime, sliced
2   cups club soda, chilled
    Crushed ice (optional)

1. In a large pitcher, combine wine, orange juice, sugar, brandy, orange liqueur, orange slices, and lime slices. Chill at least 2 hours. Add club soda before serving. If desired, serve over crushed ice. Makes 6 servings.

Per serving: 232 cal., 0 g fat (0 g sat. fat), 0 mg chol., 30 mg sodium, 25 g carbo., 1 g fiber, 1 g pro.

Gingered Beer
Start to Finish: 10 minutes

6   12-ounce cans ginger ale, chilled
6   12-ounce bottles pale ale or stout, chilled

1. In a large chilled pitcher, combine equal parts ginger ale and pale ale or stout. Pour into glasses. Replenish pitcher as needed. Makes 12 servings.

Per serving: 132 cal., 0 g fat (0 g sat. fat), 0 mg chol., 21 mg sodium, 22 g carbo., 0 g fiber, 1 g pro.

Sangria Sparklers

Lime-Tea Punch

Prep: 10 minutes   Cool: 15 minutes   Chill: 4 hours

8   individual-size black tea bags
6   cups boiling water
2   tablespoons honey
1   12-ounce can frozen limeade concentrate
1   1-liter bottle ginger ale, chilled
    Ice cubes
1   lime, cut into wedges

1. Steep tea bags in boiling water for 5 minutes; remove tea bags and discard. Let mixture cool for 15 minutes. Stir in honey until dissolved. Stir in limeade concentrate until melted. Cover and chill mixture for at least 4 hours.

2. To serve, transfer tea mixture to a punch bowl; add ginger ale and ice. Garnish each serving with a lime wedge. Makes 16 ($^2/_3$-cup) servings.

Make-Ahead Directions: Prepare tea mixture as directed in Step 1; cover and chill for up to 48 hours.

Per serving: 73 cal., 0 g fat (0 g sat. fat), 0 mg chol., 9 mg sodium, 19 g carbo., 0 g fiber, 0 g pro.

Hot Cider Surprise Punch

Start to Finish: 30 minutes

4   cups apple cider
4   cups cranberry juice
2   cups pomegranate juice
6   inches stick cinnamon
3   pieces whole star anise
2   2- to 3-inch strips orange peel*
1   2- to 3-inch strip lemon peel*
    Orange slices

1. In a 4- to 5-quart Dutch oven, combine cider, cranberry juice, pomegranate juice, stick cinnamon, star anise, orange peel, and lemon peel. Bring to boiling; reduce heat. Simmer, covered, for 20 minutes. Using a slotted spoon, remove stick cinnamon, star anise, orange peel, and lemon peel. Serve punch warm in mugs; garnish with orange slices. Makes 10 (8-ounce) servings.

***Test Kitchen Tip:** When removing orange and lemon peel, avoid using the white pith, which adds bitterness.

Per serving: 122 cal., 0 g fat (0 g sat. fat), 0 mg chol., 20 mg sodium, 31 g carbo., 0 g fiber, 0 g pro.

Creamy Fruit Punch with Lime

Start to Finish: 15 minutes

1   1$^3/_4$-quart carton strawberry ice cream
1   1$^3/_4$-quart carton peach ice cream
2   12-ounce cans evaporated milk, chilled
1   tablespoon finely shredded lime peel
$^3/_4$ cup lime juice
1   2-liter bottle ginger ale, chilled
$^1/_3$ cup sugar (optional)
    Fresh pineapple wedges (optional)
    Whole fresh strawberries (optional)

1. Stir ice creams to soften; transfer to a very large punch bowl. Gradually stir in evaporated milk, then lime peel and lime juice. Carefully stir in ginger ale. If desired, garnish glasses with pineapple wedges and strawberries. Fill glasses with punch. Makes 32 (6-ounce) servings.

Per serving: 209 cal., 9 g fat (6 g sat. fat), 46 mg chol., 64 mg sodium, 28 g carbo., 0 g fiber, 4 g pro.

Frosty Mint Cocktail

Prep: 20 minutes   Freeze: 12 hours
Stand: 30 minutes

1   cup water
$^2/_3$ cup sugar
$^1/_2$ cup loosely packed mint leaves
3   cups orange juice
1   6-ounce can unsweetened pineapple juice
$^1/_3$ cup lemon juice
1   1-liter bottle lemon-lime carbonated beverage, chilled

1. In a small saucepan, combine the water, sugar, and mint leaves. Bring to boiling. Reduce heat and simmer, uncovered, for 2 minutes. Remove from heat; strain. Discard mint leaves. Pour sugar mixture into a 2-quart square baking dish. Stir in orange juice, pineapple juice, and lemon juice. Cover and freeze for at least 12 hours or until completely frozen.

2. To serve, let frozen mixture stand at room temperature for 30 minutes. Scrape mixture with a large metal spoon to form slush. Spoon slush into 12-ounce glasses, filling glasses half full. Fill glasses with carbonated beverage. Makes 10 to 12 (12-ounce) servings.

Per serving: 134 cal., 0 g fat (0 g sat. fat), 0 mg chol., 23 mg sodium, 34 g carbo., 0 g fiber, 1 g pro.

company's
coming

Steak with Sautéed Onions

Despite a hectic schedule, don't put off the pleasure of inviting friends to share a meal. These delicious main-dish recipes are as foolproof as they are company-special.

Steak with Sautéed Onions

Start to Finish: 25 minutes

6	4-ounce beef tenderloin steaks, cut 1 inch thick
1/4	teaspoon salt
1/4	teaspoon ground black pepper
1	small red onion, cut into 6 wedges
2	cloves garlic, minced
2	tablespoons butter
1	teaspoon dried basil, crushed
1/2	teaspoon dried oregano, crushed
2	tablespoons whipping cream
6	tablespoons onion marmalade or orange marmalade
	Snipped fresh parsley (optional)

1. Sprinkle steaks with salt and pepper. In a large skillet, cook onion and garlic in hot butter over medium heat for 6 to 8 minutes or until onion is tender, stirring frequently. Remove onion from skillet; set aside.

2. Add steaks to hot skillet. Cook to desired doneness, turning occasionally. Allow 10 to 13 minutes for medium-rare (145°F) to medium (160°F). Sprinkle steaks with basil and oregano the last 2 minutes of cooking.

3. Transfer steaks to plates and keep warm. Return onions to skillet. Heat onions through. Remove skillet from heat. Stir in whipping cream. Spoon cream over steaks. Top each steak with 1 tablespoon of the marmalade. Divide cooked onions evenly among the steaks. If desired, sprinkle with parsley. Makes 6 servings.

Per serving: 271 cal., 13 g fat (4 g sat. fat), 63 mg chol., 110 mg sodium, 14 g carbo., 0 g fiber, 24 g pro.

Wine-Balsamic-Glazed Steak

Start to Finish: 30 minutes

2	teaspoons cooking oil
1	pound boneless beef top loin or top sirloin steak, cut 1/2 to 3/4 inch thick
3	cloves garlic, minced
1/8	teaspoon crushed red pepper
3/4	cup dry red wine
2	cups sliced fresh mushrooms
3	tablespoons balsamic vinegar
2	tablespoons soy sauce
4	teaspoons honey
2	tablespoons butter

1. In a large skillet, heat oil over medium-high heat until very hot. Add steak. Reduce heat to medium and cook, uncovered, for 10 to 13 minutes or to desired doneness, turning meat occasionally. Allow 10 to 13 minutes for medium-rare (145°F) to medium (160°F). If meat browns too quickly, reduce heat to medium-low. Transfer meat to platter and keep warm.

2. Add garlic and red pepper to skillet; cook for 10 seconds. Remove skillet from heat. Carefully add wine. Return to heat. Boil, uncovered, about 5 minutes or until most of the liquid is evaporated. Add mushrooms, vinegar, soy sauce, and honey; return to simmer. Cook and stir about 4 minutes or until mushrooms are tender. Stir in butter until melted. Spoon over steak. Makes 4 servings.

Per serving: 377 cal., 21 g fat (9 g sat. fat), 82 mg chol., 588 mg sodium, 12 g carbo., 0 g fiber, 27 g pro.

Honey-Ancho-Glazed Beef Tenderloin

Prep: 20 minutes   Soak: 1 hour   Grill: 35 minutes
Stand: 15 minutes

2	to 3 cups hickory wood chips
1/4	cup honey
1 1/2	teaspoons ground ancho chile pepper* or chili powder
2	tablespoons cooking oil
1	3- to 4-pound beef tenderloin roast
1	teaspoon salt
1	teaspoon ground black pepper

1. At least 1 hour before grilling, soak wood chips in enough water to cover. Drain before using.

2. In a small saucepan, combine honey and chile pepper. Cook and stir over medium-low heat until heated through. Remove from heat. Stir in oil. Brush some of the mixture over roast. Sprinkle roast with salt and black pepper.

3. In a grill with a cover, arrange preheated coals around a drip pan. Test for medium heat above drip pan. Sprinkle wood chips over coals. Pour 1 inch of water into drip pan. Place roast on grill rack over drip pan. Cover and grill for 35 to 45 minutes or until an instant-read thermometer inserted near the center of the roast registers 135°F, brushing with honey mixture occasionally during the first 20 minutes. Discard any remaining honey mixture.

4. Remove roast from grill. Cover; let stand for 15 minutes before slicing. (The temperature of the meat will rise 10°F during standing.) Makes 8 to 10 servings.

Per serving: 325 cal., 17 g fat (4 g sat. fat), 78 mg chol., 360 mg sodium, 18 g carbo., 0 g fiber, 27 g pro.

Peppery Beef with Mushrooms

Start to Finish: 25 minutes

2	to 3 teaspoons steak seasoning blend or cracked black pepper
4	beef tenderloin steaks or 2 beef top loin steaks, cut 1 inch thick
2	tablespoons butter
1	tablespoon olive oil or butter
2	4-ounce packages sliced cremini, shiitaki, or portobello mushrooms or one 8-ounce package sliced button mushrooms (3 cups)
1	large leek, thinly sliced
1/2	teaspoon dried thyme or oregano, crushed
1	5.5- to 6-ounce can tomato juice

1. Use your fingers to press the steak seasoning onto both sides of the steaks. If using top loin steaks, cut each steak in half crosswise. In a large skillet, cook steaks in hot butter over medium heat to desired doneness, turning once. For tenderloin steaks, allow 10 to 13 minutes for medium-rare (145°F) to medium (160°F). For top loin steaks, allow 12 to 15 minutes for medium-rare to medium. Transfer steaks to a warm serving platter, reserving the drippings in the skillet. Keep warm.

2. Add oil to drippings in skillet. Add mushrooms, leek, and thyme. Cook and stir for 2 minutes. Stir in tomato juice. Bring to boiling; reduce heat. Simmer, uncovered, for 2 to 3 minutes more or until leek is tender. Spoon mushroom mixture over the meat. Makes 4 servings.

Per serving: 296 cal., 20 g fat (8 g sat. fat), 86 mg chol., 419 mg sodium, 5 g carbo., 1 g fiber, 26 g pro.

Pork Chops with Gorgonzola and Pears

Prep: 10 minutes   Cook: 20 minutes

4	pork rib chops, cut 3/4 to 1 inch thick
	Sea salt, kosher salt, or salt
2	tablespoons olive oil
2	medium ripe pears, peeled, cored, and cut into 8 wedges each
2	tablespoons butter
1/4	cup dry white wine or apple juice
1/4	cup whipping cream
8	ounces creamy Gorgonzola or blue cheese, crumbled
	Freshly ground black pepper

1. Sprinkle pork chops with salt. In a 12-inch skillet, cook chops in hot oil over medium heat for 5 minutes. Turn chops and cook for 5 minutes more or until brown and juices run clear (160°F). Transfer chops to a serving platter. Drain fat from skillet.

2. In same skillet, cook pear wedges in butter over medium-high heat for 5 minutes or until brown, turning once. Add pears to platter.

3. For sauce, add wine and cream to skillet. Bring to boiling; reduce heat. Boil gently, uncovered, for 1 to 2 minutes until slightly thickened. Add Gorgonzola; whisk until cheese almost melts. Remove from heat. Serve with pork and pears. Sprinkle with pepper. Makes 4 servings.

Per serving: 618 cal., 46 g fat (24 g sat. fat), 147 mg chol., 1,105 mg sodium, 14 g carbo., 4 g fiber, 34 g pro.

Rosemary-Rubbed Lamb Chops

Start to Finish: 25 minutes

8	lamb rib chops, cut 1 inch thick
2	tablespoons olive oil
2	teaspoons snipped fresh rosemary or
1/2	teaspoon dried rosemary, crushed
1/2	teaspoon coarsely ground black pepper
2	cloves garlic, minced
1/2	cup apricot preserves or peach preserves
1/4	cup water
1	tablespoon Dijon-style mustard
1	teaspoon chicken bouillon granules
1/2	teaspoon snipped fresh rosemary or
1/8	teaspoon dried rosemary, crushed
1/4	teaspoon coarsely ground black pepper
	Fresh rosemary sprigs (optional)

1. Trim fat from chops. In a bowl, combine 1 tablespoon of the oil, 2 teaspoons fresh rosemary or 1/2 teaspoon dried rosemary, 1/2 teaspoon pepper, and garlic. Use your fingers or a pastry brush to rub or brush the mixture on all sides of the chops.

2. For glaze, in a small saucepan, combine preserves, the water, mustard, bouillon granules, 1/2 teaspoon fresh rosemary or 1/8 teaspoon dried rosemary, and 1/4 teaspoon pepper; heat and stir until bubbly. Remove from heat.

3. In a large skillet, cook chops in remaining 1 tablespoon hot oil over medium heat for 9 to 11 minutes for medium doneness (160°F), turning once. Serve chops with glaze. If desired, garnish with rosemary sprigs. Makes 4 servings.

Per serving: 289 cal., 12 g fat (3 g sat. fat), 48 mg chol., 361 mg sodium, 29 g carbo., 1 g fiber, 15 g pro.

Blackberry Salad with Pork

Prep: 25 minutes   Roast: 25 minutes   Oven: 425°F

1	12- to 16-ounce pork tenderloin
	Salt and ground black pepper
1/4	cup olive oil
1/4	cup honey
1/4	cup lemon juice
6	cups packaged mixed baby greens (spring mix)
2	cups blackberries, raspberries, and/or sliced strawberries
1	cup grape tomatoes
1/2	cup pine nuts, toasted*
4	ounces Brie cheese, cut into wedges

1. Preheat oven to 425°F. Place pork on a rack in a shallow roasting pan. Sprinkle with salt and pepper. Roast, uncovered, for 25 to 35 minutes or until an instant-read thermometer inserted in center registers 155°F. Remove from oven. Cover with foil and let stand until temperature registers 160°F. Cool slightly. Slice pork 1/4 inch thick.

2. For dressing, in a screw-top jar, combine oil, honey, lemon juice, and salt and pepper; cover and shake.

3. In salad bowls or on individual plates, place greens; top with berries, tomatoes, pine nuts, Brie wedges, and pork slices. Drizzle with dressing. Serve immediately. Makes 4 servings.

*Note: To toast nuts, place nuts in a shallow baking pan. Place in a 350°F oven for 5 to 7 minutes, shaking pan once or twice. Watch closely so nuts don't burn.

Per serving: 569 cal., 36 g fat (10 g sat. fat), 95 mg chol., 308 mg sodium, 32 g carbo., 5 g fiber, 37 g pro.

Pan-Seared Lamb Chops with Fresh Mint Salad

Start to Finish: 30 minutes

1/4	cup snipped fresh mint
1/4	cup snipped fresh Italian (flat-leaf) parsley
1/4	cup crumbled feta cheese (1 ounce)
1/4	cup toasted chopped pecans
8	lamb rib chops or loin chops, cut 1 inch thick
2	teaspoons olive oil
	Salt and ground black pepper
	Olive oil (optional)
	Lemon juice (optional)

1. In a small bowl, combine mint, parsley, feta cheese, and pecans; set aside.

2. Trim fat from chops. Rub chops with 2 teaspoons olive oil; sprinkle with salt and pepper. Heat a large heavy skillet over medium-high heat until very hot. Add chops. For medium-rare doneness, cook over medium-high heat for 8 to 10 minutes or until brown (145°F), turning chops once halfway through cooking,

3. To serve, sprinkle chops with mint mixture. If desired, drizzle olive oil and/or lemon juice over mint mixture. Makes 4 servings.

Per serving: 252 cal., 17 g fat (5 g sat. fat), 72 mg chol., 311 mg sodium, 2 g carbo., 1 g fiber, 22 g pro.

Chili-Glazed Pork Roast

Prep: 20 minutes Roast: 1¼ hours
Stand: 15 minutes Oven: 325°F

1	tablespoon packed brown sugar
1	tablespoon snipped fresh thyme or
	1 teaspoon dried thyme, crushed
1	teaspoon chili powder
1	teaspoon snipped fresh rosemary or
	¼ teaspoon dried rosemary, crushed
⅛	teaspoon cayenne pepper
1	2- to 2½-pound boneless pork top loin roast (single loin)
	Fresh rosemary sprigs (optional)

1. Preheat oven to 325°F. In a small bowl, combine brown sugar, thyme, chili powder, rosemary, and cayenne pepper. Sprinkle mixture evenly over roast; rub in with your fingers.

2. Place roast on a rack in a shallow roasting pan. Insert an ovenproof meat thermometer into center of roast. Roast for 1¼ to 1½ hours or until thermometer registers 155°F. Cover roast with foil; and let stand for 15 minutes (the temperature of the meat will rise 5°F during standing). If desired, garnish serving platter with rosemary. Makes 8 to 10 servings.

Per serving: 134 cal., 4 g fat (2 g sat. fat), 50 mg chol., 37 mg sodium, 2 g carbo., 0 g fiber, 20 g pro.

> Wine experts now suggest hosts serve the *wine they like with the food they like,* relaxing wine/food pairing rules.

Mustard-Maple Pork Roast

Prep: 20 minutes   Roast: 1¼ hours
Stand: 15 minutes   Oven: 325°F

1	2- to 2½- pound boneless pork loin roast (single loin)
2	tablespoons Dijon-style mustard
1	tablespoon maple-flavor syrup
2	teaspoons dried sage, crushed
1	teaspoon finely shredded orange peel
¼	teaspoon salt
¼	teaspoon ground black pepper
20	to 24 tiny new potatoes
16	ounces packaged, peeled baby carrots
1	tablespoon olive oil
¼	teaspoon salt

1. Preheat oven to 325°F. Trim fat from meat. In a small bowl, stir together mustard, syrup, sage, orange peel, ¼ teaspoon salt, and pepper. Spoon mixture onto meat. Place roast, fat side up, on a rack in a shallow roasting pan. Insert a meat thermometer into center of roast. Roast, uncovered, for 30 minutes.

2. Meanwhile, peel a strip of skin from the center of each potato. In a covered large saucepan, cook potatoes in enough boiling salted water to cover for 5 minutes. Add carrots; cook for 5 minutes more. Drain.

3. Toss together potatoes, carrots, olive oil, and ¼ teaspoon salt. Place in roasting pan around pork roast. Roast, uncovered, for 45 minutes to 1 hour more or until meat thermometer registers 155°F. Remove roast from oven; cover with foil. Let stand for 15 minutes before carving (the meat temperature will rise 5°F during standing). Makes 8 servings.

Per serving: 281 cal., 10 g fat (3 g sat. fat), 51 mg chol., 309 mg sodium, 29 g carbo., 3 g fiber, 19 g pro.

Pecan-Crusted Chicken

Prep: 20 minutes   Cook: 12 minutes

2	tablespoons orange marmalade
2	tablespoons pure maple syrup
1	cup finely chopped pecans
3	tablespoons all-purpose flour
¼	teaspoon salt
4	skinless, boneless chicken breast halves
2	tablespoons cooking oil
1	tablespoon butter

1. In a small bowl, stir together orange marmalade and maple syrup; set aside. In a shallow dish, combine pecans, flour, and salt. Brush marmalade mixture on both sides of chicken breast halves. Dip into pecan mixture to coat, pressing pecan mixture into chicken, if necessary.

2. In a 12-inch skillet, heat cooking oil and butter over medium heat until mixture begins to bubble. Add chicken breasts and cook for 6 minutes. Turn chicken. Cook for 6 to 9 minutes more or until golden brown and no longer pink in center (170°F). Watch closely and reduce heat if chicken browns too quickly. Makes 4 servings.

Per serving: 506 cal., 32 g fat (5 g sat. fat), 90 mg chol., 279 mg sodium, 21 g carbo., 3 g fiber, 36 g pro.

Cheese-Stuffed Chicken

Prep: 25 minutes   Bake: 50 minutes   Oven: 350°F

4	medium chicken breast halves
¾	cup shredded mozzarella cheese (3 ounces)
½	cup crumbled feta cheese
¼	cup chopped peanuts
2	slices bacon, crisp-cooked, drained, and crumbled, or ¼ cup cooked bacon pieces
	Salt and ground black pepper
	Paprika

1. Preheat oven to 350°F. Skin chicken, if desired. Using a sharp knife, make a pocket in each breast by cutting horizontally from side to side, leaving edges intact. In a bowl, combine mozzarella cheese, feta cheese, peanuts, and bacon. Spoon filling into pockets, packing lightly (pockets will be full). Place chicken, bone side down, in a 3-quart rectangular baking dish. Lightly sprinkle chicken with salt, pepper, and paprika.

2. Bake, uncovered, for 50 to 55 minutes or until an instant-read thermometer inserted in the chicken registers 170°F. Makes 4 servings.

Per serving: 457 cal., 29 g fat (10 g sat. fat), 136 mg chol., 587 mg sodium, 3 g carbo., 1 g fiber, 44 g pro.

Grilled Chicken with Cucumber-Yogurt Sauce

Prep: 20 minutes   Grill: 12 minutes

1   6-ounce carton plain low-fat yogurt
1/4   cup thinly sliced green onions
2   teaspoons snipped fresh mint
1/2   teaspoon ground cumin
1/4   teaspoon salt
1/8   teaspoon ground black pepper
1   cup chopped, seeded cucumber
4   skinless, boneless chicken breast halves
1/8   teaspoon ground black pepper

1. In a medium bowl, combine yogurt, green onions, mint, cumin, salt, and 1/8 teaspoon pepper. Transfer half of the yogurt mixture to a small bowl; set aside. For cucumber-yogurt sauce, stir cucumber into remaining yogurt mixture.

2. Sprinkle chicken breasts with 1/8 teaspoon pepper. Grill chicken on the rack of an uncovered grill directly over medium coals for 12 to 15 minutes or until chicken is no longer pink (170°F), turning once halfway through grilling and brushing with reserved yogurt mixture for the last half of grilling time. Discard any remaining yogurt mixture.

3. Serve chicken with the cucumber-yogurt sauce. Makes 4 servings.

Per serving: 159 cal., 2 g fat (1 g sat. fat), 68 mg chol., 251 mg sodium, 5 g carbo., 0 g fiber, 29 g pro.

Chicken Veneto

Start to Finish: 30 minutes

8   ounces dried fettuccine or linguine
12   ounces skinless, boneless chicken breast halves
2   tablespoons extra virgin olive oil
1/4   cup butter
3   cloves garlic, minced
1   9-ounce package frozen artichoke hearts, thawed and halved
1/4   cup coarsely chopped pistachios
3/4   cup dry white wine
1/4   teaspoon salt
2   tablespoons snipped fresh Italian (flat-leaf) parsley
  Cracked black pepper

Chicken Veneto

1. Cook pasta according to package directions. Drain; keep warm.

2. Meanwhile, cut chicken into bite-size strips. In a very large skillet, cook chicken in hot oil over medium-high heat for 3 to 4 minutes or until chicken is no longer pink. Remove chicken from skillet; discard pan drippings.

3. In the same skillet, melt butter over medium heat. Add garlic; cook and stir for 15 seconds. Remove from heat. Add artichokes, pistachios, and wine. Return to heat. Bring to boiling; reduce heat. Simmer, uncovered, for 5 minutes. Stir in salt. Return chicken to skillet. Cook for 1 to 2 minutes more or until heated through.

4. Spoon chicken mixture over pasta. Sprinkle with parsley and cracked black pepper. Serve immediately. Makes 4 servings.

Per serving: 583 cal., 25 g fat (8 g sat. fat), 82 mg chol., 325 mg sodium, 51 g carbo., 6 g fiber, 31 g pro.

130

Game Hens with Rhubarb Barbecue Glaze

Prep: 30 minutes   Cook: 20 minutes
Roast: 55 minutes   Oven: 375°F

3   1¼- to 1½-pound Cornish game hens
    Olive oil
    Salt and ground black pepper
3½ to 4 cups chopped fresh or frozen
    rhubarb
1   cup bottled tomato-base barbecue
    sauce
¼   cup water
8   ounces dried orzo
1   cup packaged shredded carrots
¼   cup sliced green onions
    Salt and ground black pepper

1. Preheat oven to 375°F. Use a long, heavy knife or kitchen shears to halve Cornish hens lengthwise, cutting through the breastbone, just off-center, and through the center of the backbone. (Or ask the butcher to halve hens.) Twist wing tips under back. Rub olive oil over the surface and in the cavity of each hen half; sprinkle generously with salt and pepper. Place hen halves, cut side down, in a 15x10x1-inch baking pan. Roast, uncovered, for 40 minutes.

2. Meanwhile, for sauce, in a medium saucepan, bring the rhubarb, barbecue sauce, and the water to boiling over medium-high heat. Reduce heat to medium-low and cook, covered, for 20 minutes or until the rhubarb loses its shape. Remove from heat; coarsely mash rhubarb in the pan. Remove and reserve 1 cup of the sauce for the orzo mixture.

3. Brush surfaces of game hens with some of the remaining sauce. Roast for 15 to 20 minutes more, brushing every 5 minutes, or until hens are glazed, no longer pink, and an instant-read thermometer inserted in thigh muscle registers 180°F.

4. Meanwhile, cook orzo according to package directions; drain. Transfer orzo to a large bowl. Stir in the 1 cup reserved sauce, shredded carrots, and green onions. Season with salt and pepper. Serve orzo mixture with game hen halves. Pass remaining sauce. Makes 6 servings.

Per serving: 375 cal., 10 g fat (2 g sat. fat), 111 mg chol., 609 mg sodium, 39 g carbo., 4 g fiber, 31 g pro.

Chicken Caribbean

Start to Finish: 25 minutes

4   skinless, boneless chicken breast halves
½   teaspoon Jamaican jerk seasoning
½   cup canned coconut milk
¼   cup orange juice
2   tablespoons snipped fresh basil
1   teaspoon finely shredded orange peel
2   cups hot cooked rice

1. Rub both sides of chicken with jerk seasoning. Grill chicken on the rack of an uncovered grill directly over medium coals for 12 to 15 minutes or until chicken is no longer pink (170°F), turning once.

2. Meanwhile, for sauce, in a small saucepan, combine coconut milk, orange juice, and 1 tablespoon of the basil. Bring to boiling; reduce heat. Simmer, uncovered, about 5 minutes or until reduced to ½ cup.

3. Stir orange peel into rice. Serve chicken and sauce over rice. Sprinkle with remaining 1 tablespoon basil. Makes 4 servings.

Per serving: 287 cal., 9 g fat (6 g sat. fat), 59 mg chol., 85 mg sodium, 25 g carbo., 0 g fiber, 24 g pro.

Chicken Medallions with Mustard Sauce

Start to Finish: 25 minutes

4   skinless, boneless chicken breast halves
    Salt and ground black pepper
2   tablespoons olive oil or cooking oil
¼   cup dry white wine
2   tablespoons crème fraiche
2   tablespoons tarragon mustard or dill
    mustard

1. Place each chicken breast half between two pieces of plastic wrap. With the flat side of a meat mallet, pound lightly to ½-inch thickness. Remove plastic wrap. Sprinkle chicken with salt and pepper.

2. In a 12-inch skillet, cook chicken breasts, two at a time, in hot oil over medium-high heat for 2 to 3 minutes or until golden, turning once. Transfer chicken to a serving platter; keep warm.

3. For sauce, carefully add wine to hot skillet. Cook and stir until bubbly, loosening any brown bits in bottom of skillet. Add crème fraiche and mustard to skillet; stir with a wire whisk until combined. Spoon sauce over chicken. Makes 4 servings.

Per serving: 255 cal., 11 g fat (3 g sat. fat), 92 mg chol., 306 mg sodium, 1 g carbo., 0 g fiber, 33 g pro.

Spicy Grilled Shrimp
Prep: 15 minutes   Marinate: 1 hour   Grill: 7 minutes

- 1½ **pounds fresh or frozen peeled and deveined extra-large shrimp**
- ¼ **cup orange marmalade**
- ¼ **cup honey**
- 2 **to 3 teaspoons Cajun seasoning**
- 1 **tablespoon olive oil**

1. Thaw shrimp, if frozen. If using wooden skewers, soak in water for 1 hour. Rinse shrimp; pat dry. For sauce, in a small saucepan, stir together marmalade, honey, and ½ teaspoon of the Cajun seasoning; set aside.

2. Place shrimp in a self-sealing plastic bag set in a shallow bowl. For marinade, in a small bowl combine oil and remaining Cajun seasoning. Pour marinade over shrimp. Seal bag. Marinate shrimp in refrigerator for 1 hour, turning bag occasionally.

3. Drain shrimp, discarding marinade. Thread shrimp onto skewers. For a charcoal grill, place skewers on the greased rack of an uncovered grill directly over medium coals. Grill for 7 to 9 minutes or until shrimp are opaque, turning once halfway through grilling. (For a gas grill, pre-heat grill. Reduce heat to medium. Place skewers on greased grill rack over heat. Cover and grill as above.)

4. Stir marmalade sauce over low heat for 2 to 3 minutes or until melted. Drizzle sauce over shrimp on skewers. Serve shrimp on skewers. Makes 4 servings.

Per serving: 430 cal., 7 g fat (1 g sat. fat), 259 mg chol., 357 mg sodium, 55 g carbo., 1 g fiber, 37 g pro.

Cajun Shrimp Pasta with Andouille Cream Sauce

Start to Finish: 40 minutes

1   pound fresh or frozen peeled, deveined large shrimp
1   pound dried bow tie pasta
1   cup chopped sweet onion (1 large)
1   tablespoon olive oil
3   to 4 teaspoons Cajun seasoning
1   10-ounce container refrigerated Alfredo pasta sauce
1/2   cup milk
4   ounces smoked cheddar cheese, shredded (1 cup)
4   ounces cooked andouille sausage, chopped
1   cup chopped tomatoes
    Grated Parmesan cheese
    Sliced green onions

1. Thaw shrimp, if frozen. Set aside. Cook pasta according to package directions; drain and return to pan. Keep warm.

2. Meanwhile, in a 12-inch skillet, cook onion in hot oil over medium heat for 5 to 10 minutes or until tender, stirring occasionally. Stir in Cajun seasoning. Add shrimp. Cook for 2 to 4 minutes or until shrimp are opaque, stirring occasionally. Reduce heat to low.

3. Stir in Alfredo sauce, milk, and cheese. Cook and stir over low heat until cheese melts. Stir in sausage and tomatoes. Add shrimp mixture to hot pasta; toss gently to coat. Sprinkle with Parmesan cheese and green onions. Makes 8 servings.

Per serving: 473 cal., 17 g fat (8 g sat. fat), 136 mg chol., 629 mg sodium, 51 g carbo., 3 g fiber, 29 g pro.

andouille sausage

Often used in Cajun cooking, andouille (ahn-DWEE) is a pork sausage seasoned with salt, pepper, and garlic, and smoked over pecan wood. Outside Louisiana's Cajun country the real thing can be hard to find. Look for it at a specialty food store. Or substitute kielbasa and add a little cayenne pepper.

Poached Salmon with Shrimp Sauce

Start to Finish: 40 minutes

6   6-ounce fresh or frozen skinless salmon fillets
4   cups dry white wine or chicken broth
1   bay leaf
1   sprig fresh parsley
1   teaspoon dried thyme
2   whole peppercorns
1/2   teaspoon salt
1/2   cup finely chopped green onions or shallots
8   tablespoons butter
    Salt and ground black pepper
2   cups whipping cream
1   8-ounce container button mushrooms, quartered or sliced
8   ounces peeled and deveined cooked small shrimp
    Lemon slices (optional)

1. Thaw fish, if frozen. Rinse fish; pat dry with paper towels. Set aside. Pour 3 cups wine into a fish poacher or large roasting pan that has a wire rack with handles.

2. Tie bay leaf, parsley, thyme, and peppercorns in a double-thick square piece of 100%-cotton cheesecloth; add to wine in pan. Stir in 1/2 teaspoon salt. Place pan over two burners on range top. Bring to boiling; reduce heat.

3. Grease wire rack; place fish on rack and lower into pan. Simmer, covered, for 6 to 10 minutes or until fish flakes easily when tested with a fork. Remove fish; keep warm.

4. Meanwhile, for sauce, in a 10-inch skillet, cook and stir onions in 1 tablespoon butter until tender. Add remaining 1 cup wine; season with salt and pepper. Bring to boiling; reduce heat slightly. Boil gently, uncovered, about 5 minutes or until sauce is reduced by half.

5. Reduce heat to medium. Add cream. Cook and stir for 7 to 10 minutes or until sauce is thickened. Whisk in 5 tablespoons butter, 1 tablespoon at a time, until melted. Remove from heat; keep warm.

6. In another skillet, cook and stir mushrooms in the remaining 2 tablespoons butter over medium heat about 5 minutes or until mushrooms are tender and liquid has evaporated. Stir mushrooms and shrimp into sauce; heat through. Serve salmon with sauce. If desired, garnish with lemon slices. Makes 6 servings.

Per serving: 787 cal., 64 g fat (30 g sat. fat), 252 mg chol., 625 mg sodium, 4 g carbo., 1 g fiber, 42 g pro.

Coconut Shrimp with Chutney

Start to Finish: 15 minutes   Oven: 400°F

1	pound fresh or frozen peeled and deveined shrimp
1	cup flaked coconut, toasted and chopped
1/2	cup seasoned fine dry bread crumbs
3/4	teaspoon curry powder
2	egg whites, lightly beaten
	Nonstick cooking spray
1/2	cup mango chutney
1/4	cup orange juice
1/4	teaspoon ground ginger

1. Thaw shrimp, if frozen. Rinse shrimp; pat dry with paper towels. Preheat oven to 400°F. Generously grease a 15×10×1-inch baking pan; set aside.

2. In a shallow bowl, combine coconut, bread crumbs, and curry powder. Place egg whites in another small shallow bowl. Dip shrimp into egg whites, then into coconut mixture, pressing it firmly onto shrimp. Place in prepared baking pan. Coat shrimp with nonstick cooking spray.

3. Bake about 10 minutes or until shrimp are opaque. Meanwhile, in a small bowl, combine chutney, orange juice, and ginger. Serve with shrimp. Makes 10 servings.

Per serving: 138 cal., 4 g fat (3 g sat. fat), 69 mg chol., 290 mg sodium, 14 g carbo., 1 g fiber, 11 g pro.

Black Walnut-Crusted Catfish with Maple Sauce

Start to Finish: 25 minutes

4	fresh or frozen catfish fillets, about 1/2 inch thick (about 1 1/2 pounds)
	Salt and ground black pepper
1/4	cup milk
1	egg
2	cups cornflakes, finely crushed
1/4	cup finely chopped black walnuts or walnuts
1	tablespoon butter
1/4	cup pure maple syrup
1/4	cup butter, softened

1. Thaw fish, if frozen. Rinse fish; pat dry with paper towels. Season fish with salt and pepper. Measure thickness of fish fillets. Set aside.

2. In a shallow dish, use a fork to beat together milk and egg. In another shallow dish, combine cornflakes and walnuts. Dip fish fillets in milk mixture, allowing excess to drip off. Dip coated fish fillets in walnut mixture, turning to coat evenly.

3. In a large skillet, melt 1 tablespoon butter over medium heat. Cook fish, half at a time, for 4 to 6 minutes per 1/2-inch thickness or until golden and fish flakes easily when tested with a fork, turning once. (Reduce heat as necessary to prevent overbrowning.)

4. Meanwhile, for sauce, in a small saucepan, bring syrup to boiling. Remove from heat and whisk in 1/4 cup butter until combined. Serve with fish. Makes 4 servings.

Note: To bake fish, prepare as directed above through Step 2. Place fish on a greased baking sheet. Bake, uncovered, in a 450°F oven for 4 to 6 minutes per 1/2-inch thickness or until golden and fish flakes easily when tested with a fork. Serve with maple sauce as directed above.

Per serving: 533 cal., 33 g fat (13 g sat. fat), 172 mg chol., 496 mg sodium, 27 g carbo., 1 g fiber, 32 g pro.

Sea Bass with Chili Oil

Start to Finish: 25 minutes

1 1/4	pounds fresh or frozen sea bass fillets
2	medium carrots
5	cups chopped cabbage (about 1 1/2 pounds)
2	tablespoons water
1	tablespoon lemon juice
1/2	teaspoon salt
1/4	teaspoon ground black pepper
2	to 3 teaspoons bottled chili oil
2	teaspoons grated fresh ginger
1	teaspoon bottled minced garlic (2 cloves)
	Bottled chili oil (optional)
	Lemon wedges (optional)

1. Thaw fish, if frozen. Rinse fish; pat dry with paper towels. Cut fish into four serving-size pieces; set aside. Using a vegetable peeler, cut the carrots into long thin ribbons (about 1 cup). In a 12-inch skillet, combine carrot ribbons, cabbage, the water, lemon juice, 1/4 teaspoon of the salt, and pepper.

2. Sprinkle fish pieces with the remaining 1/4 teaspoon salt. In a small bowl, stir together the 2 to 3 teaspoons chili oil, ginger, and garlic; spread over fish pieces. Place fish pieces on top of vegetable mixture in skillet.

3. Bring skillet mixture just to boiling; reduce heat. Simmer, covered, for 9 to 12 minutes or until fish flakes easily when tested with a fork. Transfer fish and vegetable mixture to plates. If desired, drizzle with additional chili oil and serve with lemon wedges. Makes 4 servings.

Per serving: 196 cal., 5 g fat (1 g sat. fat), 58 mg chol., 415 mg sodium, 9 g carbo., 3 g fiber, 28 g pro.

Salmon with Matzo Crust

Start to Finish: 20 minutes

1½   **6-inch squares matzo, broken up**
  2   **tablespoons snipped fresh dill or**
      1½ teaspoons dried dillweed
  3   **tablespoons olive oil or cooking oil**
  4   **4- to 5-ounce skinless salmon fillets,**
      1 inch thick
     Steamed green beans (optional)
     Lemon wedges (optional)
     Fresh dill sprigs (optional)

1. Preheat oven to 450°F. In a blender or food processor, combine matzo, dill, ½ teaspoon *salt,* and ¼ teaspoon *ground black pepper.* Cover; blend or process until coarse. Transfer to a shallow dish. Brush a shallow baking pan with oil. Brush fish with oil. Roll fish in crumb mixture; place in prepared pan. Drizzle fish with remaining oil.

3. Bake, uncovered, for 10 to 12 minutes or until fish flakes easily when tested with a fork. If desired, serve with green beans and garnish with lemon wedges and dill sprigs. Makes 10 servings.

Per serving: 340 cal., 23 g fat (4 g sat. fat), 67 mg chol., 358 mg sodium, 9 g carbo., 0 g fiber, 24 g pro.

Two-Step Crunchy
Chicken Strips

kid-friendly
dishes

Most kids have strong opinions about food. They either beg for something every day or won't touch it. What's a mom to do? Try these kid-tested recipes. They're so easy your child can help cook.

Two-Step Crunchy Chicken Strips
Prep: 10 minutes   Bake: 10 minutes   Oven: 425°F

Nonstick cooking spray
2¹/₂ cups crushed bite-size cheddar fish-shape crackers or pretzels
²/₃ cup bottled buttermilk ranch salad dressing
1 pound chicken breast tenderloins
Buttermilk ranch salad dressing (optional)

1. Preheat oven to 425°F. Line a 15×10×1-inch baking pan with foil; lightly coat the foil with cooking spray. Set aside.

2. Place the crushed crackers in a shallow dish. In another shallow dish place ranch dressing. Dip chicken tenderloins into dressing, allowing excess to drip off; dip into cracker crumbs to coat. Arrange chicken in prepared pan. Bake for 10 to 15 minutes or until chicken is no longer pink (170°F). If desired, serve with additional ranch dressing. Makes 4 to 6 servings.

Per serving: 517 cal., 21 g fat (2 g sat. fat), 66 mg chol., 1,060 mg sodium, 51 g carbo., 2 g fiber, 33 g pro.

Chili Dogs
Prep: 10 minutes   Broil: 5 minutes

8 hot dogs
8 hot dog buns, split
1 15-ounce can chili without beans
¹/₂ cup salsa
2 green onions, chopped
Shredded cheddar or Monterey Jack cheese
Coarsely crushed corn chips

1. Preheat broiler. Place hot dogs on the unheated rack of a broiler pan. Broil for 3 minutes. Turn hot dogs and broil for 2 to 3 minutes more or until hot dogs are heated through. Put hot dogs in buns; arrange on a platter.

2. Meanwhile, in a medium saucepan, combine chili and salsa. Cook over medium heat until heated through, stirring constantly.

3. To serve, put chili mixture, onions, cheese, and crushed chips in separate serving bowls. Serve with hot dogs. Makes 8 servings.

Per serving: 302 cal., 15 g fat (4 g sat. fat), 46 mg chol., 952 mg sodium, 29 g carbo., 2 g fiber, 14 g pro.

Macaroni and Cheese Chowder

Start to Finish: 25 minutes

- 1   14-ounce can reduced-sodium chicken broth
- 1   cup water
- 1   5.5-ounce package macaroni and cheese dinner mix
- 1   14.5-ounce can cream-style corn
- 1   cup chopped ham and/or cooked chicken
- 1/2 cup milk

1. In a large saucepan, bring chicken broth and the water to boiling. Gradually add macaroni from mix. Reduce heat to medium-low. Simmer, covered, for 11 to 14 minutes or until macaroni is tender.

2. Stir in cream-style corn, ham, milk, and contents of cheese packet. Cook and stir over medium heat until heated through. Makes 4 servings.

Per serving: 301 cal., 6 g fat (2 g sat. fat), 27 mg chol., 1,324 mg sodium, 48 g carbo., 2 g fiber, 16 g pro.

Pizza Soup

Start to Finish: 20 minutes

- 1   cup chopped onion
- 1   cup chopped green sweet pepper
- 1   cup sliced fresh mushrooms
- 1   cup halved, sliced zucchini
- 1   14-ounce can beef broth
- 1   14.5-ounce can diced tomatoes with basil, garlic, and oregano, undrained
- 1   8-ounce can tomato sauce with garlic and onion
- 4   ounces cooked smoked turkey sausage, thinly sliced
- 1/2 teaspoon pizza seasoning
- 1/2 cup shredded mozzarella cheese (2 ounces)

1. In a medium saucepan, combine onion, sweet pepper, mushrooms, zucchini, and 1/4 cup of the broth. Bring to boiling; reduce heat. Simmer, covered, for 5 minutes.

2. Stir in remaining broth, undrained tomatoes, tomato sauce, sausage, and pizza seasoning. Simmer for 5 to 10 minutes more or until vegetables are tender. Top each serving with cheese. Makes 6 servings.

Per serving: 119 cal., 3 g fat (1 g sat. fat), 17 mg chol., 1,018 mg sodium, 14 g carbo., 2 g fiber, 9 g pro.

Crater Taters

Prep: 20 minutes   Microwave: 10 minutes
Stand: 5 minutes

- 4   large baking potatoes (about 2 pounds total)
  Broccoli-Cheese, Ham Alfredo, Tex-Mex, or Chili-Cheese topping

1. Scrub potatoes with a vegetable brush; prick with a fork. Microwave, uncovered, on 100% power (high) for 10 to 15 minutes or until potatoes are nearly tender, rearranging once. Let potatoes stand for 5 minutes. Use a fork to cut an X in the top of each potato. Spoon desired topping onto each potato. Makes 4 servings.

Broccoli-Cheese: In a saucepan, prepare one 10-ounce package frozen cut broccoli in cheese sauce as directed on the package.

Per serving: 275 cal., 2 g fat (1 g sat. fat), 3 mg chol., 251 mg sodium, 58 g carbo., 3 g fiber, 8 g pro.

Ham Alfredo: In a saucepan, combine one 10-ounce container refrigerated Alfredo pasta sauce and 1 cup diced cooked ham. Cook on medium-low heat until mixture is hot, stirring several times with a wooden spoon.

Tex-Mex: Spoon 2 tablespoons salsa on each baked potato. Spoon 1 tablespoon dairy sour cream and/or guacamole on top of the salsa. If desired, top with some shredded cheddar cheese.

Chili-Cheese: In a medium saucepan, combine one 15-ounce can chili with beans and 1/2 cup shredded Colby and Monterey Jack cheese or cheddar cheese. Cook over medium-low heat until mixture is hot, stirring several times with a wooden spoon.

oven-baked potatoes

If your crew prefers potatoes baked in the oven, scrub potatoes with a brush, pat dry, and prick with a fork. For soft skins, rub each potato with shortening or wrap in foil. Bake potatoes in a 425°F oven for 40 to 50 minutes or until tender. To serve, roll each potato gently under your hand. Cut an X in the top, then press in and up on the ends. Use the same method to bake sweet potatoes.

Chicken Tortilla Soup

Start to Finish: 20 minutes

2   **14-ounce cans chicken broth**
2   **cups loose-pack frozen pepper stir-fry vegetables (yellow, green, and red sweet peppers, and onions)**
1   **14.5-ounce can Mexican-style stewed tomatoes, undrained**
2   **cups chopped cooked chicken**
1   **cup crushed packaged baked tortilla chips (about 2 cups uncrushed)**

Dairy sour cream, chopped avocado, and/or fresh cilantro (optional)

1. In a large saucepan, combine broth, frozen vegetables, and undrained tomatoes. Bring to boiling; reduce heat. Simmer, covered, for 3 to 5 minutes or until vegetables are tender. Stir in chicken; heat through.

2. Ladle soup into warm soup bowls and sprinkle with crushed tortilla chips. If desired, top with sour cream, avocado, and/or cilantro. Makes 4 servings.

Per serving: 247 cal., 6 g fat (1 g sat. fat), 64 mg chol., 1,266 mg sodium, 17 g carbo., 2 g fiber, 24 g pro.

Team Favorite Turkey Burger

Prep: 15 minutes   Broil: 14 minutes

- ¼ **cup fine dry bread crumbs**
- 3 **tablespoons ketchup**
- 4 **teaspoons dill or sweet pickle relish**
- ½ **teaspoon bottled minced garlic**
- ¼ **teaspoon salt**
- ¼ **teaspoon ground black pepper**
- 1 **pound uncooked ground turkey or chicken**
- ⅓ **cup low-fat mayonnaise dressing or salad dressing**
- 4 **romaine or green leaf lettuce leaves**
- 8 **tomato slices**
- 4 **whole wheat hamburger buns, split and toasted**

1. Preheat broiler. In a large bowl, combine bread crumbs, 2 tablespoons ketchup, 2 teaspoons relish, garlic, salt, and ⅛ teaspoon pepper. Add ground turkey; mix well. Shape turkey mixture into four ¾-inch-thick patties.

2. In a small bowl, combine mayonnaise dressing, remaining 1 tablespoon catsup, remaining 2 teaspoons relish, and remaining ⅛ teaspoon pepper; set aside.

3. Place patties on the unheated rack of a broiler pan. Broil 4 to 5 inches from the heat for 14 to 18 minutes or until no longer pink (165°F), turning once halfway through broiling. Place lettuce and tomato slices on the bottom halves of buns. Top with burgers. Spoon mayonnaise mixture on burgers. Add top halves of buns. Makes 4 servings.

Per serving: 343 cal., 12 g fat (3 g sat. fat), 74 mg chol., 953 mg sodium, 33 g carbo., 3 g fiber, 29 g pro.

Nacho Chicken Legs

Prep: 30 minutes   Bake: 1 hour   Oven: 350°F

- 1½ **cups bottled mild taco sauce**
- 2 **cups crushed tortilla chips**
- 12 **chicken drumsticks (about 3 pounds)**
  Cheese and Salsa Dipping Sauce

1. Preheat oven to 350°F. Line a large baking sheet with foil. Grease foil. Place taco sauce in a shallow dish. Place tortilla chips in another shallow dish. Dip each chicken drumstick into the taco sauce then into the crushed tortillas to cover. Place drumsticks on the prepared baking sheet. Bake for 1 hour or until chicken is no longer pink (180°F). Do not turn chicken pieces while baking.

2. Prepare dipping sauce and serve with drumsticks. Makes 6 servings.

Cheese and Salsa Dipping Sauce: In a small microwave-safe bowl, combine ⅓ cup salsa, ⅓ cup process cheese spread, and, if desired, 1 tablespoon snipped fresh cilantro. Microwave on 100% power (high) for 30 seconds. Stir. Microwave 30 seconds more or until cheese melts.

Per serving (chicken only): 418 cal., 21 g fat (5 g sat. fat), 118 mg chol., 612 mg sodium, 25 g carbo., 2 g fiber, 30 g pro.

Ham and Cheese Quesadillas

Start to Finish: 20 minutes

- ¾ **cup shredded Swiss, Monterey Jack, or cheddar cheese (3 ounces)**
- 4 **7- to 8-inch whole wheat, spinach, tomato, or plain flour tortillas**
- 3 **ounces thinly sliced cooked ham**
- ⅔ **cup chopped tomato**
- 2 **tablespoons sliced green onion (optional)**

1. Sprinkle cheese over tortillas. Top with ham, tomato, and green onion. Fold tortillas in half, pressing together.

2. In a 10-inch skillet, cook quesadillas, two at a time, over medium heat for 1½ to 2 minutes per side or until light brown. Cut into wedges; serve immediately. Makes 4 servings.

Per serving: 260 cal., 10 g fat (5 g sat. fat), 31 mg chol., 699 mg sodium, 29 g carbo., 3 g fiber, 13 g pro.

Tex-Mex Chicken Roll-Ups

Prep: 15 minutes   Bake: 25 minutes   Oven: 350°F

- 1 **3-ounce package cream cheese, softened**
- ¼ **cup snipped dried tomatoes**
- 1 **tablespoon snipped fresh cilantro**
- 6 **7- to 8-inch flour tortillas**
- 1 **4.5-ounce can whole green chile peppers, drained and cut into thin strips**
- 1½ **cups cooked chicken strips**
- ½ **cup shredded Monterey Jack cheese (2 ounces)**
  Salsa

1. Preheat oven to 350°F. In a small bowl, stir together cream cheese, dried tomatoes, and cilantro. Spread mixture over tortillas. Place chile strips near one edge of each tortilla. Top each tortilla with chicken and cheese. Roll up.

2. Place roll-ups in a lightly greased 3-quart rectangular baking dish. Bake, covered, for 25 to 30 minutes or until heated through. Serve with salsa. Makes 6 servings.

Per serving: 252 cal., 13 g fat (6 g sat. fat), 55 mg chol., 377 mg sodium, 17 g carbo., 1 g fiber, 16 g pro.

Barbecue Quesadillas

Prep: 20 minutes   Cook: 6 minutes per batch
Oven: 350°F

> **Nonstick cooking spray**
> 4   **7- or 8-inch flour tortillas**
> 1   **cup shredded extra-sharp cheddar cheese or Mexican cheese blend (4 ounces)**
> 1   **4-ounce can diced green chiles, drained**
> 1   **18-ounce tub refrigerated barbecue sauce with shredded chicken (2 cups)**
> 1   **cup bottled salsa**
> ¼   **cup dairy sour cream**
> ¼   **cup sliced green onions**

1. Coat one side of each tortilla with cooking spray. Place, coated sides down, on cutting board or waxed paper. Sprinkle ¼ cup of the cheese over half of each tortilla. Top with green chiles and barbecue sauce with chicken. Fold tortillas in half, pressing gently.

2. Preheat oven to 350°F. In a hot 10-inch skillet, cook quesadillas, two at a time, over medium heat for 6 to 8 minutes or until golden brown, turning once. Place quesadillas on a baking sheet. Keep warm in oven. Repeat with remaining quesadillas. Cut each quesadilla into three wedges. Serve with salsa, sour cream, and green onion. Makes 4 servings.

Turkey-Havarti Quesadillas: Prepare as above except coat the unsprayed side of each tortilla with 2 teaspoons stone-ground mustard. Substitute Havarti cheese for the cheddar and 16 ounces cooked sliced turkey for the chicken. Omit green chiles, salsa, sour cream, and green onion.

Bacon, Tomato, and Avocado Quesadillas: Prepare as above except substitute Monterey Jack cheese for the cheddar, 8 slices crisp-cooked and crumbled bacon, 2 small seeded and coarsely chopped tomatoes; and 1 seeded, peeled, and chopped avocado for the filling. Omit green chiles, barbecue sauce with chicken, salsa, sour cream, and green onion.

Per serving: 469 cal., 21 g fat (10 g sat. fat), 86 mg chol., 1,606 mg sodium, 44 g carbo., 2 g fiber, 25 g pro.

Triple-Decker Tostadas
Start to Finish: 20 minutes   Oven: 450°F

    Nonstick cooking spray
1   cup canned pinto beans, rinsed and drained
1   cup bottled salsa
4   6-inch corn tortillas
$^1/_2$ cup frozen whole kernel corn
$^1/_2$ cup shredded Monterey Jack or cheddar cheese (2 ounces)
$^1/_2$ cup shredded lettuce

1. Preheat oven to 450°F. Lightly coat a 9-inch pie plate with cooking spray; set aside. In a small saucepan or skillet, slightly mash beans. Cook and stir beans over medium heat for 2 to 3 minutes; set aside.

2. Spoon $^1/_4$ cup of the salsa into the prepared pie plate. Top with one of the tortillas. Layer half of the mashed beans, one tortilla, corn, $^1/_4$ cup of the cheese, $^1/_4$ cup salsa, one tortilla, remaining bean mixture, remaining tortilla, and remaining $^1/_2$ cup salsa.

3. Bake, covered, for 12 minutes. (Or cover with microwave-safe plastic wrap; microwave on 100% power [high] for 4 minutes, rotating once.) Uncover; sprinkle with lettuce and remaining $^1/_4$ cup cheese. Makes 4 servings.

Per serving: 219 cal., 5 g fat (2 g sat. fat), 10 mg chol., 813 mg sodium, 38 g carbo., 6 g fiber, 10 g pro.

Barbecued Chicken Pizza
Prep: 20 minutes   Bake: 19 minutes   Oven: 425°F

1   10-ounce package refrigerated pizza dough
$^1/_2$ of a 32-ounce container (about 2 cups) shredded cooked chicken in barbecue sauce*
1   8-ounce package shredded four-cheese pizza cheese
$^1/_4$ cup snipped fresh cilantro

1. Preheat oven to 425°F. Lightly grease a 15×10×1-inch baking pan. Unroll pizza dough into pan; press dough with your hands into a 12×10-inch rectangle, building up the edges. Bake for 7 minutes.

2. Spread chicken in barbecue sauce over hot crust. Sprinkle cheese and cilantro over chicken. Bake for 12 to 15 minutes more or until lightly browned. Cut into wedges. Makes 6 servings.

***Note:** Or substitute 2 cups shredded cooked chicken plus $^1/_2$ cup bottled barbecue sauce.

Per serving: 324 cal., 13 g fat (6 g sat. fat), 39 mg chol., 683 mg sodium, 33 g carbo., 1 g fiber, 20 g pro.

Turkey Taco Salad
Start to Finish: 25 minutes

    Nonstick cooking spray
12   ounces uncooked ground turkey
1   15-ounce can pinto beans, rinsed and drained (optional)
1   cup frozen whole kernel corn
1   cup bottled salsa
$^1/_4$ cup water
4   to 6 cups shredded lettuce
$^1/_4$ cup shredded cheddar cheese (1 ounce)
1   cup broken baked tortilla chips

1. Lightly coat a large nonstick skillet with cooking spray. Heat over medium heat. Cook ground turkey in hot skillet about 5 minutes or until no longer pink. Drain off any fat. Stir in beans (if desired), corn, salsa, and the water. Bring to boiling; reduce heat. Simmer, covered, for 2 to 3 minutes.

2. Line four salad bowls or plates with lettuce. Top with hot turkey mixture. Sprinkle with cheese and tortilla chips. Serve immediately. Makes 4 servings.

Per serving: 275 cal., 9 g fat (3 g sat. fat), 59 mg chol., 676 mg sodium, 29 g carbo., 3 g fiber, 23 g pro.

Chicken Tacos
Start to Finish: 30 minutes

    Nonstick cooking spray
$^1/_2$ cup chopped onion (1 medium)
1   clove garlic, minced
2   cups chopped cooked chicken
1   8-ounce can tomato sauce
1   4-ounce can diced green chile peppers, drained
12   taco shells
2   cups shredded lettuce
1   medium tomato, seeded and chopped
$^1/_2$ cup finely shredded cheddar cheese (2 ounces)

1. Lightly coat a large nonstick skillet with cooking spray. Heat over medium heat. Add onion and garlic; cook until onion is tender. Stir in chicken, tomato sauce, and chile peppers. Heat through. Divide chicken mixture among taco shells. Top with lettuce, tomato, and cheese. Makes 6 servings.

Per serving: 269 cal., 12 g fat (3 g sat. fat), 48 mg chol., 525 mg sodium, 23 g carbo., 4 g fiber, 19 g pro.

Whole Wheat Pizza with the Works

Prep: 30 minutes   Bake: 35 minutes   Oven: 375°F

      Nonstick cooking spray
 1   16-ounce loaf frozen whole wheat bread
      dough, thawed
 1/2 cup pizza sauce
 1/2 of a 6-ounce package pizza-style
      Canadian-style bacon or thinly sliced
      cooked turkey pepperoni
 1 1/2 cups thinly sliced fresh mushrooms
 1   cup roma tomato slices
 1/4 cup fresh basil leaves (optional)
 1   cup shredded Italian blend cheese or
      mozzarella cheese

1. Preheat oven to 375°F. Lightly coat a 12-inch pizza pan or a 13×9×2-inch baking pan with cooking spray. On a lightly floured surface, roll bread dough into a 12 1/2-inch round or two 7-inch rounds. Transfer dough round(s) to prepared pan; build up edges slightly. Prick the dough several times with a fork.

2. Bake for 10 minutes. Top with sauce, meat, and mushrooms. Bake for 20 minutes.

3. Add tomatoes, and if desired, basil. Sprinkle with cheese. Bake about 5 minutes or until cheese melts and edge of crust is brown. Makes 8 servings.

Per serving: 222 cal., 7 g fat (2 g sat. fat), 17 mg chol., 641 mg sodium, 30 g carbo., 3 g fiber, 13 g pro.

Tastes-Like-a-Taco Pasta Sauce

Start to Finish: 35 minutes

 8   ounces lean ground beef
 1   large onion, chopped
 1   medium green, red, or yellow sweet pepper,
      seeded and chopped
 2   cloves garlic, minced
 1   15-ounce can tomato sauce
 1   14.5-ounce can diced tomatoes, undrained
 1 1/2 teaspoons chili powder
 1/4 teaspoon ground cumin
 10   ounces dried pasta
 2   tablespoons snipped fresh cilantro
 1/2 cup shredded Monterey Jack or
      cheddar cheese

1. In a large saucepan, cook beef, onion, sweet pepper, and garlic over medium heat until beef is brown. Drain off fat. Stir in tomato sauce, undrained tomatoes, chili powder, and

cumin. Bring to boiling; reduce heat. Simmer, uncovered, for 10 to 15 minutes or to desired consistency, stirring occasionally. Season with salt and ground black pepper.

2. Meanwhile, cook pasta according to the package directions; drain. Just before serving, stir cilantro into sauce. Serve over hot cooked pasta. Sprinkle with cheese. Makes 6 servings.

Per serving: 325 cal., 7 g fat (3 g sat. fat), 32 mg chol., 562 mg sodium, 47 g carbo., 3 g fiber, 17 g pro.

Pasta Pizza

Prep: 25 minutes   Bake: 30 minutes   Oven: 350°F

      Nonstick cooking spray
 2   cups dried rotini
 2   lightly beaten eggs
 1/2 cup milk
 1   cup shredded pizza cheese blend
      (4 ounces)
 3/4 cup chopped sweet pepper and/or chopped
      zucchini
 1   14.5-ounce can Italian-style stewed
      tomatoes, undrained
 1/2 teaspoon dried Italian seasoning, crushed
 1   4.5-ounce jar sliced mushrooms, drained
      (optional)
 1/2 of a 6-ounce package sliced turkey
      pepperoni
 2   tablespoons grated Parmesan cheese

1. Preheat oven to 350°F. Lightly coat a 12-inch pizza pan with cooking spray; set aside. Cook pasta according to package directions. Drain; rinse with cold water. Drain again.

2. For pasta crust, in a large bowl, combine eggs, milk, and 1/2 cup of the pizza cheese. Stir in pasta. Spread pasta mixture evenly in prepared pan. Bake for 20 minutes.

3. Meanwhile, coat a large skillet with cooking spray. Heat over medium heat. Add sweet pepper and cook until crisp-tender. Add undrained tomatoes and Italian seasoning. Bring to boiling; reduce heat. Simmer, uncovered, for 10 minutes or until most of the liquid is evaporated, stirring occasionally. If desired, stir in mushrooms.

4. Arrange pepperoni over the pasta crust. Spoon tomato mixture over pepperoni. Sprinkle with remaining 1/2 cup pizza cheese and the Parmesan cheese. Bake for 10 to 12 minutes more or until heated through and cheese melts. Cut into wedges. Makes 6 servings.

Per serving: 242 cal., 6 g fat (2 g sat. fat), 96 mg chol., 574 mg sodium, 31 g carbo., 2 g fiber, 14 g pro.

Pizza Lover's Pasta Sauce
Prep: 25 minutes   Cook: 15 minutes

Nonstick cooking spray
1 large onion, chopped
1 medium green, red, or yellow sweet pepper, seeded and chopped
2 cloves garlic, minced
1 14.5-ounce can diced tomatoes, undrained
1 8-ounce can tomato sauce
1/2 cup thinly sliced cooked turkey pepperoni, chopped
1 4-ounce can sliced mushrooms, drained (optional)
1 teaspoon dried oregano or basil, crushed

1/8 to 1/4 teaspoon crushed red pepper
8 ounces dried pasta
1/3 cup shredded Parmesan cheese

1. Coat a large saucepan with cooking spray. Heat over medium heat. Add onion, sweet pepper, and garlic; cook until tender, stirring occasionally. Stir in undrained tomatoes, tomato sauce, pepperoni, mushrooms (if desired), oregano, and crushed red pepper. Bring to boiling; reduce heat. Simmer, uncovered, about 10 minutes or until desired consistency, stirring occasionally.

2. Meanwhile, cook pasta according to package directions; drain. Serve pasta with sauce. Sprinkle with cheese. Makes 6 servings.

Per serving: 234 cal., 4 g fat (1 g sat. fat), 20 mg chol., 572 mg sodium, 38 g carbo., 2 g fiber, 11 g pro.

Chilly Bow Ties and Tuna

Prep: 20 minutes   Chill: 4 to 24 hours

8 ounces dried bow tie pasta
$\frac{1}{3}$ cup light mayonnaise dressing or salad dressing
$\frac{1}{3}$ cup bottled reduced-calorie Italian salad dressing
$\frac{1}{4}$ cup thinly sliced green onions (optional)
2 tablespoons orange juice
$\frac{1}{4}$ teaspoon salt
$\frac{1}{4}$ teaspoon ground black pepper
1 11-ounce can mandarin orange sections, drained
1 12-ounce can chunk white tuna (water pack), drained and broken into chunks
1 cup fresh pea pods, halved
  Milk (optional)

1. In a large saucepan, cook pasta according to package directions; drain. Rinse with cold water; drain again.

2. Meanwhile, for dressing, in a large bowl, combine mayonnaise dressing, Italian dressing, green onions (if desired), orange juice, salt, and pepper.

3. Add cooked pasta to dressing. Toss well to combine. Gently stir in orange sections, tuna, and pea pods. Cover and chill for 4 to 24 hours. Before serving, if necessary, stir in a little milk to moisten. Makes 6 servings.

Per serving: 254 cal., 3 g fat (1 g sat. fat), 13 mg chol., 433 mg sodium, 43 g carbo., 2 g fiber, 13 g pro.

Chuckwagon Chicken Shepherd's Pie

Prep: 30 minutes   Bake: 30 minutes   Oven: 350°F

$2\frac{1}{4}$ cups milk
1 22-ounce package frozen mashed potatoes
$\frac{1}{4}$ cup snipped fresh parsley
$\frac{1}{2}$ teaspoon salt
1 2- to $2\frac{1}{2}$-pound purchased roasted chicken
1 28-ounce can baked beans
1 11-ounce can whole kernel corn with sweet peppers, drained
$\frac{1}{2}$ cup bottled salsa

1. Preheat oven to 350°F. In a large saucepan, heat milk over medium heat until simmering. Stir in frozen mashed potatoes. Cook over medium-low heat for 5 to 8 minutes or until heated through and smooth, stirring often. Stir in 2 tablespoons of the parsley and the salt; set aside.

2. Remove skin and bones from chicken. Using two forks, shred chicken. In a large bowl, stir together chicken, undrained beans, corn, salsa, and remaining 2 tablespoons parsley. Spoon into a 3-quart rectangular baking dish. Spoon potatoes over chicken mixture and spread evenly.

3. Bake, uncovered, for 30 to 35 minutes or until heated through. Makes 6 servings.

Per serving: 645 cal., 22 g fat (7 g sat. fat), 106 mg chol., 1,200 mg sodium, 70 g carbo., 11 g fiber, 42 g pro.

My Own Pasta Bake

Prep: 30 minutes   Bake: 20 minutes   Oven: 375°F

8 ounces dried penne
1 14-ounce can whole Italian-style tomatoes, undrained
$\frac{1}{2}$ of a 6-ounce can ($\frac{1}{3}$ cup) Italian-style tomato paste
$\frac{1}{4}$ cup tomato juice
$\frac{1}{2}$ teaspoon sugar
$\frac{1}{2}$ teaspoon dried oregano, crushed, or 2 teaspoons snipped fresh oregano
$\frac{1}{4}$ teaspoon ground black pepper
1 pound lean ground beef
$\frac{1}{2}$ cup chopped onion (1 medium)
$\frac{1}{4}$ cup sliced pitted ripe olives
$\frac{1}{2}$ cup shredded reduced-fat mozzarella cheese (2 ounces)

1. Cook pasta according to package directions. Drain; set aside.

2. Meanwhile, in a blender or food processor, combine undrained tomatoes, tomato paste, tomato juice, sugar, dried oregano (if using), and pepper. Cover and blend or process until smooth. Set aside.

3. In a large skillet, cook ground beef and onion over medium-high heat until meat is brown and onion is tender. Drain off fat. Stir in tomato mixture. Bring to boiling; reduce heat. Simmer, covered, for 10 minutes. Preheat oven to 375°F. Stir pasta, fresh oregano (if using), and olives into meat mixture. Divide pasta mixture among six 10- to 12-ounce casseroles.

4. Bake, covered, for 15 minutes. (Or spoon all of the pasta mixture into a 2-quart casserole. Bake, covered, for 30 minutes.) Sprinkle with mozzarella cheese. Bake, uncovered, about 5 minutes more or until cheese melts. Makes 6 servings.

Per serving: 330 cal., 10 g fat (4 g sat. fat), 51 mg chol., 442 mg sodium, 36 g carbo., 2 g fiber, 22 g pro.

breakfast
bonanza

With all the easy, *delicious options* for the first meal of the day, you *won't want to miss out* on breakfast. These foods are a smart choice for supper too—they save time and stretch your budget.

Beef Hash with a Spicy Kick

Prep: 30 minutes Marinate: 30 minutes
Cook: 20 minutes

1/2	cup orange juice
2	tablespoons lime juice
1	tablespoon adobo sauce (from canned chipotle peppers)
1 1/4	pounds beef sirloin or top loin steak, finely chopped
2	large onions, chopped (2 cups)
2	tablespoons minced garlic or bottled minced garlic
1	tablespoon chili powder
1	tablespoon cooking oil
1 1/2	pounds Yukon gold potatoes or red-skin potatoes, cooked and diced
1	tablespoon chopped chipotle peppers in adobo sauce
2	roma tomatoes, seeded and chopped
1/4	cup snipped fresh cilantro
	Salt and freshly ground black pepper
	Fried eggs (optional)
	Fresh cilantro sprig (optional)

1. In a plastic bag set in a bowl, combine orange juice, lime juice, and adobo sauce; add meat, turning to coat. Seal bag. Marinate in refrigerator for 30 minutes. Drain and discard marinade. Pat meat dry with paper towels.

2. In a 12-inch heavy skillet, cook onions, garlic, and chili powder in hot oil over medium heat for 5 minutes or until onion is tender. Increase heat to medium-high. Add meat to skillet; cook and stir about 2 minutes or until meat is brown. Stir in potatoes and chipotle peppers. Spread in an even layer in the skillet. Cook about 8 minutes more or until potatoes are golden brown, turning occasionally. Fold in tomatoes and cilantro; heat through. Season with salt and black pepper. If desired, serve with fried eggs and garnish with fresh cilantro. Makes 6 servings.

Per serving: 263 cal., 6 g fat (2 g sat. fat), 45 mg chol., 189 mg sodium, 28 g carbo., 4 g fiber, 24 g pro.

Baked Mediterranean Eggs

Prep: 30 minutes   Bake: 18 minutes   Oven: 400°F

- 8 **eggs**
- 1/4 **cup sliced pitted kalamata or black olives**
- 4 **pita bread rounds**
- 4 **roma tomatoes, chopped**
- 1/2 **of a small cucumber, seeded and chopped**
- 2 **tablespoons snipped Italian (flat-leaf) parsley**
- 8 **slices Canadian bacon**
- 4 **ounces crumbled feta cheese with garlic and herb**
- 1/4 **cup plain low-fat yogurt**

1. Preheat oven to 400°F. Lightly coat four 10- to 12-ounce ramekins or custard cups with *nonstick cooking spray*. Break two eggs into each ramekin. Divide olives among ramekins. Place ramekins in a 3-quart rectangular baking dish; add boiling water to dish to depth of 1 inch. Place baking dish on lower oven rack. Bake for 10 minutes. Place pita rounds on baking sheet; place on upper oven rack. Bake for 8 minutes more or until eggs are set when lightly shaken and pita rounds are heated through.

2. Meanwhile, combine tomatoes, cucumber, parsley, 1/4 teaspoon *salt,* and 1/8 teaspoon *ground black pepper;* set aside. Lightly coat a large skillet with cooking spray; cook Canadian bacon until light brown, turning once.

3. Sprinkle pita rounds with cheese. Carefully remove ramekins from water; invert onto rounds. Top each serving with some of the tomato mixture and a spoonful of yogurt. Serve immediately with Canadian bacon. Pass additional tomato mixture. Makes 4 servings.

Per serving: 536 cal., 24 g fat (9 g sat. fat), 470 mg chol., 1,624 mg sodium, 45 g carbo., 3 g fiber, 33 g pro.

Potato-Vegetable Frittata

Start to Finish: 30 minutes

- 2 **cups broccoli florets**
- 1 **red sweet pepper, cut into bite-size strips**
- 2 **tablespoons olive oil**
- 1/2 **of a 20-ounce package refrigerated Southwest-style shredded hash brown potatoes (2 1/4 cups)**
- 8 **eggs, lightly beaten**
- 1/4 **teaspoon salt**
- 1/8 **teaspoon ground black pepper**
- 2 **ounces shredded Colby and Monterey Jack cheese (1/2 cup)**
- 1 **medium tomato, chopped**

1. In a large oven-proof skillet, cook broccoli and sweet pepper in hot oil over medium heat for 2 minutes. Add hash browns. Press into an even layer; cook for 2 minutes. Stir and press again; cook 2 minutes more.

2. Preheat broiler. In a large bowl, whisk together eggs, salt, and pepper. Pour over mixture in skillet. As mixture sets, run a spatula round edge of skillet, lifting the egg mixture so uncooked portion flows underneath. Continue cooking and lifting edges until the egg mixture is almost set but still moist.

3. Broil 4 to 5 inches from heat for 1 to 2 minutes or until top is set. Sprinkle with cheese and tomato; cut into wedges. Makes 4 servings.

Per serving: 354 cal., 22 g fat (7 g sat. fat), 437 mg chol., 461 mg sodium, 22 g carbo., 3 g fiber, 20 g pro.

Salmon-Potato Bake

Prep: 20 minutes   Bake: 30 minutes
Stand: 10 minutes   Oven: 350°F

- **Nonstick cooking spray**
- 1 **16-ounce package refrigerated sliced potatoes**
- 8 **ounces Gouda or Monterey Jack cheese, shredded (2 cups)**
- 6 **ounces thinly sliced smoked salmon (lox-style), cut into bite-size strips**
- 6 **eggs, beaten**
- 2 **cups milk**
- 1/4 **teaspoon salt**
- 1/4 **teaspoon ground black pepper**

1. Preheat oven to 350°F. Lightly coat six 10- to 14-ounce casserole dishes or ramekins with cooking spray. Place dishes in a 15×10×1-inch baking pan; set aside.

2. Place potatoes in a 2-quart square microwave-safe baking dish. Add 1 tablespoon *water* to dish. Cover with waxed paper. Microwave on 100% power (high) for 2 minutes. Arrange half the potatoes in prepared dishes. Layer with half the cheese and all the smoked salmon. Top with remaining potatoes and remaining cheese.

3. In a large bowl, whisk together eggs, milk, salt, and pepper. Slowly pour over layers. Bake, uncovered, for 30 to 35 minutes or until puffed, set, and golden (press lightly in center; casseroles are done when no liquid appears). Let stand 10 minutes. Makes 6 servings.

Per serving: 352 cal., 18 g fat (9 g sat. fat), 268 mg chol., 1,127 mg sodium, 21 g carbo., 1 g fiber, 25 g pro.

Mexican Beef Hash with Eggs

Start to Finish: 30 minutes

- ¼ cup thinly sliced green onions
- 2 fresh jalapeño or serrano peppers, seeded and finely chopped*
- 2 cloves garlic, minced
- 2 tablespoons cooking oil
- 8 ounces cooked beef, chopped
- 1 teaspoon ground cumin
- ¼ teaspoon finely shredded lime peel
- 1 tablespoon lime juice
- 8 eggs
- 1 tablespoon water
  Salt and ground black pepper
- ¼ cup dairy sour cream
- ¼ cup shredded cheddar cheese (1 ounce)

1. In a large nonstick skillet, cook onion, jalapeño, and garlic in hot oil over medium heat until tender. Stir in beef, cumin, lime peel, and lime juice. Cook and stir until heated through. Divide mixture among four plates, keep warm.

2. In the same skillet, heat remaining 1 tablespoon oil over medium heat. Carefully break four eggs into skillet. When whites are set, add water. Cover skillet and cook until desired doneness (3 to 4 minutes for soft-set yolks or 4 to 5 minutes for firm-set yolks). Remove from skillet; keep warm. Repeat with remaining eggs.

3. Top each serving of beef mixture with two fried eggs. Season to taste with salt and black pepper. Top with sour cream and shredded cheese. Makes 4 servings.

***Note:** Because hot chile peppers, such as jalapeños, contain volatile oils that can burn your skin and eyes, wear plastic or rubber golves when working with chile peppers. If your bare hands do touch the peppers, wash your hands well with soap and water.

Per serving: 366 cal., 24 g fat (8 g sat. fat), 475 mg chol., 374 mg sodium, 3 g carbo., 1 g fiber, 32 g pro.

Bagel, Lox, and Egg Strata

Prep: 30 minutes   Chill: 4 to 24 hours
Bake: 45 minutes   Stand: 10 minutes   Oven: 350°F

- ¼ cup butter, melted
- 8 cups plain bagels cut into bite-size pieces (4 to 6 bagels)
- 1 3-ounce package thinly sliced smoked salmon (lox-style), cut into small pieces
- 8 ounces Swiss or Monterey Jack cheese, shredded (2 cups)
- ¼ cup snipped fresh chives

> In the morning, mix a strata and pop it into the refrigerator. With *less than an hour's* baking time, it's ready for dinner.

- 8 eggs, beaten
- 2 cups milk
- 1 cup cottage cheese
- ¼ teaspoon ground black pepper

1. Spread butter in a 3-quart rectangular baking dish. Place bagel pieces in prepared dish. Sprinkle lox, cheese, and chives over bagel pieces. In a large bowl, combine eggs, milk, cottage cheese, and pepper. Pour over layers. Press down gently with the back of a wooden spoon to moisten all of the ingredients. Cover and chill for 4 to 24 hours.

3. Preheat oven to 350°F. Bake, uncovered, about 45 minutes or until set and edges are puffed and golden. Let stand 10 minutes before serving. Makes 12 servings.

Per serving: 267 cal., 14 g fat (8 g sat. fat), 176 mg chol., 497 mg sodium, 16 g carbo., 1 g fiber, 17 g pro.

Citrus Raisin Strata

Prep: 10 minutes   Bake: 45 minutes
Stand: 15 minutes   Oven: 350°F

- 10 slices cinnamon-raisin bread
- 3 eggs, lightly beaten
- 2 cups half-and-half or light cream
- ⅔ cup sugar
- 1½ teaspoons finely shredded orange peel
- 1 teaspoon vanilla
  Vanilla yogurt (optional)

1. Preheat oven to 350°F. Tear bread into bite-size pieces; place in a greased 2-quart square baking dish. In a medium bowl, combine eggs, half-and-half, sugar, orange peel, and vanilla. Pour over bread. Bake, uncovered, about 45 minutes or until a knife inserted near the center comes out clean. Let stand 15 minutes before serving. If desired, serve with vanilla yogurt. Makes 6 servings.

Per serving: 345 cal., 14 g fat (7 g sat. fat), 136 mg chol., 233 mg sodium, 48 g carbo., 2 g fiber, 9 g pro.

Turkey Sausage Strata

Prep: 25 minutes   Chill: 6 to 24 hours
Bake: 1 hour   Oven: 325°F

1	pound bulk turkey sausage
½	cup chopped onion (1 medium)
12	slices white bread
1	9-ounce package frozen cut broccoli, thawed and well drained
1	cup shredded mozzarella cheese (4 ounces)
1	2-ounce jar sliced pimiento, drained
6	eggs, beaten
3	cups milk
¼	teaspoon dry mustard

1. In a medium skillet, cook sausage and onion over medium heat until meat is brown. Drain off fat. In a greased 3-quart rectangular baking dish, layer six slices bread, half the sausage mixture, half the broccoli, half the mozzarella, and half the pimiento. Repeat layers.

2. In a bowl, combine beaten eggs, milk, ½ teaspoon *salt,* and dry mustard. Pour over the layers in the dish. Cover; chill for 6 to 24 hours.

3. Preheat oven to 325°F. Bake, uncovered, for 1 hour or until a knife inserted near center comes out clean. Makes 12 servings.

Per serving: 238 cal., 11 g fat (4 g sat. fat), 146 mg chol., 639 mg sodium, 19 g carbo., 1 g fiber, 17 g pro.

Italian Breakfast Burritos

Prep: 25 minutes

2	cups fresh baby spinach, chopped
3	ounces prosciutto, chopped
½	cup fresh basil, snipped
1	6-ounce jar marinated artichoke hearts, drained
3	shallots, finely chopped
2	cloves garlic, minced
2	tablespoons olive oil
8	eggs
6	10-inch flour tortillas
½	cup purchased basil pesto
1½	cups shredded mozzarella cheese

1. In a large skillet, cook and stir spinach, prosciutto, basil, artichoke hearts, shallots, and garlic in hot oil over medium heat until spinach wilts.

2. In a bowl, whisk together eggs, dash *salt,* and dash *ground black pepper.* Pour over vegetables in skillet. Cook over medium heat, without stirring, until mixture begins to set on bottom and around edge. With spatula or large spoon, lift and fold partially cooked egg mixture so uncooked portion flows underneath. Continue cooking for 2 to 3 minutes or until egg mixture is cooked through and still glossy and moist. Remove from heat.

3. Wrap tortillas in white paper towels; microwave on 100% power (high) for 30 to 60 seconds or until warm. Spread each tortilla with pesto to within 1 inch of edge. Sprinkle cheese over pesto. Divide egg mixture among tortillas; roll up, tucking in ends. Makes 6 servings.

Per serving: 606 cal., 42 g fat (8 g sat. fat), 300 mg chol., 975 mg sodium, 32 g carbo., 1 g fiber, 25 g pro.

Tex-Mex Spinach Omelet

Start to Finish: 25 minutes

4	eggs
1	tablespoon snipped fresh cilantro
	Dash salt
	Dash ground cumin
	Nonstick cooking spray
1	ounce cheddar or Monterey Jack cheese with jalapeño peppers, shredded (¼ cup)
¾	cup fresh baby spinach leaves
	Corn-Pepper Relish

1. In a medium bowl, combine eggs, cilantro, salt, and cumin. Beat with a whisk or rotary beater until frothy.

2. Coat an unheated 10-inch nonstick skillet with flared sides with nonstick cooking spray. Heat skillet over medium heat.

3. Pour egg mixture into prepared skillet. Cook, without stirring, for 2 to 3 minutes or until egg mixture begins to set. Run a spatula around edge of skillet, lifting egg mixture so uncooked portion flows underneath.

4. Continue cooking and lifting edge until egg mixture is set but still glossy and moist. Sprinkle with cheese. Top with three-fourths of the spinach and half of the Corn-Pepper Relish. Using the spatula, lift and fold an edge of the omelet partially over filling. Top with remaining spinach and remaining relish. Cut omelet in half; transfer to warm plates. Makes 2 servings.

Corn-Pepper Relish: In a small bowl, combine ¼ cup chopped red sweet pepper; ¼ cup frozen loose-pack whole kernel corn, thawed; 2 tablespoons chopped red onion; and 1 tablespoon snipped fresh cilantro.

Per serving: 231 cal., 15 g fat (6 g sat. fat), 438 mg chol., 311 mg sodium, 8 g carbo., 1 g fiber, 17 g pro.

Breakfast breads are welcome at supper too. Add *toast or toasted English muffins or bagels* to the evening menu.

Oven Omelets with Artichokes and Spinach

Start to Finish: 25 minutes   Oven: 400°F

    Nonstick cooking spray
10 **eggs**
¼ **cup water**
½ **teaspoon salt**
¼ **teaspoon ground black pepper**
2 **6-ounce jars marinated artichoke hearts, drained and chopped**
4 **cups chopped fresh spinach**
¾ **cup shredded Swiss or Provolone cheese (3 ounces)**

1. Preheat oven to 400°F. Lightly coat a 15×10×1-inch baking pan with cooking spray; set pan aside.

2. In a medium bowl, use a fork or rotary beater to beat eggs, the water, salt, and pepper until combined but not frothy.

3. Place the prepared pan on an oven rack. Carefully pour the egg mixture into the pan. Bake about 7 minutes or until egg mixture is set but still has a glossy surface.

4. Meanwhile, for the filling, in a large skillet, cook artichoke hearts over medium heat until heated through, stirring occasionally. Add spinach; cook and stir until spinach wilts.

5. Cut the baked egg mixture into six 5-inch squares. Using a large spatula, remove omelet squares from pan and invert onto warm serving plates.

6. Spoon filling on half of each omelet square. Sprinkle with cheese. Fold the other omelet half over the filled half, forming a triangle or rectangle. Makes 6 servings.

Per serving: 225 cal., 16 g fat (5 g sat. fat), 367 mg chol., 342 mg sodium, 7 g carbo., 2 g fiber, 16 g pro.

BLT Pancake Clubs

Prep: 25 minutes   Bake: 12 minutes   Oven: 375°F

    Butter
2 **eggs, beaten**
1½ **cups buttermilk**
1 **tablespoon butter, melted**
1 **cup white whole wheat or whole wheat flour**
1 **tablespoon sugar**
1 **teaspoon baking powder**
½ **teaspoon baking soda**
¼ **teaspoon salt**
2 **medium tomatoes, sliced**
4 **lettuce leaves**

8 **to 12 slices thick-cut bacon, cooked and drained**
¼ **to ½ cup bottled blue cheese dressing**

1. Preheat oven to 375°F. Generously butter a 15×10×1-inch baking pan; set aside. In a medium bowl, combine eggs, buttermilk, and melted butter. In a large bowl, combine flour, sugar, baking powder, baking soda, and salt. Make a well in the center of the flour mixture. Add the buttermilk mixture; stir just until combined (do not overbeat).

2. Pour batter into prepared pan, spreading evenly. Bake for 12 to 15 minutes or until set and light brown.

3. Loosen edges of pancake with a table knife or thin spatula. With a serrated knife, carefully cut pancake into 12 equal portions.

4. For each serving, place a pancake portion on each of four plates. Top with one or two tomato slices, a second pancake, lettuce, two slices bacon, and 1 tablespoon dressing. Top with a third pancake. Pass additional dressing. Makes 4 servings.

Per serving: 427 cal., 25 g fat (9 g sat. fat), 147 mg chol., 1,163 mg sodium, 33 g carbo., 4 g fiber, 19 g pro.

Breakfast Tortilla Wraps

Start to Finish: 15 minutes

2 **strips bacon, chopped**
½ **cup chopped green sweet pepper**
½ **teaspoon ground cumin**
½ **teaspoon crushed red pepper**
¼ **teaspoon salt**
4 **eggs, lightly beaten**
½ **cup chopped tomato**
    Several dashes bottled hot pepper sauce (optional)
4 **8-inch whole wheat tortillas, warmed**

1. In a large nonstick skillet, cook bacon until crisp. Drain all but 1 tablespoon of the fat from skillet. Add green pepper, cumin, crushed red pepper, and salt. Cook for 3 minutes.

2. Add eggs to skillet. With a spatula or large spoon, lift and fold egg mixture so uncooked portion flows underneath. Continue cooking over medium heat about 2 minutes or until egg is cooked through but still glossy and moist. Stir in tomato and, if desired, hot pepper sauce. Spoon onto tortillas; roll up. Makes 4 servings.

Per serving: 193 cal., 9 g fat (3 g sat. fat), 216 mg chol., 285 mg sodium, 17 g carbo., 1 g fiber, 10 g pro.

Breakfast Pizza

Prep: 25 minutes   Bake: 10 minutes   Oven: 375°F

	Nonstick cooking spray
1½	cups loose-pack frozen diced hash brown potatoes with peppers and onion
1	clove garlic, minced
6	eggs, beaten
⅓	cup milk
1	tablespoon snipped fresh basil
½	teaspoon salt
¼	teaspoon ground black pepper
1	tablespoon olive oil
1	14-ounce Italian bread shell such as (Boboli)
1	cup shredded mozzarella cheese (4 ounces)
2	roma tomatoes, sliced
¼	cup shredded fresh basil

1. Preheat oven to 375°F. Coat an unheated large nonstick skillet with nonstick cooking spray. Heat over medium heat. Add potatoes and garlic; cook and stir about 4 minutes or until tender.

2. In a small bowl, stir together eggs, milk, 1 tablespoon snipped basil, salt, and pepper. Add oil to skillet; add egg mixture. Cook, without stirring, until mixture begins to set on the bottom and around the edge. Using a large spatula, lift and fold partially cooked egg mixture so uncooked portion flows underneath. Continue cooking and folding until egg mixture is cooked through but still glossy and moist. Remove from heat.

3. To assemble pizza, place bread shell on a large baking sheet or a 12-inch pizza pan. Sprinkle half of the cheese over the bread shell. Top with egg mixture, tomatoes, and remaining cheese.

4. Bake about 10 minutes or until cheese melts. Sprinkle with the ¼ cup shredded basil. Cut into wedges to serve. Makes 8 servings.

Per serving: 273 cal., 12 g fat (3 g sat. fat), 169 mg chol., 579 mg sodium, 29 g carbo., 2 g fiber, 15 g pro.

Breakfast Pizza

Egg-Potato Casseroles

Prep: 15 minutes Bake: 25 minutes
Stand: 5 minutes Oven: 350°F

　　 Nonstick cooking spray
2/3　cup loose-pack frozen diced hash brown
　　 potatoes with onion and peppers
1/3　cup loose-pack frozen cut broccoli
2　 tablespoons chopped Canadian-style
　　 bacon or lean cooked ham
2　 tablespoons milk
2　 teaspoons all-purpose flour
2/3　cup refrigerated or frozen egg product,
　　 thawed
3　 tablespoons shredded reduced-fat
　　 cheddar cheese
1　 teaspoon snipped fresh basil or
　　 1/4 teaspoon dried basil, crushed
1/8　teaspoon ground black pepper

1. Preheat oven to 350°F. Lightly coat two 10-ounce casseroles with nonstick cooking spray. Arrange hash brown potatoes and broccoli in casseroles; top with Canadian bacon. In a small bowl, gradually stir milk into flour. Stir in egg, half of the cheese, the basil, pepper, and dash *salt*. Pour egg mixture over vegetables.

2. Bake for 25 to 30 minutes or until a knife inserted near the centers comes out clean. Sprinkle with remaining cheese. Let stand for 5 minutes before serving. Makes 2 servings.

Per serving: 171 cal., 4 g fat (2 g sat. fat), 16 mg chol., 609 mg sodium, 17 g carbo., 1 g fiber, 16 g pro.

BMT Scrambled Eggs

Start to Finish: 20 minutes

　　 Nonstick cooking spray
1/2　cup sliced fresh mushrooms
1/4　cup thinly sliced green onions
1　 teaspoon cooking oil
4　 eggs, beaten
1/4　cup milk
1/8　teaspoon ground black pepper
1/2　cup shredded reduced-fat cheddar cheese
　　 (2 ounces) or 1/4 cup crumbled feta or blue
　　 cheese (2 ounces)
1　 slice turkey bacon or bacon, crisp-cooked
　　 and crumbled
8　 grape or cherry tomatoes, halved

1. Coat an unheated large nonstick skillet with nonstick cooking spay. Heat skillet over medium heat. Add mushrooms and green onions. Cook and stir for 5 to 7 minutes or until vegetables are tender. Stir in oil.

2. In a medium bowl, stir together eggs, milk, and pepper. Pour egg mixture into skillet. Cook, without stirring, until mixture begins to set on the bottom and around edge. Using a large spoon or spatula, lift and fold partially cooked egg mixture so uncooked portion flows underneath.

3. Sprinkle with cheese and bacon. Continue cooking over medium heat for 2 to 3 minutes or until egg mixture is cooked through but is still glossy and moist. Remove from heat immediately. Top with tomatoes. Makes 4 servings.

Per serving: 102 cal., 5 g fat (2 g sat. fat), 13 mg chol., 286 mg sodium, 5 g carbo., 1 g fiber, 11 g pro.

Gingerbread Pancakes

Start to Finish: 30 minutes

2　 cups packaged buttermilk complete
　　 pancake mix
1　 teaspoon ground cinnamon
1　 teaspoon ground ginger
1　 teaspoon ground nutmeg
2　 eggs, lightly beaten
2/3　cup milk
1/3　cup molasses
1/3　cup strong coffee
3　 tablespoons cooking oil
　　 Butter and maple-flavor syrup

1. In a large bowl, combine pancake mix, cinnamon, ginger, and nutmeg. In a medium bowl, combine eggs, milk, molasses, coffee, and oil. Add egg mixture to dry mixture all at once. Stir just until moistened (batter should be lumpy).

2. Heat a lightly greased griddle or heavy skillet over medium heat until a few drops of water dance across the surface. For each pancake, pour about 1/4 cup batter onto the hot griddle. Spread batter into a circle about 4 inches in diameter. Cook over medium heat for 1 to 2 minutes on each side or until pancakes are golden brown, turning to cook second sides when pancakes have bubbly surfaces and edges are slightly dry (watch carefully so pancakes do not overbrown).

3. Keep warm in a loosely covered oven-proof dish in a 300°F oven. If desired, serve with butter and maple-flavor syrup. Makes 9 or 10 pancakes.

Per pancake: 210 cal., 8 g fat (2 g sat. fat), 55 mg chol., 338 mg sodium, 31 g carbo., 1 g fiber, 5 g pro.

Granola-Topped French Toast

Start to Finish: 40 minutes

       3   eggs, lightly beaten
     3/4   cup milk
       1   tablespoon sugar
       1   tablespoon finely shredded orange peel
     1/2   teaspoon vanilla
     1/4   teaspoon ground cinnamon
      12   1/2-inch-thick bias slices baguette-style
           French bread
       2   tablespoons butter
       1   cup granola, coarsely crushed
           Cinnamon-Yogurt Sauce
           Maple syrup (optional)

1. In a shallow bowl, whisk together eggs, milk, sugar, 1½ teaspoons of the orange peel, vanilla, and cinnamon. Dip bread slices into egg mixture, coating both sides.

2. In a skillet or on a griddle, melt 1 tablespoon of the butter over medium heat; add half of the bread slices. Sprinkle some of the granola on top of each bread slice in the skillet, pressing gently with spatula so granola sticks. Cook for 2 to 3 minutes or until bottoms are golden brown. Turn slices over, pressing lightly with the spatula. Cook for 2 minutes more or until golden brown. Remove from pan and turn each slice so granola side is on top.

3. Repeat with remaining butter, bread slices, and granola. Serve immediately with Cinnamon-Yogurt Sauce, remaining orange peel, and, if desired, maple syrup. Makes 4 servings.

Cinnamon-Yogurt Sauce: In a small bowl, combine one 6-ounce carton plain low-fat yogurt, 1 tablespoon honey, 1/4 teaspoon ground cinnamon, and 1/4 teaspoon vanilla. Serve at once or place in an airtight container and chill for up to 24 hours. Makes about 3/4 cup.

Per serving: 501 cal., 16 g fat (2 g sat. fat), 183 mg chol., 516 mg sodium, 70 g carbo., 6 g fiber, 20 g pro.

Baked French Toast with Pears and Brie

Prep: 35 minutes   Chill: 1 to 24 hours
Bake: 40 minutes   Stand: 10 minutes   Oven: 375°F

       3   medium pears, peeled, cored,
           and thinly sliced
       2   tablespoons packed brown sugar
     1/2   teaspoon snipped fresh rosemary
       2   tablespoons butter
      14   to 16 1/2-inch-thick slices French bread
       8   ounces Brie cheese, rind removed and
           cheese thinly sliced
       2   tablespoons butter, melted
       3   tablespoons granulated sugar
       1   teaspoon ground cinnamon
    2 1/2 cups milk
       3   eggs
       1   tablespoon vanilla
     1/4   teaspoon salt
           Warm maple syrup, honey, or purchased
           cranberry conserve

1. Grease a 3-quart rectangular baking dish; set aside. In a large skillet, cook pear slices, brown sugar, and rosemary in 2 tablespoons butter over medium heat for 4 to 5 minutes or until pears are just tender.

2. In the prepared baking dish, arrange half of the bread slices in a single layer. Spoon pear mixture over bread slices; arrange Brie over pear mixture. Top with remaining bread slices in a single layer. Brush bread slices with melted butter. In a small bowl, combine granulated sugar and cinnamon. Sprinkle evenly over bread slices.

3. In a medium bowl, whisk together milk, eggs, vanilla, and salt. Slowly pour over bread slices. Cover and chill for 1 to 24 hours.

4. Preheat oven to 375°F. Bake casserole, uncovered, for 40 to 45 minutes or until edges are puffed and golden. Let stand for 10 minutes. Serve warm with syrup, honey, or cranberry conserve. Makes 8 servings.

Per serving: 405 cal., 19 g fat (10 g sat. fat), 130 mg chol., 623 mg sodium, 44 g carbo., 3 g fiber, 15 g pro.

Walnut Waffles with Blueberry Sauce

Prep: 15 minutes Bake: per waffle baker directions

1	cup all-purpose flour
1	cup whole wheat flour
¼	cup coarsely ground toasted walnuts
2	teaspoons baking powder
1	teaspoon baking soda
4	egg whites
2¼	cups buttermilk
2	tablespoons cooking oil
	Blueberry Sauce

1. Stir together all-purpose flour, whole wheat flour, walnuts, baking powder, and baking soda. In a large bowl, beat egg whites with an electric mixer on medium speed until foamy. Stir in buttermilk and oil. Gradually add flour mixture, beating by hand until smooth.

2. Preheat a lightly greased square or round waffle baker. Pour 1 cup batter onto grids (for round waffle baker use ⅔ cup batter). Close lid quickly; do not open until done. Bake according to manufacturer's directions. Use a fork to lift waffle off grids. Repeat with remaining batter. Serve waffles warm with Blueberry Sauce. Makes 8 servings.

Per serving: 224 cal., 7 g fat (1 g sat. fat), 3 mg chol., 359 mg sodium, 33 g carbo., 4 g fiber, 8 g pro.

Blueberry Sauce: In a medium saucepan, combine 1 cup fresh or frozen blueberries, ¼ cup white grape juice, and 1 tablespoon honey. Heat just until bubbles form around edges. Cool slightly. Transfer to a blender. Cover and blend until smooth. Transfer sauce to a serving bowl. Stir in 1 cup fresh or frozen blueberries. Makes about 1⅔ cups.

Freezer French Toast

Prep: 30 minutes Bake: 30 minutes Oven: 350°F

1	8-ounce package cream cheese, softened
¼	cup dairy sour cream
1	16-ounce loaf French bread
¾	cup orange marmalade
4	eggs
1	cup milk
1½	teaspoons vanilla
2½	cups finely chopped almonds (10 ounces)
	Maple syrup

1. In a medium mixing bowl, beat together cream cheese and sour cream until smooth; set aside. Trim off ends of bread loaf; cut loaf crosswise in 20 slices. Spread half the slices on one side with cheese mixture. Spread remaining slices on one side with marmalade. Sandwich slices together; set aside.

2. In a shallow dish, use a fork to beat together eggs, milk, and vanilla. Place half the almonds in another shallow dish. Dip both sides of sandwiches in egg mixture; allow excess to drip off. Coat both sides of sandwiches with almonds, adding more almonds to dish as needed.

3. Place coated sandwiches on a baking sheet lined with waxed paper; cover and freeze for 3 hours or until firm. Transfer to freezer container or bag; seal, label, and freeze up to 1 month.

4. To serve, heat oven to 350°F. Place frozen French toast on a large greased baking sheet. Bake for 30 to 35 minutes or until golden and heated through, turning once. Serve with maple syrup. Makes 10 servings.

Per serving: 562 cal., 26 g fat (8 g sat. fat), 114 mg chol., 402 mg sodium, 71 g carbo., 5 g fiber, 15 g pro.

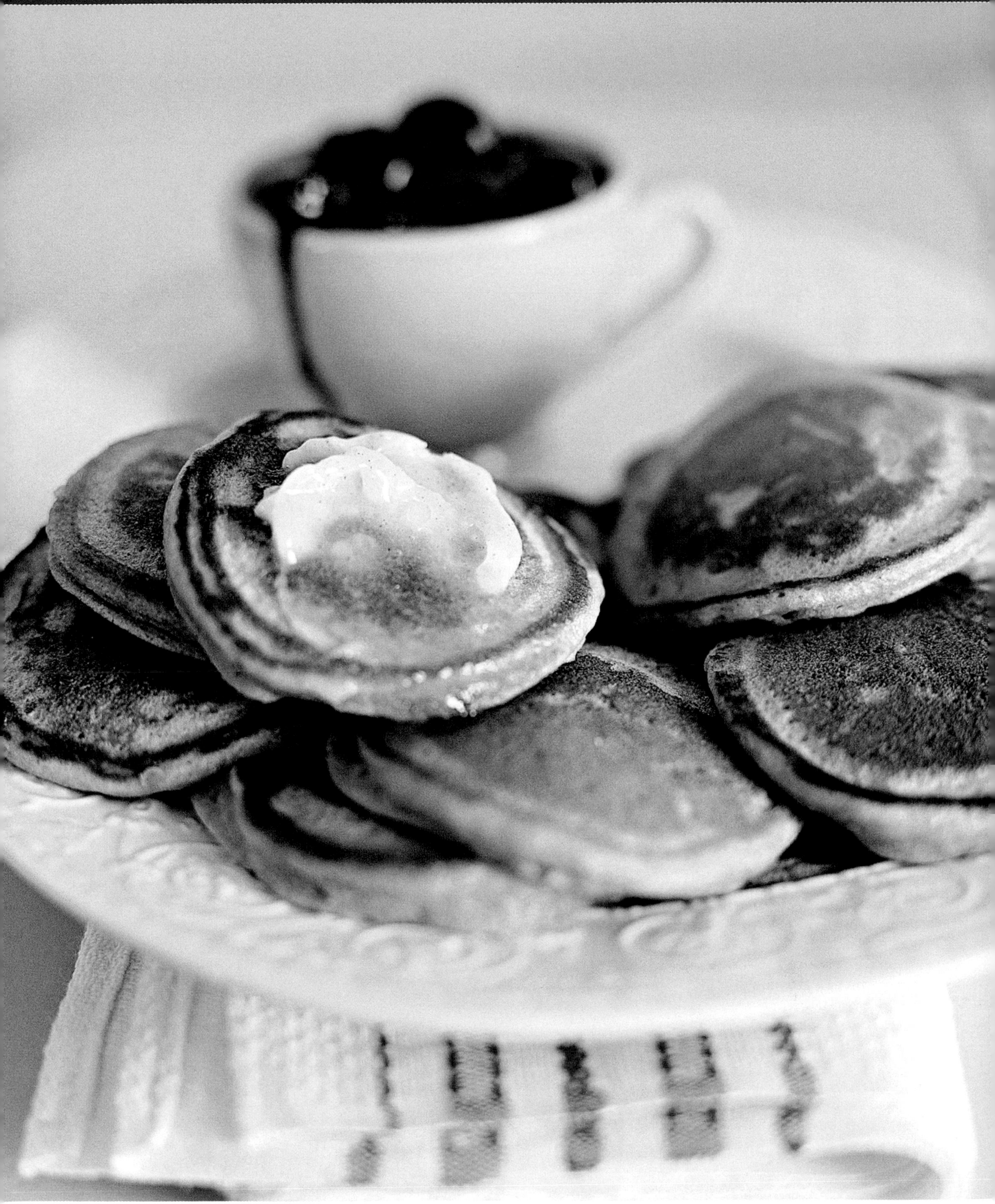

Apple Butter Hotcakes

Prep: 25 minutes   Cook: 4 minutes per batch

½	cup butter, softened
¼	cup honey
¼	teaspoon ground cinnamon
1	12-ounce package frozen pitted light or dark sweet cherries
½	cup cherry jam or cherry preserves
1	teaspoon finely shredded orange peel
1½	cups packaged regular or buttermilk pancake mix (not complete pancake mix)
¾	cup milk
2	tablespoons cooking oil
2	eggs, lightly beaten
½	cup purchased apple butter

1. For flavored butter, in a small mixing bowl, whisk together butter, honey, and cinnamon; set aside.

2. For cherry sauce, in a medium saucepan, combine frozen cherries, cherry jam, and orange peel. Bring to boiling over medium heat, stirring frequently; reduce heat. Simmer, uncovered, for 10 minutes or until sauce has thickened slightly. Cover and set aside; keep warm.

3. In a medium bowl, stir together pancake mix, milk, oil, eggs, and apple butter. Stir just until moistened (batter should still be lumpy). On a hot lightly greased griddle, spread about ¼ cup batter into a 4-inch circle. Cook over medium heat about 2 minutes on each side or until hot cakes are golden brown, turning to second sides when hot cakes have bubbly surfaces and edges are slightly dry. Serve warm with butter and desired syrup or sauce. Makes 8 to 10 hotcakes.

Per hotcake: 456 cal., 16 g fat (8 g sat. fat), 84 mg chol., 400 mg sodium, 72 g carbo., 4 g fiber, 4 g pro.

Peanut Butter Breakfast Sandwiches

Start to Finish: 30 minutes

½	cup peanut butter
8	½-inch-thick slices French bread
2	tablespoons honey
2	medium bananas
2	eggs, beaten
½	cup milk
¼	teaspoon ground cinnamon
1	tablespoon butter
½	cup fruit preserves or jam (any flavor)

1. Spread peanut butter evenly on one side of each slice of bread. Drizzle honey over peanut butter. Cut each banana in half lengthwise, then crosswise, making eight pieces total. Arrange two banana pieces on four of the prepared bread slices. Top with remaining bread slices, peanut butter sides down.

2. In a shallow bowl or pie plate, combine eggs, milk, and cinnamon. Carefully dip sandwiches into egg mixture, coating both sides.

3. In a large skillet or on a large griddle, melt butter over medium heat. Cook sandwiches in hot butter about 2 minutes on each side or until golden.

4. Meanwhile, in a small saucepan, heat fruit preserves over medium-low heat until melted, stirring frequently. To serve, cut warm sandwiches in half crosswise. Drizzle with warm fruit preserves. Makes 8 servings.

Per serving: 302 cal., 10 g fat (3 g sat. fat), 58 mg chol., 323 mg sodium, 46 g carbo., 3 g fiber, 9 g pro.

Fruit-Filled Puff Pancakes

Prep: 15 minutes   Bake: 25 minutes
Stand: 5 minutes   Oven: 400°F

	Nonstick cooking spray
2	eggs
¼	cup all-purpose flour
¼	cup milk
4	teaspoons cooking oil
	Dash salt
2	tablespoons orange marmalade
2	tablespoons orange juice or water
2	small bananas, sliced
1	cup sliced fresh strawberries or blueberries

1. Preheat oven to 400°F. For pancakes, coat four 4- to 5-inch pie plates or foil tart pans or 10-ounce custard cups with cooking spray. Set aside.

2. In a medium bowl, use a rotary beater or whisk to beat eggs, flour, milk, oil, and salt until smooth. Divide batter among prepared pans. Bake, uncovered, for 25 minutes or until brown and puffy. Turn off oven; let stand in oven for 5 minutes.

3. Meanwhile, in a small bowl, stir together marmalade and orange juice. Add banana and berries; stir gently to coat. Immediately after removing pancakes from oven, transfer to plates. Spoon some of the fruit into center of each pancake. Makes 4 servings.

Per serving: 204 cal., 8 g fat (2 g sat. fat), 107 mg chol., 119 mg sodium, 31 g carbo., 3 g fiber, 5 g pro.

Black Bean Slaw with
Soy-Ginger Dressing

simple
side dishes

You've decided on the main dish for dinner. Now you need something to go with it. Here are 21 *fast, easy salad, vegetable, and bread options* to choose from to complete your menu.

Black Bean Slaw with Soy-Ginger Dressing

Prep: 15 minutes Chill: 4 hours

- ½ of a 15-ounce can black beans, rinsed and drained
- 3 cups purchased coleslaw mix
- 1 medium green apple, cored and chopped (⅔ cup)
- ½ cup chopped red sweet pepper
- 2 tablespoons cider vinegar
- 1 tablespoon reduced-sodium soy sauce
- 1 tablespoon peanut oil
- 1 teaspoon grated fresh ginger
- 1 teaspoon honey
- ⅛ teaspoon ground black pepper

1. In a large bowl, combine black beans, coleslaw mix, apple, and sweet pepper. In a small screw-top jar, combine vinegar, soy sauce, peanut oil, ginger, honey, and black pepper; cover and shake well. Pour over cabbage mixture; toss to mix. Cover and chill for 4 hours or overnight. Makes 4 servings.

Per serving: 217 cal., 7 g fat (1 g sat. fat), 0 mg chol., 577 mg sodium, 36 g carbo., 9 g fiber, 9 g pro.

Chipotle Coleslaw

Start to Finish: 20 minutes

- ⅓ cup fat-free mayonnaise
- 1 tablespoon lime juice
- 2 teaspoons honey
- ¼ teaspoon ground cumin
- ⅛ to ¼ teaspoon ground chipotle chile pepper
- 3 cups shredded green cabbage
- ¾ cup whole kernel corn, thawed if frozen
- ¾ cup chopped red sweet pepper
- ⅓ cup thinly sliced red onion
- ⅓ cup snipped cilantro

1. In a small bowl, stir together mayonnaise, lime juice, honey, cumin, and chipotle chile pepper. In a large bowl, combine shredded cabbage, corn, sweet pepper, onion, and cilantro. Pour mayonnaise mixture over cabbage mixture. Toss lightly to coat. Serve immediately or cover and chill for up to 24 hours. Makes 6 servings.

Per serving: 55 cal., 1 g fat (0 g sat. fat), 1 mg chol., 122 mg sodium, 13 g carbo., 2 g fiber, 2 g pro.

Really Red Coleslaw

Prep: 15 minutes   Chill: up to 6 hours

- 1   10-ounce bag shredded red cabbage (about 6 cups)
- 1   medium red onion, slivered (1 cup)
- ½   cup dried tart red cherries
- ½   cup red raspberry vinaigrette
- 1   tablespoon seedless red raspberry preserves

1. In a large bowl, combine shredded cabbage, red onion, and dried cherries; set aside. In a small bowl, stir together vinaigrette and preserves. Pour over cabbage mixture and toss to coat. Serve at room temperature or chill for up to 6 hours. Makes 8 servings.

Per serving: 108 cal., 6 g fat (1 g sat. fat), 0 mg chol., 5 mg sodium, 12 g carbo., 1 g fiber, 1 g pro.

Hot-and-Sweet Pineapple Slaw

Prep: 10 minutes   Chill: 1 hour

- 1   16-ounce package shredded broccoli (broccoli slaw mix)
- 2   cups fresh pineapple chunks or one 20-ounce can pineapple chunks, drained
- 2   cups broccoli florets
- ½   cup mayonnaise or salad dressing
- 1   to 2 tablespoons adobo sauce from canned chipotle peppers in adobo sauce
- ¼   teaspoon salt

1. Rinse and drain shredded broccoli; dry thoroughly. In a bowl, combine shredded broccoli, pineapple, and broccoli florets. In a small bowl, stir together mayonnaise, adobo sauce, and salt. Add mayonnaise mixture to broccoli mixture. Toss to coat. Cover and chill for 1 to 4 hours. Toss before serving. Makes 10 servings.

Per serving: 112 cal., 11 g fat (1 g sat. fat), 6 mg chol., 145 mg sodium, 7 g carbo., 2 g fiber, 2 g pro.

Tomato-Pepper Salad

Prep: 25 minutes   Chill: 1 hour

- 3   large yellow sweet peppers, thinly sliced into rings (about 3 cups)
- 3   or 4 medium tomatoes (about 1 pound)
- ⅓   cup crumbled Gorgonzola or blue cheese
       Herb-Dijon Vinaigrette

1. In a covered large skillet, cook sweet pepper rings in boiling water for 1 to 2 minutes or just until crisp-tender. Drain and cool. Cover and chill for 1 to 24 hours.

2. To serve, cut tomatoes into wedges. On a platter, arrange tomato wedges and pepper rings. Top with cheese. Shake vinaigrette; drizzle onto salad. Makes 8 servings.

Herb-Dijon Vinaigrette: In a screw-top jar, combine 2 tablespoons olive oil, 2 tablespoons white wine vinegar or balsamic vinegar, 1 tablespoon snipped fresh chives, 2 teaspoons snipped fresh basil, 1 teaspoon sugar, ½ teaspoon Dijon-style mustard, and ⅛ teaspoon ground black pepper. Cover and shake well to mix; chill for up to 3 days. Shake well before using.

Per serving: 85 cal., 5 g fat (2 g sat. fat), 4 mg chol., 90 mg sodium, 12 g carbo., 2 g fiber, 1 g pro.

Greek Salad

Start to Finish: 15 minutes

- 6   cups packaged torn romaine and iceberg lettuce blend
- ¼   cup thin red onion wedges
- ¼   cup red sweet pepper strips
- ¼   cup crumbled feta cheese
- 2   tablespoons pitted ripe black olives, halved
- ½   cup bottled red wine vinaigrette

1. In a large bowl, toss together lettuce blend, onion, sweet pepper, feta, and olives. Drizzle with vinaigrette; toss to coat. Makes 4 servings.

Per serving: 183 cal., 17 g total fat (3 g sat. fat), 8 mg chol., 728 mg sodium, 6 g carbo., 1 g fiber, 2 g pro.

Crisp, refreshing, and *tasty*, a vegetable salad is a nutrition powerhouse and a good partner for almost any entrée.

Asian Pea Pod Salad

Start to Finish: 20 minutes

  6 cups torn romaine lettuce
  2 cups fresh pea pods, trimmed
    and halved lengthwise
 ⅓ cup bottled Italian salad dressing
  1 tablespoon hoisin sauce
  1 tablespoon sesame seeds, toasted
  4 radishes, coarsely shredded

  1. In a large salad bowl, toss together lettuce and pea pods. In a small bowl, stir together salad dressing and hoisin sauce. Pour over lettuce mixture and toss to coat. Sprinkle with sesame seeds and radishes. Makes 6 servings.

Per serving: 98 cal., 7 g fat (1 g sat. fat), 0 mg chol., 153 mg sodium, 6 g carbo., 2 g fiber, 2 g pro.

Pesto Macaroni Salad

Prep: 30 minutes   Chill: up to 2 hours

  3 cups dried elbow macaroni
  5 ounces fresh green beans, trimmed and
    cut into 1-inch pieces (about 1 cup)
  1 pound small fresh mozzarella balls,
    drained and sliced
  1 7-ounce container purchased refrigerated
    basil pesto
 ½ cup fresh basil leaves, torn
 ½ teaspoon fine sea salt

  1. Cook macaroni according to package directions; drain. Rinse with cold water; drain again. In a saucepan, cook beans, covered, in a small amount of boiling salted water for 10 to 15 minutes or until crisp-tender; drain. Rinse with cold water; drain again. In a large bowl, combine macaroni, green beans, mozzarella, and pesto. Stir in basil and salt. Chill up to 2 hours before serving. Makes 14 servings.

Per serving: 249 cal., 14 g fat (4 g sat. fat), 26 mg chol., 255 mg sodium, 20 g carbo., 1 g fiber, 11 g pro.

Grapefruit-Avocado Salad

Start to Finish: 15 minutes

  4 cups packaged fresh baby spinach
  1 grapefruit, peeled and sectioned
  1 small avocado, halved, seeded, peeled,
    and sliced

  1 cup canned sliced beets
  1 tablespoon sliced almonds, toasted
    Orange Vinaigrette

  1. Divide spinach among four salad plates. Arrange grapefruit sections, avocado slices, and beets on spinach. Top with almonds. Drizzle with Orange Vinaigrette. Makes 6 servings.

  Orange Vinaigrette: In a screw-top jar, combine 1 teaspoon finely shredded orange peel, ⅓ cup orange juice, 2 teaspoons red wine vinegar, 2 teaspoons salad oil, ⅛ teaspoon salt, and dash ground black pepper. Cover and shake well.

Per serving: 106 cal., 7 g fat (1 g sat. fat), 0 mg chol., 122 mg sodium, 11 g carbo., 4 g fiber, 2 g pro.

Italian Pasta Salad

Start to Finish: 25 minutes

  4 ounces dried whole wheat rotini, dried
    whole grain penne, or dried bow tie pasta
    (about 1½ cups)
  1 cup fresh sugar snap peas, trimmed
 ½ cup chopped red sweet pepper
 ¼ cup shredded fresh basil
  2 tablespoons pitted niçoise olives or
    pitted ripe olives, quartered
    Red Wine Vinaigrette

  1. Cook pasta according to package directions, adding the sugar snap peas for the last 1 minute of cooking. Drain well. Rinse well with cold water; drain again. In a large bowl, combine pasta mixture, sweet pepper, basil, and olives. Pour Red Wine Vinaigrette over pasta mixture; toss gently to coat. Makes 6 servings.

  Red Wine Vinaigrette: In a screw-top jar, combine 2 tablespoons olive oil; 2 tablespoons red wine vinegar; 1 clove garlic, minced; ⅛ teaspoon salt; and dash ground black pepper. Cover and shake well to mix.

Per serving: 118 cal., 5 g fat (1 g sat. fat), 0 mg chol. 75 mg sodium, 16 g carbo., 2 g fiber, 3 g pro.

shredding basil

A quick way to shred (chiffonade) fresh basil is to stack several leaves and roll them up like a cigar. Starting at one end, use a sharp knife to cut crosswise into thin slices.

Originally from Greece, *feta cheese* is crumbly with a sharp, tangy, salty flavor. It's available plain or with basil.

Greek Vegetable Salad

Start to Finish: 30 minutes

- 2 cups chopped tomatoes
- 1 cup chopped cucumber
- 1/2 cup chopped yellow, red, and/or green sweet pepper
- 1/4 cup chopped red onion
- 1 1/2 teaspoons snipped fresh thyme or 1/2 teaspoon dried thyme, crushed
- 1 teaspoon snipped fresh oregano or 1/4 teaspoon dried oregano, crushed
- 2 tablespoons white balsamic vinegar or regular balsamic vinegar
- 2 tablespoons olive oil
  Leaf lettuce (optional)
- 1/2 cup crumbled feta cheese (2 ounces)

1. In a large bowl, combine tomatoes, cucumber, sweet pepper, red onion, thyme, and oregano. For dressing, in a small bowl, whisk together vinegar and olive oil. Pour dressing over vegetable mixture. Toss gently to coat.

2. If desired, line a serving bowl with lettuce; spoon in vegetable mixture. Sprinkle with feta cheese. Makes 8 servings.

Per serving: 65 cal., 5 g fat (1 g sat. fat), 3 mg chol., 120 mg sodium, 4 g carbo., 1 g fiber, 2 g pro.

Bacon-Onion Biscuits

Prep: 30 minutes   Bake: 25 minutes   Oven: 350°F

- 4 slices bacon, chopped
- 1 large onion, chopped (1 cup)
- 3 cups all-purpose flour
- 1 tablespoon baking powder
- 1 tablespoon sugar
- 3/4 teaspoon cream of tartar
- 1/2 teaspoon salt
- 3/4 cup butter
- 1 cup milk

1. In a skillet, cook bacon and onion until bacon is slightly crisp and onion is tender. Drain and discard fat.

2. In a bowl, stir together flour, baking powder, sugar, cream of tartar, and salt. Using a pastry blender, cut in butter until mixture resembles coarse crumbs. Make a well in the center of flour mixture. Combine milk and bacon mixture; add all at once to flour mixture. Using a fork, stir just until moistened.

3. Turn dough out onto a lightly floured surface. Knead dough by folding and gently pressing dough for four to six strokes or just until dough holds together. Pat or lightly roll dough to 3/4-inch thickness. Cut dough with a floured 2 1/2-inch biscuit cutter, rerolling dough scraps as necessary. Place biscuits on a baking sheet; freeze for 1 hour. Transfer to a plastic freezer bag. Seal, label, and freeze for up to 1 month. Makes 12 biscuits.

4. To serve, preheat oven to 350°F. Place frozen biscuits 1 inch apart on an ungreased baking sheet. Bake for 25 minutes or until golden.

Per biscuit: 294 cal., 18 g fat (10 g sat. fat), 41 mg chol., 354 mg sodium, 27 g carbo., 1 g fiber, 6 g pro.

Soft Pretzels

Prep: 15 minutes   Bake: 12 minutes   Oven: 375°F

- 1 package (8) refrigerated breadsticks
- 1 egg white
- 1 tablespoon water
  Sesame seeds and/or poppy seeds

1. Preheat oven to 375°F. Lightly grease a baking sheet; set aside. Unroll breadsticks so the dough lies flat. Gently pull each breadstick into a 16-inch-long rope. Shape each rope into a pretzel by crossing one end over the other to form a circle, overlapping about 4 inches from each end. Take one end of the rope in each hand and twist once at the point where the rope overlaps. Carefully lift each end across to the opposite edge of the circle; tuck ends under edges to make pretzel shape. Moisten the ends and press to seal.

2. Place pretzels on prepared baking sheet. In a small bowl, beat egg white and the water with a fork until well mixed. Brush pretzels with egg white mixture. Sprinkle with sesame seeds and/or poppy seeds. Bake for 12 to 15 minutes or until golden brown. Makes 8 pretzels.

Per pretzel: 114 cal., 3 g fat (1 g sat. fat), 0 mg chol., 297 mg sodium, 18 g carbo., 1 g fiber, 4 g pro.

dried tomatoes

Unless dried tomatoes (not oil-pack) will be cooked, soften them before use by soaking for 5 minutes in enough boiling water to cover; drain well.

Green Bean Salad

Prep: 15 minutes   Chill: 1 hour

- 12 ounces fresh green beans, trimmed
- 8 ounces yellow and/or red cherry tomatoes, halved
- 1/2 of a small red onion, thinly sliced
  Basil-Tomato Vinaigrette

1. In a medium saucepan, cook green beans, covered, in a small amount of boiling lightly salted water about 8 minutes or just until crisp-tender. Drain; rinse with cold water and drain again.

2. In a large bowl, combine beans, tomatoes, and red onion. Drizzle with Basil-Tomato Vinaigrette; toss gently to coat. Cover and chill for 1 to 4 hours. Makes 6 servings.

Basil-Tomato Vinaigrette: In a small bowl, stir together 1/3 cup snipped fresh basil; 3 tablespoons red wine vinegar; 2 tablespoons snipped dried tomatoes; 1 tablespoon olive oil; 2 cloves garlic, minced; 1/4 teaspoon salt; and 1/4 teaspoon ground black pepper.

Per serving: 53 cal., 2 g fat (0 g sat. fat), 0 mg chol., 126 mg sodium, 8 g carbo., 3 g fiber, 2 g pro.

Great Greek Green Beans

Prep: 10 minutes   Cook: 20 minutes

- 1/2 cup chopped onion
- 1 clove garlic, minced
- 2 tablespoons olive oil
- 1 28-ounce can diced tomatoes, undrained
- 1/4 cup sliced pitted ripe olives
- 1 teaspoon dried oregano, crushed
- 2 9-ounce packages or one 16-ounce package frozen French-cut green beans, thawed and drained
- 1/2 cup crumbled feta cheese (2 ounces)

1. In a large skillet, cook onion and garlic in hot oil about 5 minutes or until tender. Add undrained tomatoes, olives, and oregano. Bring to boiling; reduce heat. Boil gently, uncovered, for 10 minutes. Add beans. Return to boiling. Boil gently, uncovered, about 8 minutes or to desired consistency and beans are tender.

2. Transfer to a serving bowl; sprinkle with cheese. If desired, serve with a slotted spoon. Makes 6 servings.

Per serving: 132 cal., 7 g fat (2 g sat. fat), 8 mg chol., 419 mg sodium, 15 g carbo., 5 g fiber, 4 g pro.

Caramelized Brussels Sprouts

Prep: 15 minutes   Cook: 21 minutes

- 5 cups small, firm fresh Brussels sprouts (about 1 1/2 pounds)
- 1/4 cup sugar
- 2 tablespoons butter
- 1/4 cup red wine vinegar
- 1/3 cup water
- 1/2 teaspoon salt

1. Prepare the Brussels sprouts by peeling off two or three of the dark outer leaves from each Brussels sprout; trim stem ends.

2. In a large skillet, heat sugar over medium-high heat until it begins to melt, shaking pan occasionally to heat sugar evenly. Once sugar starts to melt, reduce heat and cook until sugar begins to turn brown. Add butter; stir until melted. Add vinegar. Cook and stir for 1 minute.

3. Carefully add the water and salt. Bring to boiling; add Brussels sprouts. Return to boiling; reduce heat. Simmer, covered, for 6 minutes.

4. Uncover and cook about 15 minutes more or until most of the liquid has been absorbed and the sprouts are coated with a golden glaze, gently stirring occasionally. Makes 8 servings.

Per serving: 76 cal., 3 g fat (2 g sat. fat), 8 mg chol., 155 mg sodium, 11 g carbo., 2 g fiber, 2 g pro.

Roasted Asparagus

Prep: 10 minutes   Roast: 15 minutes   Oven: 450°F

- 2 pounds fresh asparagus, trimmed
- 2 tablespoons olive oil
- 1/4 cup grated Parmesan cheese
- 1/4 cup butter, softened
- 1/4 cup finely chopped radishes
- 2 tablespoon snipped fresh chives
- 1 tablespoon lemon juice

1. Preheat oven to 450°F. Place asparagus in a 3-quart rectangular baking dish. Drizzle with oil and sprinkle with cheese. Roast, uncovered, about 15 minutes or until crisp-tender, using tongs to lightly toss twice during roasting.

2. Meanwhile, in a small bowl, combine butter, radishes, chives, and lemon juice. Transfer asparagus to a warm platter. Serve with butter mixture. Makes 8 servings.

Per serving: 105 cal., 10 g fat (5 g sat. fat), 17 mg chol., 82 mg sodium, 3 g carbo., 1 g fiber, 2 g pro.

Pear-Walnut Salad with Dijon Vinaigrette

Start to Finish: 20 minutes

- 2 medium ripe pears, cored and thinly sliced lengthwise
  - Dijon Vinaigrette
- 1 medium head Boston or Bibb lettuce
- 2 ounces Gorgonzola or blue cheese, cut into wedges
- 1/4 cup walnut pieces, toasted
- 1 large yellow or red tomato, seeded and chopped

1. In a medium bowl, toss pear slices with 1/3 cup of the Dijon Vinaigrette.

2. To serve, line four salad plates or bowls with lettuce leaves. Top with pear mixture. Top each serving with cheese, walnuts, and tomato. Drizzle with remaining Dijon Vinaigrette. Makes 4 servings.

Dijon Vinaigrette: In a screw-top jar, combine 1/2 cup olive oil; 1/4 cup white wine vinegar; 1 tablespoon sugar; 1 tablespoon Dijon-style mustard; 1 clove garlic, minced; 1/4 teaspoon salt; and 1/4 teaspoon freshly ground black pepper. Cover and shake well. Serve immediately or store in refrigerator for up to 1 week. Stir just before serving. Makes about 1 cup.

Per serving: 419 cal., 36 g fat (7 g sat. fat), 11 mg chol., 414 mg sodium, 20 g carbo., 4 g fiber, 6 g pro.

Cumin-Scented Carrots

Start to Finish: 15 minutes

- 4 medium carrots, cut into 1/2-inch slices or 2 cups packaged, peeled baby carrots
- 1 tablespoon butter
- 1/2 teaspoon ground cumin
  - Salt and ground black pepper

1. In a covered medium saucepan, cook carrots in a small amount of boiling water for 7 to 9 minutes or until crisp-tender; drain.

2. Meanwhile, in a medium skillet, melt butter over medium heat. Add cumin; cook and stir for 30 seconds. Add cooked carrots, stirring to coat. Sprinkle lightly with salt and pepper. Makes 4 servings.

Per serving: 54 cal., 3 g fat (2 g sat. fat), 8 mg chol., 88 mg sodium, 6 g carbo., 2 g fiber, 1 g pro.

Sesame Asparagus

Prep: 10 minutes   Chill: 1 to 4 hours

- 1 pound fresh asparagus spears, trimmed
- 2 tablespoons reduced-sodium soy sauce
- 1/4 teaspoon toasted sesame oil
  - Sesame seeds, toasted

1. In a covered large saucepan, cook asparagus in boiling water for 1 minute. Using tongs, transfer asparagus to a large bowl of ice water. Let stand for 2 minutes. Drain well and pat dry with paper towels. Place asparagus in a large resealable plastic bag.

2. In a small bowl, whisk together soy sauce and sesame oil; pour over asparagus. Seal bag. Chill for 1 to 4 hours. Drain, discarding soy sauce mixture. To serve, sprinkle asparagus with sesame seeds. Makes 4 servings.

Per serving: 21 cal., 1 g fat (0 g sat. fat), 0 mg chol., 301 mg sodium, 3 g carbo., 1 g fiber, 2 g pro.

Green Beans and Tomatoes

Start to Finish: 20 minutes

- 1 1/2 pounds fresh green beans, trimmed
- 1 pint small tomatoes (such as yellow pear, red grape, red and/or orange cherry), halved
- 1/4 cup bottled basil vinaigrette salad dressing
  - Salt and freshly ground black pepper

1. In a large saucepan, cook beans, covered, in a small amount of boiling salted water for 10 to 15 minutes or until crisp-tender. Drain and rinse under cool water. Drain and pat dry with paper towels.

2. In a large bowl, combine green beans and tomatoes. Drizzle with vinaigrette salad dressing; toss to coat. Add more vinaigrette, if necessary. Season to taste with salt and pepper. Serve immediately or chill up to 8 hours. Makes 6 to 8 servings.

Per serving: 86 cal., 5 g fat (1 g sat. fat), 0 mg chol., 106 mg sodium, 10 g carbo., 4 g fiber, 4 g pro.

Bow Ties with Mushrooms and Spinach

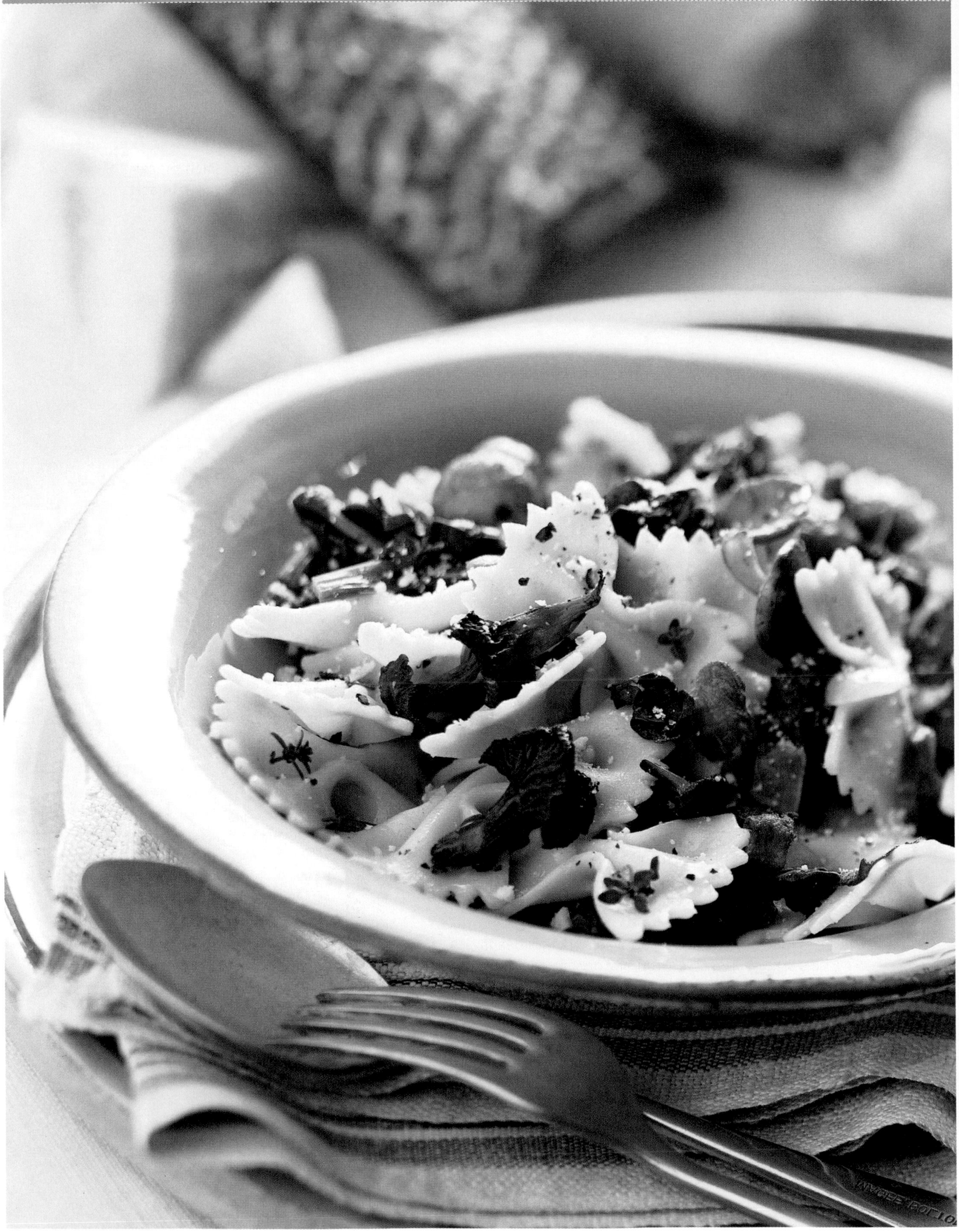

Bow Ties with Mushrooms and Spinach

Prep: 10 minutes   Cook: 10 minutes

- **6** ounces dried bow tie pasta
- **1** medium onion, chopped
- **1** cup sliced portobello or other fresh mushrooms
- **2** cloves garlic, minced
- **1** tablespoon olive oil
- **4** cups thinly sliced fresh spinach
- **1** teaspoon snipped fresh thyme
- **⅛** teaspoon ground black pepper
- **2** tablespoons shredded Parmesan cheese

1. Cook pasta according to package directions; drain.

2. Meanwhile, in a large skillet, cook and stir onion, mushrooms, and garlic in hot oil over medium heat for 2 to 3 minutes or until mushrooms are nearly tender. Stir in spinach, thyme, and pepper; cook for 1 minute or until heated through and spinach is slightly wilted. Stir in cooked pasta; toss gently to mix. Sprinkle with cheese. Makes 4 servings.

Per serving: 219 cal., 5 g fat (1 g sat. fat), 2 mg chol., 86 mg sodium, 35 g carbo., 4 g fiber, 9 g pro.

Saucepan Baked Beans

Prep: 10 minutes   Cook: 10 minutes

- **1** 16-ounce can pork and beans in tomato sauce
- **1** 15-ounce can navy or Great Northern beans, rinsed and drained
- **¼** cup ketchup
- **2** tablespoons maple syrup or packed brown sugar
- **2** teaspoons dry mustard
- **¼** cup purchased cooked bacon pieces or 2 slices bacon, crisp-cooked and crumbled

1. In a medium saucepan, combine pork and beans, navy beans, ketchup, maple syrup, and dry mustard. Bring mixture to boiling; reduce heat. Simmer, uncovered, about 10 minutes or to desired consistency, stirring frequently. Stir in bacon. Makes 6 servings.

Per serving: 211 cal., 3 g fat (1 g sat. fat), 5 mg chol., 870 mg sodium, 39 g carbo., 8 g fiber, 11 g pro.

Sautéed Spinach with Bacon and Mustard

Start to Finish: 15 minutes

- **4** slices bacon, cut into 1-inch pieces
- **2** 10-ounce bags prewashed spinach
- **1** tablespoon butter
- **1** tablespoon Dijon-style mustard
- **¼** teaspoon crushed red pepper

1. In a very large skillet, cook bacon over medium heat until crisp. Drain bacon on paper towels, reserving 1 tablespoon drippings in skillet. Gradually add spinach to skillet, stirring frequently with metal tongs. Cook for 2 to 3 minutes or until spinach is just wilted. Remove spinach from skillet to a colander; hold over sink and press lightly with the back of a spoon to drain.

2. In the same skillet, melt butter over medium heat; stir in mustard and crushed red pepper. Add drained spinach; toss to coat. Reheat spinach if necessary. Top with bacon. Serve immediately. Makes 4 to 6 servings.

Per serving: 135 cal., 11 g fat (4 g sat. fat), 18 mg chol., 340 mg sodium, 5 g carbo., 3 g fiber, 7 g pro.

Sautéed Spinach with Bacon and Mustard

sweet-treat
desserts

1-2-3 Cheesecake

Something sweet at the end of a meal always seems to make the time at the table more satisfying. Treat your family to one of these easy, pleasing sweets tonight.

1-2-3 Cheesecake

Prep: 25 minutes   Bake: 70 minutes   Cool: 1 hour
Chill: overnight   Oven: 275°F

- 1   cup sugar
- 4   8-ounce packages cream cheese, softened
- 3   eggs
- 1   teaspoon finely shredded lemon peel or
      1 teaspoon vanilla (optional)
      Sliced fresh plums, peaches, or nectarines
      (optional)
      Shredded lemon peel (optional)

1. Preheat oven to 275°F. Line the outside of an 8-inch springform pan with heavy foil. Grease the bottom and sides inside the pan; set aside.

2. In a very large mixing bowl, beat sugar and cream cheese with a sturdy handheld or freestanding electric mixer on medium to high speed for 8 to 10 minutes or until mixture is smooth and sugar is dissolved, scraping sides of bowl twice.

3. Stir in eggs just until combined. Pour batter into prepared pan; place in a shallow roasting pan. Place roasting pan on the oven rack. Pour very hot water into roasting pan to a depth of 1 inch.

4. Bake, uncovered, for 70 to 75 minutes or until center appears nearly set when pan is gently shaken.

5. Carefully lift springform pan from water bath; let cool on wire rack for 15 minutes. Run a thin metal spatula around the edge of the cheesecake to loosen from pan. Cool for 45 minutes more. Cover; chill overnight.

6. To serve, remove sides of the pan. If desired, top with sliced fruit and shredded lemon peel. Cut cheesecake into wedges. Makes 10 servings.

Per serving: 413 cal., 33 g fat (20 g sat. fat), 163 mg chol., 290 mg sodium, 22 g carbo., 0 g fiber, 9 g pro.

Cherry-Wine Poached Apples

Prep: 15 minutes   Cook: 30 minutes

- 2   medium cooking apples (such as Granny Smith, Braeburn, Pink Lady, or Jonagold)
- 1   cup Riesling wine or unsweetened grape juice
- 1   cup frozen unsweetened pitted dark sweet cherries
- ¼   cup water
- 1   3-inch sprig fresh rosemary

1. Using a melon baller, remove the core through the bottom of each apple. Peel apples, leaving stems intact. Place apples in a medium saucepan. Add wine, cherries, the water, and rosemary. Bring to boiling; reduce heat. Simmer, covered, about 10 minutes or just until apples are tender, turning occasionally to coat apples with liquid.

2. Using a slotted spoon, transfer apples to serving dishes. Simmer cooking liquid, uncovered, about 20 minutes or until reduced to 1 cup. Remove from heat; cool slightly. Strain liquid, discarding cherries and rosemary. Spoon liquid over apples on serving plates. Serve warm or cover and chill for up to 24 hours. Makes 2 servings.

Per serving: 166 cal., 0 g fat, 0 mg chol., 1 mg sodium, 23 g carbo., 2 g fiber, 1 g pro.

Raspberry-Peach Crisp

Prep: 30 minutes   Bake: 45 minutes
Cool: 45 minutes   Oven: 375°F

- 4   cups sliced fresh peaches or frozen unsweetened peach slices, thawed
- 2   tablespoons granulated sugar
- 1   tablespoon quick-cooking tapioca
- 2   tablespoons red raspberry preserves
- ⅔   cup quick-cooking rolled oats
- 2   tablespoons whole wheat flour
- 2   tablespoons packed brown sugar
- ½   teaspoon ground cinnamon
- 2   tablespoons butter
   Vanilla low-fat yogurt or vanilla frozen yogurt (optional)

1. Preheat oven to 375°F. For fruit filling, thaw fruit, if frozen; do not drain. In a large bowl, combine peach slices, granulated sugar, tapioca, and raspberry preserves. Place fruit mixture in a 2-quart square baking dish.

2. For the topping, in a medium bowl, combine oats, whole wheat flour, brown sugar, and cinnamon. Using a pastry blender, cut in butter until crumbly. Sprinkle topping over fruit.

3. Bake for 45 to 50 minutes or until bubbly. Cool on a wire rack for 45 minutes; serve warm. If desired, serve with vanilla yogurt. Makes 8 servings.

Per serving: 159 cal., 4 g fat (2 g sat. fat), 8 mg chol., 22 mg sodium, 31 g carbo., 4 g fiber, 3 g pro.

Berry Pudding Cakes

Prep: 20 minutes   Bake: 20 minutes   Oven: 400°F

   Nonstick cooking spray
- 2   eggs, lightly beaten
- ¼   cup granulated sugar
- 1   teaspoon vanilla
   Dash salt
- 1   cup milk
- ½   cup all-purpose flour
- ½   teaspoon baking powder
- 3   cups fresh berries (such as raspberries, blueberries, and/or sliced strawberries)
- 2   teaspoons powdered sugar (optional)

1. Preheat oven to 400°F. Lightly coat six 6-ounce individual quiche dishes with nonstick cooking spray. Arrange in a 15×10×1-inch baking pan; set aside. In a medium bowl, combine eggs, granulated sugar, vanilla, and salt; whisk until light and frothy. Whisk in milk until combined. Add flour and baking powder; whisk until smooth.

2. Divide berries among prepared quiche dishes. Pour batter over berries. (Batter will not cover berries completely.) Bake about 20 minutes or until puffed and golden brown. Serve warm. If desired, sift powdered sugar over each serving. Makes 6 servings.

Per serving: 149 cal., 3 g fat (1 g sat. fat), 74 mg chol., 84 mg sodium, 26 g carbo., 3 g fiber, 5 g pro.

topper toasting

To toast coconut or nuts, preheat oven to 350°F. Place coconut or nuts in a shallow baking pan. Bake for 5 to 10 minutes or until toasted, stirring once or twice. Watch closely to be sure they aren't getting too brown. Cool slightly before using.

Golden Cake with Apricot-Almond Topping

Prep: 15 minutes   Bake: 40 minutes
Cool: 10 minutes   Oven: 350°F

1	2-layer-size package yellow cake mix
1	15-ounce can unpeeled apricot halves in light syrup
$2/3$	cup unsweetened pineapple juice
2	teaspoons cornstarch
$1/2$	cup toasted coarsely chopped almonds
2	tablespoons shredded coconut, toasted

1. Preheat oven to 350°F. Prepare cake mix according to package directions. Bake in a greased and floured 10-inch tube pan for 40 to 45 minutes or until a toothpick inserted near the center comes out clean. Cool on a wire rack for 10 minutes. Remove cake from pan; cool.

2. Rinse and drain apricots. Cut apricots into strips; set aside. In a small saucepan, combine pineapple juice and cornstarch. Cook and stir until thickened and bubbly; cook and stir for 2 minutes more. Stir in nuts and apricots. Cool slightly. Spoon warm topping over cake. Sprinkle with coconut. Makes 16 servings.

Per serving: 240 cal., 11 g fat (2 g sat. fat), 41 mg chol., 220 mg sodium, 34 g carbo., 1 g fiber, 3 g pro.

Cinnamon-Glazed Poached Pears

Prep: 20 minutes   Cook: 50 minutes
Cool: 30 minutes   Chill: 2 hours

  4   medium Bartlett pears
1½   cups pomegranate or cranberry juice
  1   cup water
  2   tablespoons honey
  6   inches stick cinnamon or ¼ teaspoon
        ground cinnamon

1. Cut a thin slice from the bottom of each pear so pears stand up. If desired, use a melon baller to remove the core through the bottom of each pear.

2. In a large saucepan, combine juice, the water, honey, and cinnamon. Bring to boiling, stirring to dissolve honey. Add pears. Return to boiling; reduce heat. Cook, covered, about 10 minutes or just until pears are tender. Remove pan from heat and let cool for 30 minutes. Transfer pears and liquid to a large bowl, turning pears a few times to coat with liquid. Cover and chill for 2 to 24 hours.

3. Remove pears from liquid; cover and chill until ready to serve or, if desired, pears may stand at room temperature while syrup is being reduced. Strain liquid; discard stick cinnamon, if using. Transfer liquid to a medium saucepan. Bring to boiling; simmer gently, uncovered, about 40 minutes or until reduced to ¼ cup. Watch mixture closely at the end to prevent overcooking. To serve, drizzle reduced liquid over pears. Makes 4 servings.

Per serving: 177 cal., 0 g fat, 0 mg chol., 16 mg sodium, 47 g carbo., 5 g fiber, 1 g pro.

Strawberry-Pretzel Parfaits

Prep: 20 minutes   Chill: up to 4 hours

  1   8-ounce tub light cream cheese,
        softened
  1   tablespoon milk
  1   teaspoon vanilla
  1   cup coarsely crushed pretzels
        (about 2¼ ounces)
1½   cups sliced fresh strawberries

1. In a small bowl, stir together cream cheese, milk, and vanilla until smooth. In four 8-ounce parfait glasses or drinking glasses, layer half the pretzels, half the cream cheese mixture, and half the strawberries. Repeat layers. Serve immediately or cover and chill for up to 4 hours before serving. Makes 4 servings.

Per serving: 188 cal., 9 g fat (5 g sat. fat), 27 mg chol., 507 mg sodium, 20 g carbo., 2 g fiber, 8 g pro.

Honey-Ginger Compote

Prep: 20 minutes   Chill: 4 hours

  ¼   cup apple juice, apple cider, or
        unsweetened pineapple juice
  2   teaspoons honey
  1   teaspoon finely chopped crystallized ginger
  1   teaspoon lemon juice
1½   cups assorted fruit (such as cubed melon,
        halved grapes, raspberries, pitted sweet
        cherries, cubed peaches, cubed pears,
        cubed mango, sliced kiwifruit, and/or
        chopped pineapple)
  2   tablespoons low-fat vanilla yogurt

1. In a small saucepan, combine apple juice, honey, crystallized ginger, and lemon juice. Cook and stir over medium heat until boiling. Transfer to a small bowl; cover and refrigerate for 4 to 48 hours.

2. To serve, in a medium bowl, toss together assorted fruit. Spoon into tall stemmed glasses or dessert dishes. Pour apple juice mixture over fruit. Spoon yogurt on top of fruit mixture. Makes 2 servings.

Per serving: 103 cal., 0 g fat, 0 mg chol., 10 mg sodium, 27 g carbo., 1 g fiber, 1 g pro.

Apricot-Peach Cobbler

Prep: 10 minutes   Bake: per package directions

  1   15-ounce can unpeeled apricot halves
        in light syrup
  1   7.75-ounce packet cinnamon swirl biscuit
        mix (such as Bisquick complete)
  1   21-ounce can peach pie filling
  1   teaspoon vanilla
        Vanilla ice cream (optional)

1. Preheat oven to temperature called for on biscuit mix package. Drain apricot halves, reserving syrup. Prepare biscuit mix according to package directions, except use ½ cup reserved apricot syrup in place of the water. Bake according to package directions.

2. Meanwhile, in a medium saucepan, combine pie filling, drained apricots, and any remaining apricot syrup. Heat through. Remove from heat; stir in vanilla. Spoon fruit mixture into bowls. Top with warm biscuits. If desired, serve with ice cream. Makes 6 servings.

Per serving: 284 cal., 4 g fat (0 g sat. fat), 0 mg chol., 346 mg sodium, 59 g carbo., 2 g fiber, 3 g pro.

Salted Peanut Bars

Prep: 25 minutes   Chill: 1 hour

Nonstick cooking spray
4   cups dry-roasted or honey-roasted peanuts
1   10.5-ounce package tiny marshmallows
$\frac{1}{2}$ cup butter
1   14-ounce can sweetened condensed milk ($1\frac{1}{3}$ cups)
1   10-ounce package peanut butter-flavor pieces
$\frac{1}{2}$ cup creamy peanut butter

1. Line a 13×9×2-inch baking pan with heavy foil. Coat foil with nonstick cooking spray. Spread half of the peanuts evenly in prepared baking pan.

2. In a 3-quart saucepan, combine marshmallows and butter; heat and stir over medium-low heat until melted. Stir in sweetened condensed milk, peanut butter pieces, and peanut butter until smooth. Quickly pour peanut butter mixture over peanuts in pan. Sprinkle remaining peanuts over peanut butter mixture. Gently press peanuts into peanut butter mixture.

3. Chill about 1 hour or until firm; cut into pieces. Store, covered, in refrigerator. Makes 60 pieces.

Per piece: 144 cal., 10 g fat (3 g sat. fat), 7 mg chol., 128 mg sodium, 12 g carbo., 1 g fiber, 4 g pro.

Peanut-Apple Crunch Balls

Prep: 25 minutes   Stand: 30 minutes

$\frac{1}{3}$ cup chunky peanut butter
$\frac{1}{4}$ cup butter
2   tablespoons honey
1   cup rice and wheat cereal flakes, crushed slightly
1   cup bran flakes, crushed slightly
$\frac{1}{3}$ cup finely snipped dried apples
2   tablespoons finely chopped peanuts
$\frac{1}{8}$ teaspoon apple pie spice
2   ounces white baking chocolate (with cocoa butter), chopped
$\frac{1}{4}$ teaspoon shortening

1. In a medium saucepan, combine peanut butter, butter, and honey. Cook over low heat just until melted and nearly smooth, whisking constantly. Stir in cereals, apples, peanuts, and apple pie spice until well mixed. Divide mixture into 18 portions. Using slightly wet hands, shape mixture into balls. Let stand on a baking sheet lined with waxed paper about 15 minutes or until firm.

2. In a small saucepan, combine white chocolate and shortening; cook and stir over low heat until melted. Drizzle balls with melted white chocolate. Let stand about 15 minutes or until topping is set (if necessary, chill balls until white chocolate is firm). Makes 18 balls.

Per ball: 94 cal., 6 g fat (2 g sat. fat), 1 mg chol., 76 mg sodium, 9 g carbo., 1 g fiber, 2 g pro.

Apple and Peanut Butter Crisp

Prep: 20 minutes   Bake: 30 minutes   Oven: 375°F

6   medium red and/or green cooking apples, cored, peeled, if desired, and thinly sliced
2   tablespoons all-purpose flour
1   tablespoon brown sugar
$\frac{2}{3}$ cup quick-cooking rolled oats
2   tablespoons all-purpose flour
2   tablespoons brown sugar
$\frac{1}{4}$ cup peanut butter
2   tablespoons chopped peanuts

1. Place apple slices in a 2-quart square baking dish; set aside. In a small bowl, stir together 2 tablespoons flour and 1 tablespoon brown sugar until well combined. Sprinkle over apple slices in dish; toss to coat.

2. Bake, covered, in a 375°F oven for 15 minutes. Meanwhile, in a medium bowl, combine rolled oats, 2 tablespoons flour, and 2 tablespoons brown sugar. Using a fork, stir in peanut butter until mixture resembles coarse crumbs. Stir in peanuts.

3. Uncover apple mixture; sprinkle with oat mixture. Bake, uncovered, for 15 to 20 minutes more or until apples are tender and topping is golden. Serve warm. Makes 8 servings.

Per serving: 174 cal., 6 g fat (1 g sat. fat), 0 mg chol., 51 mg sodium, 28 g carbo., 4 g fiber, 4 g pro.

peanut butter

We love peanut butter for sandwiches and no-bake sweets, but its earliest uses were in stews (Africa) and sauces (China). Peanut butter took the United States by storm when it was sold at the Universal Exposition in St. Louis in 1904. Vendor C. H. Sumner sold more than $700 of the spread from barrels during the exposition. The first shelf-stable peanut butter in jars appeared in 1922.

Warm Chocolate Bread Pudding

Prep: 15 minutes Bake: 15 minutes Oven: 350°F

   Nonstick cooking spray
2   cups firm-texture white bread cubes
²/₃   cup milk
¼   cup granulated sugar
¼   cup miniature semisweet chocolate pieces
2   eggs
1   teaspoon finely shredded orange peel or
     tangerine peel
½   teaspoon vanilla
     Frozen light whipped dessert topping or
     powdered sugar (optional)

   1. Preheat oven to 350°F. Lightly coat four 6-ounce custard cups or ³/₄-cup soufflé dishes with cooking spray. Place bread cubes in the custard cups.
   2. In a small saucepan, combine milk, granulated sugar, and chocolate. Cook and stir over low heat until chocolate melts; remove from heat. If necessary, beat smooth with a wire whisk.
   3. In a medium bowl, beat eggs; gradually stir in chocolate mixture. Stir in orange peel and vanilla. Pour egg mixture over bread cubes; press bread with the back of a spoon to moisten.
   4. Bake for 15 to 20 minutes or until tops appear firm and a knife inserted near the centers comes out clean. Cool slightly on a wire rack. If desired, top with whipped topping or dust with powdered sugar. Makes 4 servings.
   Per serving: 170 cal., 4 g fat (2 g sat. fat), 1 mg chol., 143 mg sodium, 26 g carbo., 2 g fiber, 5 g pro.

Double Chocolate Brownies

Prep: 10 minutes Bake: 15 minutes Oven: 350°F

¼   cup butter
²/₃   cup granulated sugar
½   cup cold water
1   teaspoon vanilla
1   cup all-purpose flour
¼   cup unsweetened cocoa powder
1   teaspoon baking powder
¼   cup miniature semisweet chocolate pieces
     Sifted powdered sugar

   1. Preheat oven to 350°F. Lightly coat the bottom only of a 9×9×2-inch baking pan with *nonstick cooking spray*,
   2. In a medium saucepan, melt butter; remove from heat. Stir in granulated sugar, the water, and vanilla. Stir in

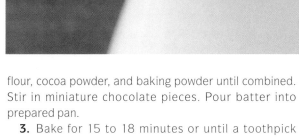

flour, cocoa powder, and baking powder until combined. Stir in miniature chocolate pieces. Pour batter into prepared pan.
   3. Bake for 15 to 18 minutes or until a toothpick inserted near the center comes out clean. Cool on a wire rack. Remove from pan. Cut into bars. Sprinkle with powdered sugar. Makes 16 brownies.
   Per brownie: 113 cal., 4 g fat (2 g sat. fat), 8 mg chol., 37 mg sodium, 17 g carbo., 0 g fiber, 1 g pro.

Double Chocolate Brownies

Peaches and Ice Cream Sandwich Bars

Prep: 25 minutes   Freeze: 4¼ hours
Stand: 10 minutes

10	to 14 rectangular ice cream sandwiches
2	pints peach or mango sorbet, softened
1	8-ounce carton dairy sour cream
1	cup whipping cream
¾	cup sifted powdered sugar
2	cups fresh blueberries or raspberries

1. Place ice cream sandwiches in a 13×9×2-inch baking pan or 3-quart rectangular baking dish, cutting to fit. Spread sorbet on top of ice cream sandwiches. Cover and freeze for 15 minutes or until sorbet is firm.

2. In a medium bowl, combine sour cream, whipping cream, and powdered sugar. Beat with electric mixer on medium speed until mixture thickens and holds soft peaks. Spread on top of sorbet.

3. Cover and freeze for 4 to 24 hours or until firm. Let stand at room temperature for 10 minutes before serving. Sprinkle fresh berries over whipped cream mixture. Makes 12 servings.

Per serving: 354 cal., 16 g fat (10 g sat. fat), 52 mg chol., 49 mg sodium, 51 g carbo., 1 g fiber, 3 g pro.

Berry Patch Ice Cream Dessert

Prep: 30 minutes   Bake: 25 minutes
Freeze: 4 to 24 hours   Stand: 15 minutes
Cool: 30 minutes   Oven: 325°F

1	19- to 22-ounce package fudge brownie mix
1	quart vanilla ice cream
2½	cups fresh or frozen berries (such as raspberries, blueberries, or halved strawberries)
¼	cup chocolate ice cream topping or raspberry syrup

1. Preheat oven to 325°F. Lightly grease two 8×1½-inch round baking pans; line bottom of each pan with waxed paper. Grease waxed paper; set pans aside. Prepare brownie mix according to package directions; divide batter evenly between prepared pans.

2. Bake for 25 minutes. Cool in pans on wire racks for 10 minutes. Loosen edges, invert, and carefully remove brownie rounds from pans. Peel off waxed paper. Cool completely on wire racks. Wrap each brownie round in plastic wrap. Place one of the brownie rounds in an airtight freezer container and freeze for another use. Store remaining brownie round at room temperature for several hours or overnight.

3. Line an 8×1½-inch round pan with plastic wrap, allowing excess to extend over edge; set aside. In a large bowl, use a wooden spoon to stir ice cream just until softened. Carefully fold in 1 cup of the berries. Spread ice cream mixture evenly in prepared pan. Cover and freeze for 4 to 24 hours.

4. To serve, place brownie round on a serving plate. Lift ice cream layer and plastic wrap from pan. Invert ice cream layer onto brownie; peel off plastic wrap. Top with remaining 1½ cups berries. Drizzle with chocolate topping. Let stand for 15 minutes before serving. Makes 10 servings.

Per serving: 350 cal., 19 g fat (8 g sat. fat), 58 mg chol., 141 mg sodium, 44 g carbo., 3 g fiber, 4 g pro.

Super-Easy Ice Cream Sandwiches

Prep: 15 minutes   Freeze: 6 hours
Stand: 10 minutes

1	pint strawberry ice cream
½	cup chopped malted milk balls
12	soft chocolate, chocolate chip, or oatmeal cookies
6	tablespoons fudge ice cream topping

1. In a large bowl, stir ice cream with a wooden spoon to soften. Stir malted milk balls into ice cream. Spoon ice cream on the flat side of six of the cookies. Spread about 1 tablespoon of fudge ice cream topping on flat side of remaining six cookies. Place each cookie, fudge side down, on ice cream. Wrap each ice cream sandwich in plastic wrap; freeze for 6 hours or until firm. Let stand about 10 minutes before eating. Makes 6 servings.

Per serving: 677 cal., 33 g fat (21 g sat. fat), 76 mg chol. 559 mg sodium, 99 g carbo., 1 g fiber, 8 g pro.

Ginger Peach Freeze

Ginger Peach Freeze

Prep: 10 minutes   Freeze: 3 hours

  1   cup water
  1   cup sugar
  3   tablespoons lemon juice
  1/4   teaspoon ground ginger
  1   16-ounce package frozen unsweetened
       peach slices
       Fresh peach slices (optional)

   1. In a medium saucepan, combine the water, sugar, lemon juice, and ginger. Bring to boiling. Remove from heat; add frozen peaches. Let stand about 30 minutes or until peaches are thawed and mixture has cooled.
   2. Transfer peach mixture, half at a time, to a blender. Cover and blend until smooth. Pour mixture into a 2-quart rectangular baking dish. Cover and freeze for 3 to 4 hours. Break up mixture with a fork and serve. If desired, garnish with fresh peach slices. Makes 8 servings.
   Per serving: 119 cal., 0 g fat (0 g sat. fat), 0 mg chol., 1 mg sodium, 31 g carbo., 1 g fiber, 0 g pro.

Ice Cream with Orange-Praline Sauce

Start to Finish: 15 minutes

  1   12-ounce jar caramel ice cream topping
  1/2   cup orange marmalade
  2/3   cup coarsely chopped pecans, toasted
  1/2   gallon vanilla, cinnamon, pumpkin, or
       eggnog ice cream

   1. In a small saucepan, stir together caramel ice cream topping and orange marmalade; cook over medium-low heat until marmalade melts, stirring occasionally. Stir in pecans; heat through. Spoon warm sauce over scoops of ice cream. Makes 10 servings.
   Make-Ahead Tip: Cover and chill sauce for up to 24 hours. Just before serving, in a small saucepan, reheat sauce over low heat, stirring occasionally.
   Per serving: 484 cal., 24 g fat (13 g sat. fat), 109 mg chol., 156 mg sodium, 61 g carbo., 1 g fiber, 7 g pro.

Lemon Cheesecake Mousse

Start to Finish: 10 minutes

- 1   8-ounce package cream cheese, softened
- 1/2   cup frozen lemonade concentrate, thawed
- 1/2   teaspoon vanilla
- 1   8-ounce container frozen whipped dessert topping, thawed
  Purchased gingersnaps (optional)

1. In a medium mixing bowl, beat cream cheese with an electric mixer on medium to high speed for 30 seconds. Beat in lemonade concentrate and vanilla. Fold in whipped topping. Divide among six dessert dishes. If desired, serve with gingersnaps. Makes 6 servings.

Per serving: 282 cal., 20 g fat (15 g sat. fat), 42 mg chol., 13 mg sodium, 21 g carbo., 0 g fiber, 3 g pro.

Surprise Chocolate Bites

Prep: 20 minutes   Bake: 10 minutes per batch
Oven: 350°F

- 1   18-ounce roll refrigerated sugar cookie dough
- 1/3   cup unsweetened cocoa powder
- 2/3   cup creamy peanut butter
- 2/3   cup powdered sugar
  Granulated sugar

1. Preheat oven to 350°F. Place cookie dough and cocoa in a large resealable plastic bag; knead to combine. In a bowl, stir together peanut butter and powdered sugar until combined. With floured hands, roll the peanut butter mixture into thirty balls, using 1 teaspoon mixture for each.*

2. To shape cookies, take 1 tablespoon of cookie dough and make an indentation in the center. Press a peanut butter ball into indentation and form dough around ball to enclose it; roll ball gently in your hands to smooth it out. Repeat with remaining dough and peanut butter balls.

3. Place balls 2 inches apart on ungreased cookie sheets. Flatten the balls slightly with the bottom of a glass dipped in granulated sugar. Bake for 10 to 12 minutes or until set. Transfer cookies to wire rack; cool. Makes 30 cookies.

*Note: For easier handling, freeze the peanut butter balls for 30 minutes. Flatten the balls slightly to form disks, then press cookie dough around them.

Per serving: 118 cal., 6 g fat (1 g sat. fat), 5 mg chol., 87 mg sodium, 15 g carbo., 0 g fiber, 2 g pro.

Red, White, and Blue Parfaits

Start to Finish: 15 minutes

- 1   8-ounce carton vanilla low-fat yogurt
- 1/4   teaspoon almond extract or 1/2 teaspoon vanilla
- 1/2   of an 8-ounce container frozen light whipped dessert topping, thawed
- 3   cups fresh raspberries and/or cut-up fresh strawberries
- 3   cups fresh blueberries

1. In a large bowl, stir together yogurt and almond extract. Fold in whipped topping. In six 12-ounce glasses, layer berries and yogurt mixture. Serve immediately or cover and chill for up to 1 hour. Makes 6 servings.

Per serving: 129 cal., 3 g fat (2 g sat. fat), 2 mg chol., 26 mg sodium, 21 g carbo., 8 g fiber, 3 g pro.

Coffee Brownies

Prep: 20 minutes   Bake: 40 minutes   Oven: 350°F

- 1   16.5-ounce package refrigerated sugar cookie dough
- 2   eggs, lightly beaten
- 1   19.5-ounce package milk chocolate brownie mix
- 1/2   cup cooking oil
- 1/3   cup coffee-flavor liqueur or cool strong coffee
- 1   cup semisweet or bittersweet chocolate pieces

1. Preheat oven to 350°F. Press sugar cookie dough into the bottom of a 13x9x2-inch baking pan; set aside.

2. In a large bowl, stir together eggs, brownie mix, oil, and liqueur until just combined. Spread over sugar cookie dough. Sprinkle with chocolate pieces.

3. Bake brownies for 40 minutes or until edges are set. Cool completely in pan on a wire rack. Cut into bars. Makes 24 bars.

Per serving: 279 cal., 15 g fat (3 g sat. fat), 23 mg chol., 159 mg sodium, 36 g carbo., 1 g fiber, 3 g pro.

3. Bake for 30 to 35 minutes or until a knife inserted near the center comes out clean. Remove custard cups from baking dish. Cool to room temperature. Chill for 2 to 24 hours. If desired, top with dessert topping and coffee beans. Makes 6 servings.

Per serving: 141 cal., 5 g fat (2 g sat. fat), 113 mg chol., 73 mg sodium, 17 g carbo., 0 g fiber, 7 g pro.

Chocolate-Peanut Ice Cream Cake

Prep: 20 minutes   Bake: 8 minutes
Cool: 15 minutes   Freeze: 5½ hours
Stand: 20 minutes   Oven: 350°F

    2   cups purchased chocolate cookie crumbs
    ½   cup butter, melted
    ¼   cup sugar
    1   quart vanilla ice cream
 1½   cups chocolate-covered peanuts, chopped
    1   quart chocolate ice cream
        Chocolate-Peanut Butter Sauce

1. Preheat oven to 350°F. For crust, in a medium bowl, combine cookie crumbs, melted butter, and sugar. Press crust mixture onto the bottom and 1 to 2 inches up the side of a 9×3-inch springform pan. Bake for 8 to 10 minutes or until crust is set. Cool on a wire rack for 15 minutes. Freeze for 30 minutes.

2. Let vanilla ice cream stand at room temperature for 15 minutes. In a large bowl, use a wooden spoon to stir vanilla ice cream just enough to soften. Spoon softened ice cream into frozen crust, spreading ice cream evenly. Sprinkle with chocolate-covered peanuts. Freeze about 1 hour or until firm.

3. Let chocolate ice cream stand at room temperature for 15 minutes. In a large bowl, use a wooden spoon to stir chocolate ice cream just enough to soften. Spoon softened chocolate ice cream on top of chocolate-covered peanuts, spreading ice cream evenly. Cover and freeze for 4 hours.

4. Using a thin metal spatula, loosen crust from side of pan; remove side of pan. Let ice cream cake stand at room temperature for 20 minutes to soften slightly.

5. To serve, cut into wedges; top with Chocolate-Peanut Butter Sauce. Makes 12 servings.

Chocolate-Peanut Butter Sauce: In a small saucepan, combine one 12-ounce jar fudge ice cream topping and 3 tablespoons creamy peanut butter. Cook and stir over medium-low heat until heated through.

Per serving: 596 cal., 35 g fat (17 g sat. fat), 86 mg chol., 368 mg sodium, 66 g carbo., 4 g fiber, 10 g pro.

Mocha Custards

Prep: 20 minutes   Bake: 30 minutes   Cool: 1 hour
Chill: 2 hours   Oven: 325°F

 2¼   cups milk
    ⅓   cup sugar
    3   tablespoons unsweetened cocoa powder
    1   tablespoon instant coffee crystals
    3   eggs, lightly beaten
 1½   teaspoons vanilla
        Frozen whipped dessert topping, thawed
        (optional)
        Coffee beans (optional)

1. Preheat oven to 325°F. In a medium saucepan, combine milk, sugar, cocoa powder, and coffee crystals. Cook and stir just until sugar and coffee are dissolved.

2. In a medium mixing bowl, gradually whisk hot mixture into eggs. Add vanilla. Place six 6-ounce custard cups in a 3-quart rectangular baking dish. Place on the oven rack. Pour egg mixture into the custard cups. Carefully pour boiling water into the baking dish to a depth of about 1 inch.

Better Homes and Gardens®

Whether you're looking for timesaving recipes, a simple no-fuss meal, or a wide variety of options, Better Homes and Gardens® books have the answer.

A great way to experience the taste and variety of America's favorite cookbook brand.

Fast Fix Family Food has more than 200 family-approved, quick and easy recipes to please everyone in the family.

5-Ingredient Favorites is full of recipes for everything from appetizers to hearty main course meals—all with the flavor of home cooking.

365 Last-Minute Meals features 365 delicious, fast recipes that make it easy to answer the never-ending question "What's for dinner?" with a meal everyone will love.